Shifting Borders and a Tattered Passport

Armand L. Mauss

Armand L. Mauss
foreword by Richard Bushman

SHIFTING

BORDERS

and a

TATTERED

PASSPORT

*Intellectual Journeys
of a Mormon Academic*

THE UNIVERSITY OF UTAH PRESS
Salt Lake City

The Defiance House Man colophon is a registered trademark
of the University of Utah Press. It is based on a four-foot-tall
Ancient Puebloan pictograph (late PIII) near Glen Canyon, Utah.

16 15 14 13 12   1 2 3 4 5

LIBRARY OF CONGRESS CATALOGING-IN-PUBLICATION DATA
Mauss, Armand L.
  Shifting borders and a tattered passport : intellectual journeys
  of a Mormon academic / Armand L. Mauss.
      p. cm.
  Includes bibliographical references (p.   ) and index.
  ISBN 978-1-60781-204-3 (cloth : alk. paper)
  1. Mauss, Armand L. 2. Mormons—California—Biography.
3. United States—Intellectual life—20th century. 4. Church of Jesus
Christ of Latter-Day Saints—United States—History—20th century.
5. Mormon Church—United States—History—20th century. I. Title.
  BX8695.M333A3 2012
  289.3092—dc23
  [B]
                                             2012025407

Index by Andrew L. Christenson.
Printed and bound by Sheridan Books, Inc., Ann Arbor, Michigan.

To Ruth

with eternal love and gratitude

Contents

WHEN THE INTELLECTUAL HISTORY OF LATE-TWENTIETH-CENTURY MOR-monism is written, Armand Mauss will occupy a preeminent position. Scores of names will figure in that history, scholars in a wide variety of fields beginning with history and extending into literature, political science, theology, philosophy, law, and sociology. But Mauss will be set apart as one of a handful who concep-tualized the course of Mormon history in our time. Many scholars explore new areas and organize narratives to clarify the course of events. Few can character-ize the underlying patterns that order those events. Mauss's book *The Angel and the Beehive* provided that kind of ordering. Even though disputed, as all strong ideas are, Mauss's underlying theme, the oscillating swings from assimilation to retrenchment and back, is now a conception that every serious student of Mor-monism must engage.

One of the many revelations in Mauss's memoir is the account of how he came to his theory as an outgrowth of his own professional development that matured over a number of years. His account can be thought of as a case study of how a Mormon scholar adapts ideas from his secular professional work to a church subject. Mormons do not often see the purely professional side of the people who write their histories and debate their theology. They see them on Sunday, as it were, when they are talking Latter-day Saint (LDS). They have only a skimpy idea of what they do the rest of the week in their professional lives. *Shift-ing Borders* unveils Mauss at his weekday work, helping us to understand where *The Angel and the Beehive* came from.

We learn how Mauss rather heroically kept at his graduate work in sociology at the University of California at Berkeley while raising a family, teaching in a community college, and holding responsibilities at church. Along the way he tells us of his association with leading sociologists of what came to be called the Berke-ley Circle, headed by Charles Y. Glock, their chief mentor, and featuring such luminaries as Rodney Stark. These scholars, notably Stark, took on the leading thesis about religion in modern times, namely, the prediction that religion was doomed to extinction. Eventually, secularism would weaken and then dissipate active religious faith. Stark and his colleagues pointed to the fact that in the late twentieth century, this was not happening as predicted. Far from dissipating, religion was reasserting itself, albeit in a new form. The old-line religious denominations were faltering, to be sure, but new religious movements (NRMs) were thriving. A good part of the theoretical work of the Berkeley Circle was to explain how new religions managed to grow in the face of supposedly lethal secular forces.

Mauss entered into this religious ferment because he happened to be at Berkeley for his graduate work and because his Mormon background gave him access to one of the most hardy of the NRMs. Mauss took up the conception of social tension and made it work for Mormonism. The Berkeley theorists postulated that successful movements stood apart from conventional religions. They were not bland versions of standard orthodoxies but deviants, distinguished in rather demanding ways from the world around them. Their appeal and strength came from these strains with the ambient culture. However, if they went too far from social norms, the strain would become more than adherents could bear and the movement would decline. Success depended on keeping the strain level at just the right pitch.

Mauss's contribution to Mormon scholarship and to sociological theory was to argue that over time, Mormonism had adjusted the degree of strain with the rest of the world. It did not just stake out its position and hold it but relieved the strain when it rose too high and then heightened it again when Mormonism seemed to be sinking into conventionality. Into that framework he placed the course of Mormon history over the twentieth century. Following the official demise of polygamy, Mormonism sought to assimilate for the first half of the century, but when those amazing Mormons went too far toward acceptance by the 1950s, the strain level was raised by emphasizing differences again. The latest chapter in this theoretical formulation, written by Mauss after the publication of *The Angel and the Beehive,* has Mormonism reversing course once more and moving back toward assimilation by relieving the strain just a little. This ongoing adjustment phenomenon had not been recognized by sociologists before Mauss discovered it in Mormonism. Now it has become a significant corollary to the theory of new religious movements.

Mauss's major work in Mormon sociology came late in his professional career, after he had proved his scholarly competence working on other subjects. The Latter-day Saint audience for Mormon scholarship may not realize that scholars outside of the church system live in a professional world where they are fighting for survival as fiercely as rising entrepreneurs putting a business together or lawyers bucking for partner in a firm. Although his dissertation had dealt with Mormon racism, he put that aside when he began to publish. Mauss proved himself with pioneering work on alcoholism, on the student protests of the 1960s, and on religious groups like the "Jesus Freaks" and the Vineyard Christian Fellowship. His best Mormon work, including publication of a much-expanded version of his PhD dissertation as *All Abraham's Children,* came long after he had earned tenure and a full professorship at Washington State University.

Along the way, however, he was always interested in Mormon applications. For a time he hoped that his skills in survey research and analysis might be put to use by the church. In the 1960s and 1970s, he participated on a committee studying inactivity, especially in the Aaronic priesthood, and for a time thought he had made an impact. He proposed the idea that people act according to how they envision their future identities more than how they think of themselves in the present. Inactive Aaronic priesthood holders would be more likely to return to church activity if they could envision a future for themselves there. Using this reasoning, Mauss persuaded church leaders to adopt the term *prospective elders.* After this early success, however, his role as a consultant was reduced, and he had fewer opportunities to contribute. It is now apparent that he pioneered the use of survey-research techniques that were eventually widely used by the research wing of the Correlation Department.

During parts of Mauss's life, LDS intellectuals did not always enjoy an entirely comfortable place in the church. Devoted as he was, he was sometimes summoned by leaders to account for some of his scholarly publications on Mormon matters. Church leaders, not familiar with the ways of intellectuals and a little skeptical, did not immediately recognize these publications' potential usefulness. The hardest thing for ordinary Mormons to appreciate is the battle intellectuals are called upon to fight to make sense of the world. Their very effectiveness as intellectuals grows out of their commitment to ideas and evidence. Whereas most people want simple, clear conclusions in harmony with their own preconceptions, scholars have to deal with the evidence and hammer out ideas. The advice to "forget it" when they come across a troubling idea is precisely what they cannot do. Their work would be useless if they did not take these pains. Inevitably, there will be misunderstandings. Scholars seem stubborn and proud, whereas laypeople seem complacent and unaware. Even when both parties act with goodwill, it takes time to achieve mutual understanding.

As with all intellectuals, Mauss had his private battles to fight as well. His greatest early struggle was with "the social construction of reality," a notion that was sweeping the scholarly world at the time of his intellectual formation in graduate school. The words *social construction* mean that each society puts together its own version of reality rather than finding a fixed and unchangeable reality out there somewhere. Independent reality may exist with God, and be known by faith, but humans have no direct access to it via reason and science. Every truth we know comes through a human mind embedded in a society of some kind. We have to accept the principle that every conception of reality is contingent on the conditions in the society where that conception originates. One can imagine the impact of this realization on a young Mormon scholar who had been raised on belief in absolute truth. One of the most intriguing passages in the memoir is the account of how Mauss coped with this crisis.

Mauss always stood at the shifting border between the university and the church, ready to step across on to the church side whenever he could make a difference. As he moved more into the realm of Mormon scholarship, he also took on institutional causes. During a crucial decade on the *Dialogue* board of directors, he helped to save the journal when it was foundering financially and organizationally. He worked to moderate the journal's tone and institute checks and balances in its governance. Later he offered his services gratis to teach in the Claremont Graduate University's Mormon studies program when it was first getting off the ground, and he remains active in the Latter-day Saint Council there. He is the model good citizen in the realm of Mormon intellectual life.

I taught a course with Armand Mauss at Claremont. He had a reputation among the students as a demanding teacher. He required a pile of reading and insisted on mastery of it. He had not yielded to the grade inflation that has infected virtually every college in the country in recent decades. If a student earned only a C in his estimation, that was the grade he or she received. But the students loved him. They knew he was honest. He would speak nothing he did not truly believe based on the evidence. He did not dress up the story to make it more attractive. Most of all, they knew that behind the tough exterior, there was a kind heart. He was interested in their welfare.

Students came to trust his judgment—and he had judgments about everything. He always had a lot to say. Once again, he has a lot to say in this memoir. We catch a glimpse here, as well as anywhere, of a Mormon scholar and intellectual at work in our time.

RICHARD BUSHMAN
New York City
March 2012

I BEGIN THIS MEMOIR WITH A DEGREE OF TREPIDATION. IT IS A RISKY EN-
terprise for more than one reason. Any autobiographical venture makes its author
vulnerable in ways that do not occur in other genres. One obvious risk is that
the author loses fairness and balance in his or her narrative in favor of unduly
self-serving interpretations, a constant temptation that I have done my best to
curtail here—though the reader will have to be the final judge. A second risk is
the exposure of the author's ego as he or she removes the veil over many personal
tastes, prejudices, and even misfeasance that need not be revealed in more detached genres. In academic and scholarly writing, which has been my main forte
until now, I have rarely felt that anything personal was at stake. To the extent that
my work was conceptual or theoretical in nature, I could depend on logical argument, often supported by references to theories and data in the published work
of other scholars. To the extent that my work depended on facts and data, I could
find security in the empirical methodology of my craft, which (assuming correct
execution) would minimize the risk of serious error in drawing my conclusions.
In any case, as long as the focus was on theories, methods, and data, it was not
on me as a scholar or as a protagonist. That is ideally the academic way. Indeed,
even a novelist or writer of fiction is typically not writing about himself and need
not feel exposed to scrutiny *as a person*—except, perhaps, for those daring novelists who occasionally attempt "semifictionalized" autobiographies and thus open
themselves to uncharitable criticisms for *both* their semifictional *and* their autobiographical efforts!

My sense of personal vulnerability is heightened by a professional flaw that is
especially embarrassing for one who has dwelled as often as I have in the halls of
academic history: I have not kept a journal or diary in which I have recorded my
life's experiences on a daily, weekly, or any other regular basis—a failing I deeply
regret as I undertake this autobiographical effort. I did keep a haphazard diary
during my two years as a Mormon missionary, but it is embarrassingly superficial,
with only four or five lines a day on very small pages. I have also submitted periodically to various interviews of one kind or another about my experiences, but

not nearly enough through the years to provide more than sketchy overviews of a few important developments. Much about my career can also be found among my personal papers now archived at the Utah State Historical Society. Yet all too much of what I shall report here will draw upon personal memory, which (considering that I am now in my eighties) might leave a lot to be desired—though I understand that long-term memory in older people is more reliable than short-term memory.

Even if that is so, it is a mixed blessing for an old man to rely on a long memory: The disadvantage is that he is not likely to recall important details of events in the distant past, or at least his *perceptions of them as they occurred*—especially his very youthful perceptions. On the other hand, the reader has the benefit of the author's *years of reflection* on those events, which sometimes provide a much fuller understanding and appreciation for them. Ideally, of course, both the earlier and the more mature perceptions—and how they differ—would be offered by the conscientious autobiographer, but at this stage all I can do is apologize for having been such a poor diarist and do my best to compensate with support for my recollections from other sources still available to me (including friends or colleagues with whom some of the events were shared). Given this predicament, I think of my efforts here far more as *reminiscences* than as history. Of course, my reminiscences are also supported wherever possible by such primary and secondary documentation as might be relevant and available.

I am well aware that much that I have included here will be of interest mainly to other academics, especially the occasional discussions of abstract sociological theories and debates underlying some of my publications. These will be found mainly in chapters 2 and 3, but to a somewhat lesser extent also in chapters 4 and 5—and even elsewhere now and then. To those readers who might find these sections tedious, I can only apologize and hope that the other material in those chapters—and in the book more generally—will eventually vindicate the readers' persistence in trying to follow the more theoretical and technical passages.

In using the imagery of "travels and journeys" in this account, I am implicitly placing much of my experience in the intellectual "borderlands" between institutional Mormonism and other worlds. One consequence of traveling often through these borderlands is an accumulated sense of marginality in both worlds. I do not mean that I feel marginal to the LDS religion. To the contrary, I feel deeply steeped in that religion—and far more knowledgeable about it than is the vast majority of the church's membership. Rather, I think of myself as "marginal" in the following senses. First, although I have participated for half a lifetime in the broad and amorphous body of scholars who have published on LDS history and culture, I have done so from outside the inner circle of institutional scholars employed by the church, who have been far more privy than I to the ecclesiastical politics that have influenced the nature and direction of sponsored research. I count many of them as brilliant friends and colleagues—and occasionally valuable informants—but I have never been one of them.

Second, I have almost always been an active leader or teacher at the local level in the LDS Church, including stints of several years each in the roles of bishop's counselor, branch president, and high priest leader, but I have never been part of what is usually considered the "hierarchy" at the stake, regional, or general level. I have numerous close friends and relatives who have served at all those levels, and who have often helped me to see the church and its workings through their eyes, but I have been spared the self-sacrifice—and the occasional compromises of intellectual independence—that go with callings in the hierarchy.

Finally, especially in my more mature years, I have felt keenly the social and intellectual marginality that is the typical fate of those who try to straddle the intellectual and the devotional plots in the ecclesiastical garden. I have learned to take personal responsibility for my own intellectual and spiritual nourishment, rather than looking to the church for all that, and I have come to accept the reality—with equanimity but without condescension—that most of my fellow Saints do not understand why I read what I read or write what I write.

Throughout the book, I document some of my experiences by referring to unpublished papers that I have collected over the years. A decade or so ago, I archived many of these papers at the Utah State Historical Society, where they are readily available to anyone wishing to review them. There are yet other personal papers, however, that I am still retaining in my files at home. I would be willing to make most of these available on request to interested or curious readers, but I have retained them for the time being. Eventually, these too will be placed in the historical society's archive.

Acknowledgments

AN INCONSPICUOUS BUT DETERMINING PRESENCE THROUGHOUT THIS book is Ruth E. Hathaway, my steadfast and intrepid wife and partner of more than six decades. Without her, this memoir would not have been possible, if only because the career from which it draws would not have been possible. Beyond that obvious acknowledgment, however, I will be eternally in her debt for her loyalty and support during all these years, and particularly during periods in our lives when my choices and decisions created burdens and complications for her. Among her most valued and indispensable contributions was her willing acceptance of the main share of parental responsibilities for our large family, which she always managed with skill and equanimity, earning the lifelong adoration of our children. This memoir is dedicated to her.

In the career reviewed here, many friends, academic and otherwise, are remembered by name with appreciation for the support, guidance, and inspiration they have provided me at important junctures. Countless others also remain in my debt, though unnamed. Then, in the actual production of this book, I have benefited by the contributions of many other scholars and colleagues, starting with editor Peter DeLaFosse and those associated with him at the University of Utah Press, particularly my skillful copy editor, Annette Wenda, who so patiently tolerated my many last-minute changes. Their encouragement was a constant source of support and inspiration to me. The favorable responses from the four external referees solicited by the press were, of course, crucial in the decision to adopt and publish this memoir. Many other colleagues read parts or all of this manuscript, offering very helpful critiques and observations. Chief among these were Richard L. Bushman, author of the insightful foreword, and Levi S. Peterson, himself one of Utah's most gifted biographers and autobiographers, with whom I shared so many important experiences at *Dialogue,* and whose laudatory comments on the book's cover will have attracted many potential readers.

Prologue

The LDS scholar has his citizenship in the Kingdom, but carries his passport into the professional world—not the other way around.

—Neal A. Maxwell

ELDER NEAL A. MAXWELL RECOGNIZED—BETTER THAN MOST MORMON
leaders of the twentieth century—the predicament of scholars who grow up
deeply steeped in the teachings of the Church of Jesus Christ of Latter-day
Saints.[1] At first, we understand the church to be God's kingdom on earth, but
then, as young adults, we venture into the alien intellectual territory of the secular, scientific world. Maxwell was fond of using the metaphor of journeys and
passports to describe such ventures. In one of his analogies, Jerusalem represents
the world of spiritual truth and learning, whereas Athens represents that of secular scholarship. LDS scholars, he insisted, "should have our citizenship in Jerusalem and have a passport to Athens" and should ultimately "draw more deeply on
our Hebrew roots than our Greek roots."[2] In referring thus to those two ancient
capitals, he was obviously recognizing that Mormons, at least those of American
or European origin, are products of a cultural and intellectual heritage deriving
from both of those classical traditions.

What follows here is a reminiscence of my own journeys between these two
worlds and why my "passport," though it has never expired, has nevertheless become somewhat tattered from frequent use. Not only has the intellectual establishment in Athens sometimes seemed wary of accepting my passport when I have
entered as a scholar in religious (especially Mormon) studies, but I have often
found suspicion about the authenticity of my passport even when I have tried to
negotiate it in Jerusalem itself—in the Mormon ecclesiastical kingdom—a kingdom, furthermore, in which the borders have seemed more narrow and heavily
guarded at some times than at others. Although I was never persona non grata in
any of my sojourns, I learned that some intellectual territories in which I traveled
were considered terra non grata in my home capital—or at least terra incognita—
requiring that my passport receive special scrutiny whenever I was coming home
from one of those locations. But enough metaphor. Join me as I recapitulate some
of my journeys.

My long intellectual life has occurred in a dialectical relationship with many cultural and ecclesiastical changes in the LDS world. Growing up outside of Utah, I became aware early in life that being religious had not only a devotional component but also an intellectual one, to which I sometimes resorted in defending my religion against the jests and jabs of friends at school. My appreciation for the intellectual component in my religion was strengthened by my experience as a young missionary for the church in the late 1940s, when the standard proselytizing approach appealed far more to the investigator's intellect, and less to his emotions, than contemporary missionary programs do. Even as a university student seeking advanced degrees, I saw the church and its leadership as supportive of intellectual inquiry about both doctrinal and organizational matters, so I was not prepared for the retrenchment process that set in during the 1960s and 1970s, as more and more overt pressure was exerted by certain church leaders to restrain the independent public speaking and writing of its own scholarly members, even the most devout among them. As the limits of acceptable topics and discourse narrowed with the passage of time, I occasionally bumped up against them as I sought space where my work might be regarded as constructive rather than subversive. In general, I seem to have found some such space, but in the process I became rather jaded as I recognized increasingly the importance of the human, bureaucratic features of the church as a complex organization.

Throughout my interactions with church leaders and members, I succeeded in avoiding formal disciplinary action over my published work, but I did experience a variety of formal and informal expressions of displeasure by leaders and members from time to time, all the way to the start of the new century. Nor have my critics always been the most orthodox. Sometimes I have found myself at odds even with my fellow travelers among the "alternate voices," but almost always with goodwill. Criticisms from various sources, however, have been occasionally interspersed also with expressions of appreciation, even from certain church leaders. Such has occurred especially in recent years, as the leadership has gradually changed through normal generational turnover and by a growing appreciation for the potential of well-meaning, independent scholars to be helpful to the church and its public image. The following account will indicate how and why my intellectual passages between the church and the world have been affected by a variety of ecclesiastical leaders and a changing leadership culture.

The first chapter provides a biographical overview, with emphasis on my adult years. Then the major events and experiences in my adult life are unfolded in several subsequent chapters, which are arranged more or less chronologically, with some overlap.

Chapter 1 | NOT A BORING LIFE

I AM A SUBJECT AND CITIZEN BY BIRTH OF THE SPIRITUAL KINGDOM IDEN-
tified in the prologue, having been "born in the covenant" to devout Mormon
parents. They, in turn, came from recent European convert families who had emi-
grated to Utah around 1890. My maternal line is entirely Swedish, the product of
Linds and Westlunds. My paternal line, Jewish until an expedient conversion to
Catholicism about 1650, came out of the German Pfalz region of what was then
western Bavaria but has frequently also been known as the Alsace-Lorraine territory of France, as it is, in fact, at the present time. My German-speaking people
left Europe in 1866 and had a prosperous twenty-year sojourn in Nebraska before their conversion to Mormonism and their move to Utah. There my Mauss
grandfather married a woman from an English convert family named Wright.[1] I
calculate that this background makes me only a third-generation Mormon, so I
can claim no deep roots in the Mormon pioneer nobility that founded Utah after
the early years of religious persecution. I have no ancestors named Smith, Young,
Pratt, Richards, Kimball, Romney, Tanner, or the like.

Nevertheless, I am Utah born, and I have always identified with my Utah
heritage. While I was yet a toddler, my parents left Utah and their families to
become part of the great Mormon diaspora that occurred between the two world
wars. In 1931, as the Great Depression was well under way, my father moved us to
Southern California, and then, five years later, to Oakland in the San Francisco
Bay Area. My upbringing was thus almost entirely in California, where I had a
rich public school education in a setting of considerable ethnic and religious diversity for its time. Since my parents were practically the only ones in their respective families to leave Utah, and we made very few trips back to visit, I grew up
without really knowing any of my cousins, and (with few exceptions) my aunts
and uncles were virtual strangers. This was especially the case on my father's side,
for his parents died while I was still small, and such visits as we made to Utah
tended to focus on mother's long-living Swedish folks. Later on, in middle age,
I made a deliberate effort to cultivate relationships with my Utah kin—to my
great delight, I would add—but I reached maturity mostly without the company

of relatives and surrounded by non-Mormons. That made my upbringing quite different from that experienced by most Utah Mormons, including my cousins.

My father, Vinal G. Mauss, was a self-made man who left school after the tenth grade in order to help support his family of nine siblings. He idolized his parents and spoke often of the warm and loving family life in which he had grown up, but it was a family that had only modest expectations for the children. Free agency, mutual support, humor, and a reluctance to pass judgment were more important values than worldly achievement in that family. Hard work was, of course, a necessity for that entire generation of Americans, immigrants or not, and opportunities for upward mobility in that economy came mainly from one's own ingenuity, ambition, good luck, or some combination of these. Rough-hewn though he was, somehow my father embraced a vision of how life might be better for him, and after his LDS mission to Japan in the early 1920s,[2] he launched his own lifelong program of self-improvement, starting with a year or two at LDS Business College. That much specialized training prepared him for accounting jobs (then called "bookkeeping") and led later to a successful career as a broker in real estate and insurance. Meanwhile, he served in several church callings, eventually as bishop of the Oakland Ward. It was this life and career that he put on hold (at age forty-nine and at great personal cost) to accept a call from the LDS Church to return to Japan as mission president—a responsibility that then covered the entire Far East. For me, as his eldest of three children, his life exemplified the values of faith, religious devotion, patience, charity, and tolerance, in addition to those I mentioned above as part of his family's general heritage. Yet he seemed to exceed his own family's expectations in his persistent striving for a better material life and in a quest for new ideas and opportunities that might make that improvement possible. Among my father's attributes that influenced me the most in my life were his persistence and his refusal to be discouraged by setbacks in the pursuit of important goals. To the extent that I have acquired any of his other attributes, they have been, alas, slow in coming and rather incomplete.[3]

My mother, Ethel Louise Lind, was very different but admirable in her own ways. Her immigrant parents, especially her formidable Swedish mother, were determined that their children would be equipped for success and respectability in the newly adopted country. Through careful scrimping, saving, and sacrifice, her parents managed to purchase eight acres of land in south Salt Lake County within about the first decade of their marriage. Mother grew up as the second eldest in a family of four daughters and one son. All were pushed constantly by their competitive matriarch to learn the ways of polite society and to achieve beyond the usual expectations for the youth of their generation. All of them attended the University of Utah for at least two years, and the daughters all became schoolteachers before marriage. Most resumed that same career later in life as well. The son pursued a successful career at the managerial level in the grocery business. All of the daughters showed great musical talent and were in some demand as vocal performers. My mother, in particular, began a serious career that might have led her into grand opera. She had leads in operas performed at the university under Professor Thomas Giles, including most notably the role of Delilah in Saint-Saëns's *Samson and Delilah* in the early 1920s. During 1925 and 1926 she competed successfully in contests sponsored by the National Federation of Music Clubs, first regionally and then at national contests held in Chicago and Philadelphia.[4] At one of the national contests, presumably in 1926, she won a scholarship to the Eastman Opera School in Rochester, New York.[5] Her Old Country parents, however, for all their upward striving, insisted that instead she come back to Utah and find a husband. She found one in my father, who had the patience and the emotional and intellectual stability to deal gently with her insecurities, unfulfilled musical ambitions, and emotional responses to stress. He, for his part, benefited by her refinement, superior education, loyalty, and devotion to church and family. Actually, so did I. I shall always be grateful to my mother for instilling in me a love for classical music and a love of learning for its own sake. Some of my happiest childhood memories are of her reading to me, then teaching me early to read, and frequently answering questions that I had not even asked about life and the world.

A Child of the Great Depression and the Wars

My mother and father were married in 1927. I came along a year later and my sister two years after that. Through a dispute with a domineering boss, my father lost a relatively secure job in Salt Lake City two years after the onset of the 1929 economic crash. With considerable reluctance, especially on Mother's part, they decided to relocate in California, where there seemed to be somewhat more economic opportunity. They left behind a dream home that they had been able to acquire as newlyweds in the Highland Park area of Salt Lake City with the help of Mother's resourceful Swedish parents. For Mother especially, giving up that home was yet another deeply felt loss after the musical career she had set aside for her marriage. For the first five years after our move to Southern California in 1931, we lived in a series of cheap rentals while Father struggled from one temporary job to another to provide a hand-to-mouth existence for the family. The great Long Beach earthquake of 1933 gave him one of his few jobs of any duration as a member of the salvage and cleanup crew. He tried and failed to launch a family restaurant business, with Mother as his first cook. He finally got hired at the cash register of a grocery firm and worked his way up to a clerical position on a traveling inventory crew in that business. After our move to northern California in 1936, he continued that line of work, and he was never again without regular employment. As my sister and I got a little older, Mother renewed her aspirations for a career in music and began periodic lessons with various voice coaches.

Her main coach during this period was one Mark Robinson, who lived in Provo, Utah, before moving to the Los Angeles area. I know nothing about his career as a singer, if he ever had one, but he was active as a choir director in LDS circles during the 1930s and 1940s. For Mother, however, his main importance was that he was a disciple (and sometime student) of Dr. Douglas Stanley, a New York medical doctor and voice coach who had invented a controversial new method by which singers could learn to project their voices by controlling the position of the tongue and opening the throat. Mother had never met Stanley personally, but she was an avid reader of his book *The Voice* and convinced of the efficacy of his method. Mother learned as much as she could about this "new method" from Mark Robinson and used it in teaching her own students (including me and my sister on occasion).[6]

In 1940, as the economy improved, Father was finally able to purchase a home again, and Mother, ten years after her second child was born, delivered her third, a baby brother. His arrival was a joyous event, but it also put an end, once and for all, to Mother's dreams of an extradomestic career in music. Thereafter, she contented herself with coaching younger vocal talent and with periodic performances at special events under local LDS auspices. Yet Mother never seemed the same to me, never again so hopeful and energetic, as when her dreams of the operatic stage were alive, unrealistic though they might always have been. My younger brother recalls a childhood richly nurtured by his mother's love and attention, much as I had also enjoyed as a small child, but during his childhood I was a teenager, and my own relationship with Mother then entered a rather turbulent period. At times, it seemed as though she could never forgive me for having reached puberty! In retrospect, however, I have come to understand and sympathize far more with the predicament of a talented and sensitive woman, longing for an artistic career that could never be fulfilled, delivering an unexpected child on the verge of middle age, and dealing with two teenagers, including a boy who was fully her match in willfulness!

Indeed, I remember myself as a willful and difficult child, always testing the boundaries that my parents tried to establish. The prospect of corporal punishment, common in their generation, always lurked as a resort in their discipline, but it was almost never used, even in some egregious cases of disobedience on my part. Yet they never gave me reason to doubt their ultimate love and support, and I took advantage of their forbearance. My parents also had very different approaches to parenting. My father was the soul of patience, always preferring unemotional reasoning and persuasion. Mother, when challenged, became indignant and emotional, sometimes responding with a slap, but more often with vindictiveness and a temporary withdrawal of affection. Her love at times seemed conditional, but it was always restored eventually. Nor were my parents always consistent in family rules, or in their enforcement, so I had plenty of opportunities to play off one against the other. During my school years, they trusted me to roam with my buddies for hours at a time, wherever I wished to go in the surrounding neighborhoods, and even in the city at large, which was not considered particularly hazardous in those now-distant days of safe and well-ordered California cities.

Somehow I reached age eighteen without getting into any serious trouble, and after high school graduation I took a job driving a small delivery truck for an auto parts company while trying to decide whether to go on a mission for the church or stay home and marry the latest girl with whom I had become enamored. As luck or Providence would have it, a lover's quarrel prompted the young woman to leave me for a visit of several weeks to her grandparents in Utah. My father, then also my ward bishop, aided and abetted by the stake president—and with ample prodding from my mother—moved with astonishing and uncharacteristic alacrity to get me an almost immediate mission call from the church. I was still only eighteen. By the time my girlfriend returned, my mission call was in hand and an elaborate farewell program at church had been scheduled. Our amorous relationship did not survive my mission, to the ultimate and enormous benefit of us both, and the mission proved a major turning point in my life.

THE MISSION EXPERIENCE

My mission call was not a total surprise.[7] After all, it had been anticipated in family conversations for my entire life. It was expected of Mormon boys in my generation. I had become ambivalent about it only because of my romantic attachment and because of the uncertainty during my teen years that I would be available, given that our country was at war and all the boys just older than I were being drafted for military service. World War II ended, however, as I entered my final year of high school, and the romance was eventually put on hold. So a mission it was. I was a religious boy despite my rebellious tendencies, and I had been reared in a California Mormon community that had richly nurtured me socially, intellectually, and spiritually. The Oakland Ward, where I had lived for more than the previous decade, had a membership drawn from the working and lower-middle classes, with very few members of greater social status. All were hardworking, earnest, and (for the most part) religiously devout. From among them had come my most important ecclesiastical leaders, teachers, and youth counselors—all devoted volunteers, of course. I could not and would not let them down.

After two weeks (or less) of orientation and instruction during March 1947 at the small mission training home in Salt Lake City, I was set apart as a missionary by Levi Edgar Young, of the First Council of Seventy. I traveled with several other missionaries for four days and nights by railroad to Cambridge, Massachusetts, headquarters of the church's New England Mission—which then covered all the maritime provinces of Canada as well as the six US states of that region. I arrived as a strongly committed, if ignorant, Mormon boy, still with many juvenile traits and not yet fully sobered by my new responsibilities. The mission president, William H. Reeder, had had a career as a judge in municipal and juvenile courts. He took immediate umbrage at my youthfully jocular manner and determined to keep an eye on me. He eventually assigned me to work with a mature companion named Warren Turner in Torrington, Connecticut, where there had not been any missionaries for some time. After several weeks of tracting, we found only a teenage girl to be interested in our message. (She eventually joined the church but only some years later).[8] Among my most important experiences in that town was an encounter with a Protestant minister (Episcopal vicar, as I recall, though he might have been Congregational—my memory is not clear on this). Over the resistance of my senior companion, we called at the parsonage or rectory, as the residence was usually called, and we were greeted by a dignified clergyman who reluctantly invited us in. What followed, at least from my viewpoint, was a debacle that had a profound impact on my faith, to say nothing of my ego. The vicar dealt with us kindly. He recognized and seemed to value our sincerity and intellectual naïveté as he listened patiently to my recitation of the conventional Latter-day Saint understanding of the organization of the primitive Christian church, complete with proof-text verses from the New Testament.

When I had finished, he said he had a few questions, which raised my hopes until I realized that his "questions" all had to do with such matters as the historical sources on which I had based my presentation, my understanding of the various functions of ecclesiastical roles within the primitive church, and my grasp of the meaning of certain terms in ancient Greek (starting with *ecclesia*). Then came a thirty-minute tutorial on the historical and linguistic difficulties of figuring out how closely the organization and functions of the primitive Christian church resembled any modern model, LDS or otherwise. I was stunned and humbled. I had had no idea that so much knowledge was available outside of LDS literature on subjects of such great importance to the LDS religion itself.[9] That entire experience left me with two resolutions that have guided my intellectual explorations ever since: I would never again enter a controversy so ill-equipped to defend my own convictions, and I would never again consider one interpretation of the scriptures—by my religion or any other—as the only authoritative word on anything. The first resolution meant that I would spend as much of my free time as possible in local libraries during my mission, and with the second resolution, I was fated, from that point on, to live in a certain intellectual tension with the conventional understandings of some of my fellow Mormons and our leaders.

After only a couple of months in Torrington, I was transferred to Franklin, New Hampshire, and a new mission president was sent to replace Judge Reeder (much to my relief). The successor was S. Dilworth Young, also of the First Council of Seventy (like his cousin who had set me apart). "Uncle Dil" (as we called him only *after* release from our missions!) had had a professional career with the Boy Scouts of America before his call to full-time church service. He knew boys, and he knew how to cultivate our loyalty and devotion. As a grandson of Brigham Young on both his paternal and maternal lines, and with a wife, Gladys, from the storied Pratt family, he was deeply steeped in the lore of early Mormon historical events, locations, and leaders in New England, and he favored us with stories of what and who had been important in some of the very towns where he sent us to work. At times it seemed that we were walking the very roads where those nineteenth-century leaders had walked and were recapitulating their experiences as the Lord's servants, giving us a strong spiritual—even mystical—identification with them.

We were not prepared, however, nor were our families back home, to learn of President Young's decision to give us an even more authentic taste of early Mormon missionary work: We were soon informed that during all but the winter months we would travel the highways and byways of the countryside by foot, as did the missionaries of old. That is, we would give up our apartments in town for seven months or so each year and travel homeless throughout the rural areas of New England, which had been largely neglected for decades in favor of urban proselytizing. Virtually all of us young men agreed to try the new program, for Young inspired such confidence that we would have followed him anywhere. My sketchy missionary diary indicates that about half of my entire mission was spent in this "country tracting," as we called it.[10] We each carried a small valise containing changes of underwear, socks, shirts, and missionary literature, along with a large umbrella, not only for the sudden summer rains of New England but also as protection against suspicious dogs. We would visit the homes in each village and all farmhouses along our route, seeking audience for our message—and preferably even the free use of a town hall or church to which we could invite interested investigators for small meetings. To the frequent question "Where are you boys staying?" we would be prepared to respond that we were traveling in the New Testament mode, "without purse or scrip," depending on the people for our food and lodging. Truth to tell, though, we did resort to begging on several occasions, usually at a motel that was not full, and I recall that in several extreme situations, with our faith wavering, we even paid for a night's lodging when ten o'clock arrived with no other prospects.

Yet it is a credit to good old-fashioned New England hospitality that in my experience, we failed on only a very few nights to get offers of meals and lodging during my entire mission. On three or four occasions, this meant improvising some kind of shelter in the woods or in a remote barn, and we often washed up in small streams. Many of the villages were connected by telephone through "party lines," so by simultaneously ringing all the phones on the line, the people in one village could forewarn those in the next village of our pending arrival. On a couple of occasions, a delegation with pitchforks met us as we entered a village and warned us just to keep walking through town without stopping. We soon learned also that we could avoid a night in jail for "vagrancy" by carrying enough money for a night's lodging, as required by local ordinances, even though we would usually not actually have to spend the money. This country tracting was not easy, but it had a way of "separating the men from the boys." It yielded many a faith-promoting story, and for me six converts from those villages, plus a solid conviction that I had been doing the Lord's work (a "testimony," in Mormon-speak). Such a system would not work now, some sixty years later, for Yankee hospitality has long since given way to well-grounded urban suspicion and cynicism throughout our society. The missionary boys today are different, too. Neither they nor their parents would likely accept the hazards and discomforts of missionary work in that mode. Most with whom I served in New England, though, were military veterans, much older than nineteen or twenty, for whom country tracting was not particularly daunting after bloody combat in war.

There was much about our experience in this mission that was freelancing and unconventional, especially compared to the tightly trained and supervised missionaries of today. There was no standard teaching approach like the so-called Anderson Plan that was introduced a few years later (and its many successors since). We taught "as the Spirit moved us," adapting strategies and messages as seemed appropriate in given cases. A couple of examples (of many that could be offered) will have to suffice here: During 1947 the church was celebrating the centennial of the Saints' first arrival into the Salt Lake Valley, attracting a certain amount of favorable national publicity (including Brigham Young on the cover of *Time* that summer). One July morning my companion David R. Kezerian and I happened into a general store in a small New Hampshire town seeking to buy postage stamps. While waiting in line, we overheard a conversation between the proprietor and an anguished customer, who was bemoaning the fact that he was in charge of the lunch program soon to take place at the local Rotary Club meeting, but an important speaker had just canceled a promised appearance. I had noticed a nearby rack containing *Time* with the picture of Brigham Young, so I stepped over and picked up a copy, walked quickly back to the counter, and interrupted the conversation to introduce myself and ask whether the Rotary Club might be interested in a presentation about this magazine article. It did not take long for the Rotary official to accept our offer, with much relief, and to promise a free lunch in the bargain for my companion and me. Each of us spoke for about fifteen minutes, relating the great westward Mormon trek to the New England origins of Joseph Smith, Brigham Young, and the rise of Mormonism. Word got around afterward, and we were given several other offers during that summer to speak at Rotary Clubs and other civic groups in nearby small towns (with regular offers also of overnight food and lodging!).

In country tracting, we obviously had a lot of flexibility in our schedules and full control over how we spent our time. During the summer of 1948, I was serving in eastern Massachusetts with Ardean W. Watts, a gifted musician who eventually had a distinguished career at the University of Utah and in the Utah Symphony. Ardean had brought a tuning wrench with him on his mission, and he would sometimes offer to tune pianos at halls or homes in order to gain access. On some of these occasions, I would sing hymns to his accompaniment, which usually softened up our hosts and their friends to listen to our message and offer us their hospitality. Late that summer, we decided to write a missionary hymn together. I created the rhyming lyrics for four stanzas and a chorus, and Ardean wrote the music. Titling it "The Lord Has Called Me to Serve Him," we sent it off to President Young at the mission home in Cambridge, asking if we could organize a chorus to sing the hymn at the next mission conference. Rather than castigating us for the time we had wasted on the hymn in place of tracting, he gathered his family and mission home staff around the piano to try it out,[11] and later that fall it was indeed sung by a mission chorus under the baton of Elder Watts. To my knowledge, it has been sung in public only twice since then—at the fiftieth anniversary and reunion of President Young's missionaries on May 17, 1997, and at the July 1999 annual Sunstone Symposium in Salt Lake City.[12] Although Ardean and I have taken different paths in our religious journeys, we have remained devoted friends since those youthful days when we came together to offer our beloved mission president a token of our devotion to him and to the cause of Zion.

At the end of my mission, I had to do some serious thinking about my future. I thought about the teaching profession, since I had come to enjoy the teaching and public preaching I had done during my mission. Yet I had also acquired from my mother a love for music, especially classical music, even though I had disappointed her by dropping my piano lessons in favor of sports and girls during high school. My musical education thereafter had consisted mainly of voice coaching from my mother supplemented by singing in choirs at school and at church. Nevertheless, at Mother's urging, I arranged to visit Dr. Douglas Stanley (mentioned earlier in this chapter) during a tour of New York City with Dwain Bracken immediately after we were released from our missions in New England. For ten dollars, Stanley gave me a half hour of voice testing and consultation, and he permitted me to stay on some three hours to witness several lessons with some of his regular students.[13] He seemed to think I had some potential for opera, but it became clear to me, from the entire experience, including conversations with some of his students, how totally my life would be preoccupied by preparing for, and living through, an operatic career. There would be very little of my time and energy left for family, church, or anything else. I was simply not prepared to make such an all-consuming investment. Once back home in California, in any case, all such thoughts became moot when I decided to go with my family to Japan.[14]

An Unexpected Sojourn in Japan

After a hiatus of twenty-four years, the Japan Mission of the LDS Church was officially reopened in 1948 under Edward L. Clissold, who had earlier been president both of the temple in Hawaii and of the missionary work among the Japanese Hawaiians. During the war, he had been called to active duty out of the naval reserve. After the war, as an officer in the administration of the American occupation, his connections enabled him to help round up the scattered Mormon flock in Japan and to start preparations for a resumption of LDS missionary work. When he was asked by the church in 1947 to head the newly formed mission, he accepted the call with the understanding that he would be able to serve only a short term before returning to his affairs in Hawaii. After he arrived in Japan early in 1948, Clissold proved extremely capable and valuable in purchasing and renovating a mission home and grounds in a nice part of Tokyo and in getting the first batch of missionaries processed and assigned throughout the country. He left a strong foundation on which his successor could later build an extensive missionary program with church branches and districts all over the country. That successor was to be my father, Vinal G. Mauss.[15]

Within weeks of my return from my own mission in early 1949, my father, still bishop of the Oakland Ward, received a call from the president of the church asking him to accept an assignment as president of the newly opened mission in Japan.[16] I had been planning to enter the University of California as a freshman in the fall, having as yet had no college education. However, faced with the choice of staying in California or living in Japan for a while, I did not take long to decide that I would accompany my father and the family.[17] I went with no clear idea of what I would do there, or how long I would stay, but I couldn't resist the prospect of such an adventure, and I assumed that I would find some way to continue my education. As matters turned out, my sojourn in Japan lasted four and a half years, from the summer of 1949 to the very end of 1953. During that time, I managed to graduate from a highly regarded Jesuit university, serve two and a half years of a four-year enlistment in the United States Air Force, find a bride, and produce two children (with a third on the way).

Each of my many experiences in Japan is a somewhat complicated story in its own right, but here I will offer only a brief overview of them. First, however, some general context. I arrived in Japan just four years after the end of the war. A few bomb craters and other signs of the war's devastation were still apparent in Tokyo, but in large part the postwar government of Japan, under the determined guidance of General Douglas MacArthur and the US Occupation Forces, had restored to Japan the well-ordered civil society for which it was once (and still remains) justly renowned. Of course, US military personnel and agencies of all kinds were still highly visible during the entire occupation, but Japanese civil institutions and commerce were already starting to thrive. Foreigners of all kinds, not only Americans, were coming and going for diplomatic assignments, business ventures, educational experiences, employment as civilians in the occupation, or other purposes. My first objective was to find a college or university where instruction was offered in English. I soon learned of Sophia University, a Jesuit institution of long-standing in Japan, which had added, just before my arrival, an International Division in which courses were taught in the English language each day during afternoons and evenings. In correspondence with the registrar at the University of California, I was assured the Sophia was indeed an accredited university whose credits could readily be transferred later to UC.[18] My father paid my tuition for the first semester. For the rest of the year, I succeeded in working off the tuition with a clerical job in the office of the dean of the International Division. I majored in the history of the Far East and minored in philosophy (as all students of the Jesuits were expected to do). My experience with the Jesuits had an important influence on my life, and I will refer to that influence later.

My main source of income came eventually from a part-time job in the mornings at an army intelligence agency that was debriefing repatriated Japanese soldiers who had been trapped by the Soviets in Manchuria at the end of the war and held for four years in slave labor. The survivors returned to Japan with a wealth of knowledge about the Soviet industries at which they had been required to work, and my job was to write up reports in smooth English from the bilingual interviewers who had done the interrogations. For about the first two years, then, most of my time was devoted to my courses at Sophia and to my army job. I was also studying the Japanese language constantly and trying it out as often as possible on the patient and courteous natives. This pleasant and intellectually fulfilling life was suddenly interrupted by a letter I received in early 1951 from my California draft board requiring me to return home and report for service in the war that had erupted during the previous summer in Korea.

In exploring my options, I learned that my army job, my two years of college, and my growing knowledge of the Japanese language made me an attractive recruit for the US Air Force. For a commitment of four years, I was offered an enlistment under very favorable circumstances without having to leave Japan. These circumstances also included a waiver of basic training, permission to live off base in a Japanese neighborhood, a promotion in rank every three months (up to staff sergeant), and my tuition at Sophia. Accordingly, I simply started wearing a uniform, left my army job, began work at the 6004th Air Intelligence Service Squadron in another part of Tokyo, and continued my studies at Sophia. For the next two and a half years I enjoyed working alongside four Japanese consultants to an air force intelligence project on the Soviet Union, all of whom had been high-ranking Japanese military officers: Generals Issaku Imagawa and Takashi Aoki and Colonels Masakata Suzuki and Saburo Kato. All were highly educated, and Suzuki was a cultured poet and calligrapher. My wife, Ruth, and I were even entertained in their homes on a few occasions, and we kept in touch by mail with most of them for several years after our return to the United States. One of the most interesting things about getting to know them, however, was their alternative explanation for the causes of the recent war between our two countries.

During my earliest months in Japan, before my military connection, I frequently accompanied the regular LDS missionaries in their work and to the various Sunday schools that they were establishing among the Japanese converts.

I continued doing so (with diminishing frequency) for a year or so, despite my other obligations. Since I was living at the mission home, I became well acquainted with Tatsui Sato, a recent convert who was employed in translating all the LDS scriptures into contemporary Japanese. He was my earliest guide as I sought to navigate the gulf between the American and Japanese ways of understanding religious concepts. I also associated often with many of the first-wave missionaries of those days. One of these, Paul C. Andrus, had already become quite fluent in Japanese, with an especially strong grasp of the highly systematic grammar of that language, and he became my first language teacher.[19] I shall always be grateful to him for providing the solid foundation upon which my more formal study of the language at Sophia could be built.

My main connection with the church, however, was not through the mission to the Japanese but through the rather extensive parallel church program for LDS servicemen throughout the Far East. Organized in branches and districts, like any other mission, this program was able to serve both military and civilian members who were coming and going in Japan in rather large numbers. Even before I entered the air force, I was made president of the large LDS Service Branch in central Tokyo and eventually president also of the Central Honshu Service District of which that branch was a part. This branch had a membership of some two hundred, consisting of all the LDS military and civilian Americans and other foreigners known to be residing in the Tokyo area. About half that number attended the various Sunday meetings held in the large Army Chapel Center near the Japanese Diet Building (equivalent of the US Capitol). LDS members living in outlying military housing centers distant from the Army Chapel Center attended Sunday schools dependent on the main branch. As such a young man, I found that presiding over the auxiliaries and outlying Sunday schools for the men, women, and families in that branch, military and civilian, proved a rather complex matter, but it was an enormously rich and broadening experience. It certainly highlighted the ultimately egalitarian nature of the LDS priesthood: while branch president, I never held a military rank higher than staff sergeant, but I led many in my branch who were commissioned officers up to and including the rank of full colonel.

Yet my most important experience in the LDS servicemen's program was meeting Ruth Elinor Hathaway, a petite young blonde from southeastern Idaho who had also joined the US Air Force and been sent to a duty station in Tokyo. One Sunday evening in October 1950, she appeared in the audience as I was conducting a sacrament meeting, and I noticed immediately her broad, fetching smile, set off by charming dimples on either side. It did not take me long to make her acquaintance, and we soon became as inseparable as our respective military circumstances would permit. Our relationship deepened just as I finished a college course in poetry and as the country exploded in the cherry blossoms of spring.[20] We were married on May 2, 1951, in the nondenominational military chapel center where our usual church meetings were held.[21] My father, the mission president, officiated. We honeymooned in Nikko, known for years as a favorite honeymoon spot on the shores of Lake Chuzenji. Then we rented a small cottage on the edge of the mission-home compound, and both continued with our jobs in the air force until pregnancy provided the grounds for Ruth's early discharge from the service.

When we left Japan at the end of 1953 for reassignment in the state of Washington, we had two children and one more on the way. I had no idea what a jewel I had discovered in snatching Ruth, or what a loyal and long-suffering partner she would be for the next six decades and more. My intellectual life had expanded enormously from my experiences at a Jesuit university and my regular association with numerous Japanese friends, some of whom were LDS converts, of course, but many others were not. My religious life had been enriched by witnessing firsthand the nurturing power of LDS community life for servicemen and -women in an exotic locale far from home. Truly, my years in Japan had made me a more sophisticated, tolerant, and appreciative man, much more aware of the power of ideas that would always be in competition with those from my own LDS upbringing.[22] In some ways, the drastic changes in my life were symbolized by my two ocean voyages: The voyage *to Japan* with my father and family took two weeks on the luxury liner *President Cleveland,* with lavish amenities, a layover in Hawaii, and a summer Pacific Ocean as smooth as glass. The *return voyage,* on the military transport USNS *James O'Hara,* fortunately took a little less time, for we went across the northern Pacific in midwinter (with a stop at Adak Island), on a roiling sea, with a pregnant wife and two children, all seasick much of the time.

BACK TO CALIFORNIA

On leaving Japan, I still had a year and a half left of my four-year military obligation, which I served at Fairchild Air Force Base while living with my family in nearby Spokane, Washington. My church work during that time took the form mainly of service as a counselor in the stake-mission presidency, overseeing the work of local members serving as part-time missionaries. My most important assignment was actually to teach a four-week "school" for the stake missionaries, for which I developed a course in LDS doctrine and proselytizing procedures.[23] My remaining duties for the air force continued to be interesting, but my discharge in June 1955 ended our short transitional stay in Spokane. Then we were off to California, which I still considered home, not only because of my earlier life there but also because my parents, who had left Japan several weeks ahead of us in 1953, were now living in Walnut Creek, a growing suburb of Oakland and Berkeley. We lived for the first few months with my parents (until the fall of 1955) while I sought full-time employment and regular housing. I soon found a job as a night watchman and janitor at a nearby junior college, which permitted me to continue my education during the day. My father eventually provided the down payment on a modest "starter home" for us in Walnut Creek and cosigned the mortgage (anything to get us and our fussy babies out of his house!). During the summer term of 1955, I enrolled as a graduate student at UC-Berkeley in pursuit of a general secondary teaching credential and a master's degree in Asian and US history. Our next twelve years in Walnut Creek brought five more children (a total of eight), nose-to-the-grindstone work and studies, and continued church work, including a stint of five years in the bishopric of the Walnut Creek Ward. In subsequent pages, I will have occasion to comment further on the extent and significance of some of these important developments.

Under these circumstances, my first priority had to be supporting my family, continuing my graduate studies only as time, energy, and funds permitted. Fortunately, my military service had entitled me to supplement my income while in school with modest stipends under the so-called GI Bill. After two years in my night job as janitor, with various other odd jobs on the side, I succeeded in earning a master's degree and a credential permitting me to teach in the public schools of California at grades seven through community college. Finally, I was able to give up the night job! During the next five years, I was fortunate to teach in the public schools of Lafayette, California, beginning with grade seven, and eventually in the higher grades at the local Acalanes High School—I say fortunate because academic expectations were very high in those school districts on the parts of both students and parents. My first five years in the teaching profession would not have been nearly so pleasant in nearby Oakland, but in Lafayette, my courses in history and English were quite demanding in both the quantity and the quality of work from the students, and I delighted in feeding them concepts and historical anecdotes not included in the normal curriculum. Years later, in 2003, I was invited to the fortieth anniversary of one of their high school graduating classes, and I was both amazed and gratified at the number of students who approached me with accounts of what they remembered from my classes those many decades earlier. I have often thought that I might well have enjoyed a satisfying and relatively stress-free life if I had simply lived out a career as a high school teacher rather than getting involved in the intellectual pressures and politics that

I eventually encountered in my university career. Yet there was no denying that I was soon bored with the intellectual level that I had to maintain for such young students, and I longed for the opportunity to give greater expression especially to my intellectual interest in religious issues, which was, of course, not possible in public schools.

After five years in the Lafayette schools, I was fortunate to find a position in a nearby community college. Diablo Valley College (DVC) was the very same institution where I had earlier worked two years as night custodian, and now I was returning there as a member of the faculty in the social sciences! The teaching load of five classes (fifteen semester hours) did not seem especially heavy, even when I often supplemented it with another course or two in the evenings at other colleges in the area. Unlike the constant and relentless classroom time required in secondary schools, my professional time as a college teacher was all my own, as long as I met my scheduled classes (usually three times a week each). By arranging my class schedule carefully, I was able to liberate many hours in the afternoons and evenings to drive the twenty miles into Berkeley for graduate classes in pursuit of my next degree. With that arrangement, I was able to complete all my doctoral studies and examinations, except for the dissertation, in 1966. Meanwhile, I did not stint on my obligations to DVC. I taught a full load, did my share or more of the routine committee work, agreed to run twice (though unsuccessfully) as chairman of the social science division, headed a major academic symposium open to the public, and even took a demanding role in a Saroyan play staged by the faculty. I had a pleasant collegial relationship with the college administration and with most of my teaching colleagues, *except* for a segment of the social science faculty. In that segment I encountered for the first time how nasty faculty politics could be and, to my surprise, an undercurrent, very near the surface, of anti-Mormon prejudice.

This faction, some half dozen of the social science faculty, had a vision of the community college as part of a great egalitarian movement that would bring an Ivy League education to the children of the masses through reorganizing DVC into small "cluster colleges" (colleges within a college, as it were), where students would share the same small courses and tutorials and organize their academic lives around relationships with a nurturing and caring small faculty available to them all day long. This academic idealism simply ignored the reality that most of these students were at DVC because they were not academically eligible for admission to the university; their interests in college were entirely pragmatic and utilitarian, not intellectual; and DVC, like most other community colleges, was a commuter campus, at which the parking lot was virtually deserted by four o'clock each day. The last thing students wanted to do was to hang around campus for nurturing by the faculty.

I openly opposed the kind of hand-holding pedagogy of these faculty colleagues, as well as their proposal for reorganizing the college—a proposal that, in any case, would not have been approved by the administration or governing board.[24] That was strike one against me. Strike two was my aspiration for a PhD and an eventual position at a university as well as my publications in scholarly journals. This labeled me as "research-oriented," as contrasted with the purely "teaching-oriented" types like themselves, devoted entirely to caring for the students.[25] In the academic mythology common then (and even now), devotion to research or original scholarship and devotion to good teaching were inversely related. Some of these colleagues were further infuriated by my success in getting travel money from the administration of President William Niland to present my papers at academic conferences. Strike three was my conservative political tendencies, which became apparent as I was seen occasionally reading William F. Buckley's *National Review*. For two or three of my antagonists, my religion was all of a piece with the rest of my retrograde thinking. At the end of my DVC career, as I was leaving for my first university position, I asked for a private conversation with Bill Tarr, the colleague who had been my most visible antagonist (as, I suppose, I must have been his). I wanted to "bury the hatchet" and leave that faculty on a note of reconciliation, if possible. When I asked Bill what I had done to cause him to dislike me so much, he replied candidly (if privately) that he had never liked Mormons and that a few of our colleagues shared his feelings. That explained much of the animus in our relationship, but I took comfort from the fact that most of my colleagues were sorry to see me go and staged a nice farewell party, at which I was given an attractive and customized trophy with an appreciative engraving.

UTAH CALLS

In the summer of 1967, I left DVC and Walnut Creek after twelve eventful years in that area, during which time my three oldest children had grown from toddlers to teenagers and five younger ones had been added. I accepted a new position that had been offered me by Utah State University (USU) in Logan. At academic conferences during late 1966 and early 1967, I had seriously explored the university job market for the first time and was pleased to see that opportunities, though shrinking in number, were still plentiful. At two such conferences, I was strenuously urged by members of the Sociology Department at Brigham Young University to apply there. Given my recent exposure to the emerging intellectual environment in the Church Education System (CES), I was reluctant but might still have applied to BYU if I had not gotten wind of the so-called spy scandal that occurred there during 1966, in which Ernest Wilkinson, university president, and a couple of apostles had importuned a group of students to report professors with seemingly liberal or leftist political views.[26] In retrospect, I have always thought my discovery of that scandal was very fortunate, for had I gone to BYU, I would almost certainly have found myself in trouble, perhaps politically (for I was not nearly as conservative as Wilkinson and his apostolic allies), but surely for certain of my other boundary-testing proclivities, intellectual and otherwise. So I succeeded in negotiating a position as associate professor at USU, even though my PhD dissertation was not finished. Yet as I arrived at USU, I had cause to wonder if, after all, I had arrived at a BYU campus in Logan: I will never forget my astonishment at having a general faculty convocation opened with prayer at the start of the fall 1967 academic quarter!

The move to Logan was a mixed blessing. Our family was well received in the Fourth Ward of the LDS Church, and our two eldest children had some good experiences in the local high school. In some ways, however, the community seemed uncertain about a family of *California* Mormons, for this was the period when the news out of California was all about hippies, the counterculture, campus unrest, and various other leftist frolics. Professionally, USU was a comfortable introduction for me to academia at the more complicated university level, and it was a decent university, actually distinguished in a few fields, especially those related to agriculture. Its Department of Sociology, Social Work, and Anthropology, however, was not one of its stronger departments, and its chairman, Theral R. Black, had told me from the outset that he was hoping that I, along with some other newly recruited faculty, could help him improve the standards there, both in teaching and in expectations for research and publication.[27] I did not doubt Black's sincerity or aspirations, but I soon learned that he was captive of a group of old-timers in the department who regarded me as more of a threat than as a harbinger of a brighter future. A fourth of my teaching load consisted of the standard course in introductory sociology, which was taught in a large lecture hall with small weekly "breakout" sections for discussion. I used the same lecture material, textbook, and examinations that I had used for the same course at DVC. At the end of the first quarter, the system I had used successfully in that California *junior* college yielded so many low grades that some of the male students were in danger of losing their athletic eligibility. My hapless chairman took so much heat from coaches, administrators, and even local parents that he felt obliged to insist that I recalculate my grades based on a normal curve.[28] My unwillingness to do that soured my relationship with him from then on, but my course thereafter drew more capable students, and I continued to teach it for the next two years, along with several other courses at the upper-division level.

My lectures and visuals were eventually selected for a federally funded project of the university's media center to preserve them on videotape for future use in a variety of venues. From January through June 1969, we filmed (taped) some twenty fifty-minute lectures in introductory sociology, complete with illustrative photos, drawings, and even popular music. The director and videographer was Robert W. Donigan, a member of the speech faculty and an audiovisual expert.[29] It was an interesting learning and teaching experience for me, and my video lectures replaced me at the lectern during my final quarter at USU.[30] During one or two of my quarters at USU, I agreed also to teach this course at the USU Uintah Basin Center for Continuing Education in Roosevelt, Utah, near a Native American reservation.[31] These were small classes, where I did not resort to the video lectures, for many of the students needed the live interaction and special academic help. The most challenging aspect of this extension teaching, however, was not the students but the sometimes harrowing airplane flight to Roosevelt each week! My grading standards finally received vindication when I was asked by the college dean, M. Judd Harmon, to serve on a committee for a comparative study of grade distributions in the various departments of the college.[32] One of the findings was, indeed, that our sociology department, on average, had been giving its students unduly high grades compared to those in most of the other departments.[33]

However one might evaluate my contributions to the Department of Sociology, Social Work, and Anthropology during my two years at USU, I must say that my most interesting and enjoyable experiences there were not in that department itself but rather in the Department of History, located in the same building ("Old Main"). The chairman of that department, S. George Ellsworth, was a senior scholar whom I had known briefly during his sojourn in my home ward in Oakland during early 1949 while he was completing his PhD at UC-Berkeley. We were also both founding members of the new Mormon History Association. Indeed, Ellsworth, along with Leonard Arrington and a couple of others at USU, could be considered the founding fathers of the MHA. Although Arrington was in the Department of Economics, I would see him from time to time. In due course, I became acquainted with at least four of the new young history professors, especially Douglas Alder (later president of Dixie College), Stan Cazier (later president of USU), Gary Huxford, and Blythe Ahlstrom.

It was, in fact, through my friendships in the History Department at USU that I was invited by Doug Alder and others to join a new academic project during my second year there. Under a federal government initiative to upgrade the training of high school teachers, the History Department received a grant from the US Department of Education to provide an intensive academic year (plus summers) for selected high school social studies teachers. The intention of the program was that the teachers would apply to USU as the venue for this program and earn master's degrees in the process of updating their knowledge of the latest developments in the scholarly literature of history and the other social sciences. I was selected by my colleagues in the History Department to teach a couple of sociology courses as part of this project and to work particularly with any of the participants who wanted their master's degrees to emphasize sociology. A portion of my faculty time (a fourth or a half, as I recall) was allocated to this project, so that I taught correspondingly less in the Department of Sociology, Social Work, and Anthropology during that year. At least three of the students in the program elected to work with me on their master's papers. All three undertook original survey research projects, one on student values, one on gratification deferral among high school students, and one on racial attitudes in the surrounding Logan area.[34] The third of these papers was published in a local academic journal.[35]

Gratifying though my associations were with the USU history professors and their Department of Education graduate students, my relationships with my older sociology colleagues grew increasingly strained over my grading and my work with a couple of sociology graduate students on thesis topics that were regarded as too sensitive.[36] Against this background, I was offered no salary increase for my second year, though virtually all other department members were. A special handicap for me and other members of that department was the difficulty in those days of getting access to data-processing equipment, since faculties in chemistry and the other "hard" sciences were given priority. I knew I would never finish my dissertation without such access, which would otherwise be available to me only by traveling to Berkeley, where I still had graduate student status. All things considered, therefore, I went back on the job market again and was fortunate to receive an offer from the Department of Sociology at Washington State University, starting in the fall of 1969. My history colleagues, especially Leonard Arrington, tried to persuade me to stay at USU, but I could not see an acceptable future for me there.[37]

I must concede in retrospect that much of the difficulty with my sociology colleagues could be attributed to my own personal style, which at that time was quite candid, sometimes to an abrasive degree, and self-promoting. I had brought that attitude with me from California, where it was much more functional than in the more reserved and modest academic culture of northern Utah. In my disagreements over grades and other policies in my department, I was not very gracious, and at times I must have communicated, however inadvertently, my feeling that the "old guard" in that department was a bunch of yokels standing athwart my efforts to promote progress. Yet my two years at USU were for me a time of professional growth and enhanced understanding about the university system. Also, for the first (and last) time in my career, I was surrounded by Mormons at my place of work, and in that environment, I had to learn to keep the LDS religion separate in my mind from the Mormon individuals with whom I associated—some of whom happened to have high church positions, and not all of whom were friendly to me. This kind of psychological separation—of my religion from certain individuals who shared it—proved to be an important capability for the rest of my life.

The Final Career Move to Washington

The move to Washington State University (WSU) in Pullman was very advantageous for my academic career. The Department of Sociology there was modern in every respect, even to the point of having its own data-processing department, equipment, and consultants. Given such resources, I was able to complete the statistical analyses and writing for my dissertation within a few months, so I finally had the PhD by the end of my first year at WSU. The department also had several senior professors of national stature, and by the usual measures it was generally considered among the top fifteen or twenty sociology departments in the nation.[38] It was led by an exceptionally entrepreneurial chairman, Melvin L. DeFleur, who had succeeded in getting a lucrative "department development grant" from the National Science Foundation in the very year that I arrived. Among other things, this grant financed the recruitment of a few more senior faculty and the facilities for an "urban research station" on the waterfront in Seattle, almost three hundred miles to the west! Though a dubious expenditure of federal funds, this grant made the department a very favorable professional environment. Pullman was (and is) in a rather remote location surrounded by very productive wheat fields and quite conservative townsfolk, so it turned out to be a very good place both for rearing a family and for getting work done.[39] There was one LDS ward in Pullman and a student branch.[40] The ward was heavily populated by people connected to the university in various ways, including faculty members, of course, but that did not give the ward the kind of liberal or progressive culture, either religiously or politically, that one might have expected in a university setting, perhaps partly because so many of the LDS faculty were part of the WSU College of Agriculture and so few were on the faculties of the humanities or the social sciences.

Since I remained at WSU for the next thirty years before my formal retirement, my main career accomplishments occurred during that period. Accordingly, all the remaining chapters here, in various ways, recount and interpret the experiences I had during and after my career in Pullman, so very little needs to be singled out for discussion at this point. A brief overview should suffice, pending the additional information in later chapters.[41] My teaching covered all academic levels from freshman through doctoral students. I chaired my share of master's thesis committees and PhD dissertation committees. The best students at WSU, graduate and undergraduate, were as good as the best anywhere, but graduate students of high caliber were not numerous, at least not compared to the cohort with which I was familiar at UC-Berkeley.[42] The cohorts of undergraduates who passed through my hands in those thirty years showed declines each year in both linguistic and cultural literacy, so that those in my classes during the 1990s were noticeably less well prepared for college than their parents had been in the 1970s, not only in academic skills but also in attitudes toward academic standards and expectations. As a good departmental citizen, I took my turns serving on various committees, chaired the graduate admissions committee for several years, and even was assistant chairman of the department for a while. I found departmental politics even more pervasive and aversive than at USU. I got along well with most of my colleagues most of the time, but since my retirement, I have remained in regular and valued contact with only one, Michael Patrick Allen, a superb quantitative methodologist, with whom I shared most views on departmental politics but not on national politics.

In the WSU Sociology Department, expectations were high but reasonable for faculty research and publication. I found no difficulty in meeting them comfortably. My research and writing in the field of religion, especially in Mormon studies, were tolerated as long as I was willing to devote most of my time and energy where they were most needed, that is, in mainstream sociology. In my case, this meant teaching and research primarily in the fields of deviant behavior and social problems (which partly overlapped) and in the study of social movements. I found ways to extend the latter focus to cover religious movements, including Mormonism. Just how I combined these various threads of the sociological fabric in my publications will become clear in later chapters. Another strong expectation in that department, especially for senior faculty, was "grantsmanship"—seeking and securing grants from federal, state, and private sources to support one's research.

Such support yielded stipends for graduate students as research assistants, summer salaries for participating faculty, new equipment, and other resources—to say nothing of benefits to the university itself, which appropriated almost half of the face value of every federal grant to cover its "overhead" in administering the grant and accounting for the funds. During the 1970s and 1980s, studies of the etiology and prevention of alcohol and drug abuse were high on the agenda of federal agencies, such as the National Institute for Alcohol Abuse and Alcoholism.[43] Also, especially as a Mormon, I could see the potential value of research that might result in policies and methods to reduce alcohol use and abuse. Accordingly, I decided to seek grants to support such research, first at the state and then at the federal levels. I also agreed to join a collaboration with colleagues in the Department of Psychology to create a new graduate training program through which students preparing for professional roles in the treatment of alcoholism could receive master's degrees with expertise in psychology, sociology, and the relevant physiology. Half of my teaching time was devoted to this interdisciplinary enterprise for some five years or more. In this training program, I collaborated mainly with Professor Warren Garlington of the Department of Psychology.

Aside from the teaching, my research began with small grants from the State of Washington. Already in 1970, I had visited the new urban research station that the WSU Sociology Department had set up on the Seattle waterfront. As I walked around that classical "skid road" neighborhood, I noticed that it contained several so-called rescue missions established by both denominational and nondenominational religious organizations. The idea suddenly occurred to me that a study of those missions would permit me to combine my interest in religious organizations with an investigation of their programs for combating alcohol abuse.[44] Later, another state grant enabled me actually to launch and evaluate a new rehabilitation program in collaboration with staff at a large Lutheran mission in the area.[45] I even extended the research into a systematic evaluation of the efficacy of replacing the "drunk tanks" of the Seattle Police Department with professional treatment programs located outside the city.[46] All these projects supported graduate research assistants, some of whom produced doctoral dissertations from their work and with most of whom I published jointly authored articles in professional journals.[47] My main research initiative, however, occurred in partnership with another valued WSU colleague and professor of psychology, Ronald H. Hopkins. We collaborated on a large three-year grant from the National Institute for Alcohol Abuse and Alcoholism to evaluate the effectiveness of a newly developed model program for the public schools to prevent youthful resort to alcohol (the "Here's Looking at You" program). This project too led to several dissertations and publications with the graduate research assistants who worked with us, as will be apparent from the cv in the appendix at the end of this memoir.[48]

With all of that, and more that will go unmentioned, I came to feel that I had "paid my dues" in the grantsmanship game.[49] I had long since achieved full-professor rank, and I longed to go back to religious studies, especially on Mormons. So gradually, during the 1980s, I began to phase out all my professional activities related to deviant behavior, social problems, and alcohol studies in favor of increasing attention to religious movements in general and Mormons in particular. A year's sabbatical leave in the Department of Religious Studies at UC–Santa Barbara during 1985 helped me greatly in making this transition. I had not received much professional gratification from my work on substance abuse and other social problems, since none of my research seemed to have any influence on public policy and none of the prevention or treatment programs I had evaluated seemed to have any impact on alcohol or drug use. Nevertheless, from my studies of the *political contexts* in which those programs were developed and promoted, I learned a great deal that proved useful to me in the study of social and political *movements,* much of which turned out to be applicable also to religious movements, including Mormonism. This aspect of my work will also be explored in a later chapter.

SOME PROFESSIONAL ACTIVITIES IN THE PUBLIC ARENA

A few times in my career, I was sought out as a professional expert on Mormons in court cases where a defendant, litigant, or other principal happened to be a Latter-day Saint and where his or her religion might be relevant to understanding or evaluating the person's behavior. Most of those cases, as they turned out, were settled without going to trial, so I never needed actually to testify. In one dramatic case, however, I did get significantly involved as a witness for the defense. This was the espionage case against Richard W. Miller, an agent working out of the Los Angeles FBI office who was accused of selling classified documents to a female Soviet agent with whom he had become sexually involved. As a Mormon with a large family, his adultery had resulted in a divorce and his excommunication from the LDS Church, but he continued to maintain contact with the Russian woman and apparently did give her some classified documents. He had been under surveillance by FBI agents from the San Francisco office (where the woman in question was residing), and eventually, in October 1984, he was arrested and charged with several crimes related to espionage. The subsequent investigation and trial went on for more than a year.[50]

Ruth and I were on sabbatical leave in Santa Barbara during 1985, and among our circle of friends in Southern California was E. Gary Smith, who happened to be the family attorney for Richard Miller and his wife. When Miller was arrested, Smith helped him get connected to a pair of well-known local criminal attorneys, who had made their careers mainly as prosecutors but who ultimately agreed to defend Miller.[51] Two lines of argument seemed to undermine the case against Miller. First, he was well known by his FBI colleagues as a kind of bumbler with grandiose aspirations to achieve a career coup that would vindicate his self-conception as an outstanding agent, and his association with the Russian agent had been simply a misguided effort to infiltrate her organization (the KGB) as an FBI "plant." He had thus never intended to betray the FBI. Second, his only confession of malfeasance had been extracted under emotional duress by his local FBI bureau chief, who happened to be a Mormon bishop (though not in the Miller family's ward) and who had used his ecclesiastical rank and knowledge of Mormon theology and the prescribed LDS penance process to induce from Miller a confession as a start on his spiritual journey of repentance and return to the Mormon fold.

My role as an "expert witness" was to explain to the court how a devout but disgraced Mormon like Miller might have been vulnerable to such an inducement from a prestigious spiritual leader as a means of starting him back into the good graces of his church and family. This apparent merging of spiritual and bureaucratic authority on the part of the bishop–bureau chief, though not the key issue in the case, was at least significant enough in the minds of the jurors that during their deliberations they asked for my testimony to be read to them for reconsideration.[52] The judge, the defense, and the prosecution all took my testimony very seriously and dealt with me respectfully.[53] Though I tried to remain detached and analytical in responding to examination and cross-examination, the potential significance of the religious bonds between Miller and his chief was clear to all. The trial lasted for several weeks, ending eventually in a deadlocked jury and a mistrial in November 1985, as one or two jurors held out against the majority's "guilty" verdicts—much to the astonishment of nearly all concerned, including the defendant.[54] The FBI and the prosecution were embarrassed by this outcome, since they had been hoping to make a public example of Miller as the first agent in history to have betrayed the FBI, but it took two more trials for the government to get even the satisfaction of a greatly reduced sentence.[55] I am sure the whole process was a nightmare for Miller and his family. It was difficult to muster a lot of sympathy for him, but it was an interesting experience for me, and as close as I would ever want to get to a criminal trial!

Beyond that public episode, I will add only that during my WSU career I also got requests occasionally to do special jobs on the side in the form of "public interest" programs. These were usually funded by the National Endowment for the Humanities through various local institutions. The most important of these occurred during the period 1973–76 through the UCLA Extension Division. The Western Center for Program Development in the Humanities had been established there under the auspices of the National Endowment for the Humanities, and one of its projects was the creation of public programs for presentation in the small towns of America. Program themes were based on common human problems and issues. I was among several scholars hired on generous stipends to create such a program and take it on the road to small towns from Nome, Alaska, to Maui, Hawaii, from Julesburg, Colorado, to Coronado, California, and several towns in between. I teamed up with Professor Shigeo Kanda, a scholar in religious studies, and our theme was titled "The Self and the System," for which we created lectures, readings, colored slides, and even a film in mime to illustrate concepts for discussion. An audience member in our first small town evaluated the program as something "created by a bunch of hippies in California." Indeed, although well intentioned, these UCLA projects (and not just mine) actually came across as somewhat condescending in some of the small towns—as though experts from Los Angeles were "bringing culture to the boonies," as another critic put it. However, many of the townspeople thus served, at least the more sophisticated among them, seemed to appreciate our visits. The creative process in which I was involved (including drafting sketches for the various vignettes in the film) was an interesting change of pace from university classes, and to be sure, I was able to use the extra money to help cover the costs of keeping two young sons on LDS missions. I also worked on two or three similar programs on a smaller scale inside the state of Washington under the auspices of the state humanities council.

Family Life in Pullman and Since

Finally, a few words about our family life and religious participation during our thirty years in Washington. Perhaps partly because of its remoteness from urban amenities, Pullman turned out to be a great place to rear a family. Politically and culturally, Pullman (like most of eastern Washington) was far more conservative than the California Bay Area but less so than Logan had been. Mormons were a small minority in Pullman but a strong presence in the WSU College of Agriculture and in certain related disciplines. Mormons were also a rather controversial presence, sometimes suspected of a kind of "religious nepotism," as it were, in university relationships. This was especially the case while Louis L. Madsen (recently from USU in Logan), a prominent Mormon, was dean of the agriculture college. The religious culture in the local Mormon ward and stake was also quite conservative and parochial when we arrived, although it became less so with the passage of time and the growth of the Mormon population in the area. It took some time for the local Saints to become comfortable with me as a sociologist, partly because of some early missteps and failings of my own and partly because some of the old-time sociologists who had joined the WSU faculty in earlier years had turned out to be defectors from the faith. However, by the time we had been in Pullman for a few years, my relationships with the LDS community in general had become quite warm, especially with a certain portion of that community that was intellectually adventurous. I shall have more to say about that in a later chapter as well.

Both Pullman the town and the local Mormon ward proved to be a good place for our six sons and two daughters. All graduated from Pullman High School, and five of our sons left on their missions from that ward. In partnership with my stalwart wife, we managed to keep the family organized and functioning well, thanks in large part to our regular "family home evening" meetings.[56] In general, it was a successful effort, for all our children exhibit to this day the values that we tried to instill. As the family grew up, and expenses multiplied, they earned money by taking over one of the local newspaper agencies, with all its delivery routes, under Ruth's management, and this enterprise kept our boys employed. Eventually, Ruth gained more regular employment, first as a dispatcher for the local police department and later in important clerical positions at Washington State University. Besides all of that, she also found time somehow to earn a bachelor's degree at the university.

By 1982 we had an empty nest and a much simpler life. All of our children had gone back to California for their education, in which we provided financial help only in emergencies. Each of them financed his or her own education, five to the bachelor's level or beyond and three to community and technical college degrees. All have been gainfully employed and entirely self-supporting since then and have produced some accomplished children of their own. Although my family life proved quite successful in general, I have reflected many times on my own inadequacies as a husband and father, sometimes with serious regrets. I did not give any of my children as much regular and personal "face time" as they deserved. Nor in the discipline of my own six boundary-testing sons did I have the patience and forbearance of my father, for I did resort several times to a strapping on the behind. Nevertheless, to this day, ours is a tight-knit family with regular and convivial reunions and with many fond and humorous memories of our days in Pullman.

Since five of our children (and their descendants) eventually settled in or near Orange County, California, it was not difficult for Ruth and me to decide on retirement in that county. In the spring of 1999, we moved to a very pleasant planned community in Irvine. We have enjoyed participating in our local LDS ward and stake, where I serve on the stake public affairs council for interfaith relationships and respond periodically to reporters from various parts of the country who seek my observations on Mormon matters for their newspaper or magazine articles. I am also a consistent and conscientious home teacher in my ward, as I have always been elsewhere. Home teaching is a Mormon practice that I truly believe in. In our local Irvine LDS community generally, we find more of a "live and let live" culture than we experienced in either Logan or Pullman, but no less warm and friendly. Having encountered us only as an elderly and retired couple, our local church friends and leaders seem unsure about how to fit us into the ongoing history of their religious community, but they try.

My main preoccupations in retirement have continued to be academic in nature, writing books, articles, and encyclopedia pieces on Mormon history and culture. Two enterprises, in particular, have claimed my time and energy since formal retirement: a decade of service on the *Dialogue* board of directors (ending in 2008), including four years as chairman, and active participation (since 2004) on the LDS Council for Mormon Studies in the School of Religion at the Claremont Graduate University (CGU). A chapter is devoted to my involvement in each of those two enterprises later in this memoir. Now, however, against the general background provided in this first chapter, I will return to reflections on the major developments in my earlier intellectual and professional life, starting with my young adult years after having returned from Japan.

Chapter 2 | Earning the Passport as a "Defender of the Faith"

The Creation of a Young Mormon Apologist

As I reflect upon the first three decades of my life, I see the emergence of a young intellectual with the pretensions of a religious apologist.[1] The process did not follow a smooth and straight trajectory. It included some obstacles, lapses, and setbacks—for immature people often make rash and foolish choices. As a child in California, I benefited from a strong school system and many other opportunities for growth, despite the surrounding economic depression of the time. I also encountered periodic challenges to my LDS upbringing, both through the world's various temptations and through the occasional anti-Mormon slur or altercation. My mission to New England, starting in 1947, greatly enhanced both my intellectual development and my religious faith, as the previous chapter indicates. So did my years of church work with LDS servicemen in Tokyo. My sojourn in Japan, while intellectually broadening in many ways, also exposed me to the rigors of Jesuit apologetics at Sophia University, which I came to admire.

I returned from Japan with a wife and a family and aspirations for a teaching career of some kind, which would, of course, require some graduate work. My first years of graduate school at UC-Berkeley (1955–57) were devoted primarily to studies for the master's degree and the teaching credential. In those days, I had no inkling that my studies would ever include Mormon history, though I recall some wonderful "brown-bag" discussions of Mormon matters with a group of LDS graduate students who would meet regularly for lunch during the week. These discussions introduced me for the first time to an academic perspective (as contrasted with a devotional or apologetic one) in the study of my own religion. I first discovered this group when Paul Hyer, a fellow student in a graduate course I was taking on Japanese history, invited me to bring a lunch and meet with them the next day.[2] For a couple of years thereafter, I met with this lunch group of LDS graduate students whenever I was on campus at lunchtime. As I recall, only six or eight students came regularly, and they represented a variety of disciplines. The ones I remember by name (besides Paul Hyer) were Russell Horiuchi and Lee Farnsworth (both of whom, like Paul, eventually joined the BYU faculty); Joe (R. Joseph) Monsen (eventually a professor of economics at the University of Washington); John Martinez (who later changed his name to Juan and identified with the Chicano movement then developing in California); George Strobel (a CES faculty member then on sabbatical for a year or so); Leon Mayhew (then still an undergraduate, who eventually became a dean at UC-Davis); Calvin Wood; and Earl Remington. There were a few others.

Our discussions ranged far and wide on a variety of theological and social issues in LDS history and in the life of the LDS Church. The general outlook of the discussions was quite orthodox, but there were occasional excursions into heterodoxy. Given the paucity of available academic literature on Mormons at that time, we sometimes engaged in critiques of official church books and authors. We always welcomed each other's discoveries of new articles, ideas, or quandaries in LDS history. We were free with our opinions and never felt constrained by a sense that certain matters simply should not be discussed by faithful Latter-day Saints, but we probably never reached the level of stridency that apparently occurred sometimes in the University of Utah's "swearing elders" group.[3] I recall how excited we were when Thomas F. O'Dea's book *The Mormons* finally appeared on the otherwise nearly vacant landscape of scholarly literature on Mormons.[4] This was the first balanced study of the Saints and an occasion for great excitement in our brown-bag group, especially since the author was not a Mormon. Now, in the twenty-first century, as we rummage through the wealth of sixty years' accumulated scholarly literature of all kinds on the Mormons, it must be difficult for today's young scholars to appreciate the emptiness of the field that my generation faced.

In any case, this two-year introduction to graduate school was interrupted when, in the spring of 1957, shortly before my twenty-ninth birthday, I accepted a call to serve as a counselor in the bishopric of the Walnut Creek Ward, then a large suburban ward located some twenty miles east of Oakland and Berkeley. I had been gone from California for most of the previous decade, having left on my mission in 1947, followed by a stint overseas in both student and military roles until 1955. I therefore received my call to the bishopric with mixed feelings: On the one hand, it validated my emerging self-conception as a faithful servant of the church, starting on a path leading toward later callings to much higher office. On the other hand, the call would require a hiatus in my graduate education (five years, as it turned out), which I had started only two years earlier. Whether consciously or unconsciously, I think I also partially welcomed the bishopric service as an excuse to take a break from the rather frenetic period though which I had been living—in preparation, I had assumed, for an eventual teaching career and a rather conventional family life. In 1957, by the time I was twenty-nine, I had finished a church mission in New England, served four years in the US Air Force, earned both bachelor and master's degrees with a General Secondary Teaching Credential, married, and produced five children. I was tired. The bishopric call did not exactly give me a rest, but it gave me a break and a change of pace. I decided just to teach school for a while and to live a somewhat more normal family life in the suburbs, with an occasional graduate course on the side.

My five years as a bishop's counselor actually proved very busy and eventful in such a growing and changing ward and stake in those days. I served under a devoted and conscientious bishop, Mark R. Bickley. Other counselors who passed through that bishopric during my time included M. Taylor Abegg, Wells B. Wilkinson, and John L. Hilton, all of whom are now deceased. Coincidentally, during the 1960s, Bickley was transferred out of California to Spokane, from whence I had left in 1955 to come to Walnut Creek. There he served again as bishop, then stake president, and finally stake patriarch. Though he has passed ninety years, and is handicapped by poor vision, he and I remain in regular e-mail contact, sometimes reminiscing about our Walnut Creek days together and the teamwork and camaraderie we enjoyed.

I have reflected many times upon my intellectual development up to that stage in my life and how all of that interacted with my spiritual and religious development. Where the church was concerned, I had developed a strong commitment and loyalty, despite periodic lapses from proper observances. During several years in Japan as president of a large LDS servicemen's branch—and then of a servicemen's district—I had begun to see how the church was ideally supposed to work in the lives of its members, as well as how it did *not* work—or, at least, how it needed to be adapted to special conditions outside the Mormon corridor of the American West. My subsequent years in the Walnut Creek bishopric gave me many additional experiences with the same predicament: how to make the church work as intended despite local anomalies and individual failings among leaders and members. In the process, I developed a healthy respect for certain organizational realities and a wariness about the unquestioning implementation of policies handed down from on high to deal with local needs and circumstances. I was already beginning to see that perhaps I was not the kind of unquestioning "good soldier" who would rise steadily in the church's hierarchy. Yet from then until now, I have always thought of myself as loyal to the church and have never ceased wishing for its success.

Institutional loyalty, of course, is not the same thing as religious beliefs. During this early period of my life, I thought of myself as quite orthodox, questioning little or nothing in traditional Mormon doctrines, and generally intrigued to learn all I could about the origin and development of those doctrines. I think I fancied myself as a "defender of the faith," a concept that I had appropriated from the Jesuits who were my teachers at Sophia University. The Jesuit Order, of course, had been given that designation ("Defenders of the Faith") by a pope, largely on the basis of that order's effectiveness during the Counter-Reformation. In those days at Sophia, I did not know much about the various tactics used by the early Jesuits, but I did admire the intellectual armament that they had employed in debates during the Reformation period and since, and particularly the codification and systematization of their apologetics in the college philosophy courses that I took under their tutelage.[5]

In the 1940s and 1950s, the LDS "defenders of the faith" for me were the several LDS general authorities who had gained worldly academic credentials, such as James E. Talmage, John A. Widtsoe, and Milton R. Hunter, all of whom had written articles and books clearly in the genre of apologetics, but with considerable intellectual heft.[6] The rising star in this company, however, was Hugh W. Nibley, who (unlike those others) was never an important church leader but a somewhat eccentric BYU scholar who had specialized in ancient history while earning his PhD at UC-Berkeley in 1938. He joined the BYU faculty in 1946 and soon began publishing articles and books on the Book of Mormon and other LDS scriptures, in which he persuasively mobilized evidence from ancient history, literature, and culture to demonstrate the authenticity of those scriptures. His publications always included a cascade of footnotes from specialized sources (in various languages) that were accessible to but few other scholars, especially in the Mormon world.[7] During the early 1950s, his work was serialized in the official church magazine, *Improvement Era,* and in 1957 one of his books became the official Melchizedek priesthood lesson manual.[8] Incidentally, Nibley's work was not the only scholarly material used for priesthood lesson manuals in the 1950s. During 1952, 1953, and 1954, the manuals were studies of the ancient Christian Church by James L. Barker.[9]

A more local hero for Latter-day Saints in the San Francisco Bay Area during the 1940s and 1950s was Thomas Stuart Ferguson, an attorney who practiced and resided in Oakland while I lived there in the 1930s and 1940s and then lived eventually in the adjoining Berkeley Stake. Still later, in the 1950s, he was a pioneer and founding member of the Walnut Creek Stake and was, in fact, a high councilor in that stake during much of the time that I lived there. Ferguson, a bright and enterprising young man, became intrigued with the possibilities that archaeological research might verify the authenticity of the Book of Mormon and thereby "prove" that Joseph Smith was a true prophet, commissioned by God to restore the ancient Church of Christ. He was an early advocate for Mesoamerica as the actual setting for the Book of Mormon story.[10] He formed friendships with several LDS scholars also interested in the archaeology of the Western Hemisphere, such as M. Wells Jakeman and Milton R. Hunter, whom he had known as fellow graduate students at UC-Berkeley in the 1930s, and with successful entrepreneurs, such as J. Willard Marriott Sr. Through those friendships, he was instrumental in bringing about the establishment of the Archaeology Department at BYU and especially the associated institute there known as the New World Archaeological Foundation (NWAF).[11] He had no professional credentials of his own in archaeology, but he spent a great deal of his time in leading archaeological expeditions to Latin America, financed by himself and others. Eventually, he succeeded in getting official funds (in the low six figures) from the LDS Church itself (through President David O. McKay) to support the work of the NWAF. He seemed to enjoy regaling the Saints in "firesides" and other informal gatherings with his discoveries of evidence tying the Book of Mormon to ancient civilizations, especially in Mesoamerica. I recall many a sermon on such topics whenever he came to our ward sacrament meetings as the high-council visitor.[12]

However, by the time I left Northern California in 1967, we were no longer hearing much from Ferguson, who, in fact, was going through a crisis of faith. Decades of archaeological work by the NWAF had failed to produce anything that non-Mormons would consider evidence tying ancient civilizations to the Book of Mormon, but the "final straw," one might say, was the discovery and analysis, starting in 1967, of fragments of the papyrus from which Joseph Smith had purportedly translated the Book of Abraham from ancient Egyptian. That episode is a fascinating story in itself but beyond the scope of my account here. Suffice it to say that the undermining of Smith's translation claims by modern Egyptologists,[13] plus Ferguson's own frustration at failing to find the archaeological "proof" that he had sought for the Book of Mormon, all combined to create an intellectual and spiritual trauma for Ferguson. Given the mixed evidence that has emerged from Ferguson's biographers and family members, it is difficult to determine whether he ever really recovered his spiritual moorings as a Latter-day Saint.[14] In any case, both Ferguson's work itself and the archaeological approach to Book of Mormon scholarship more generally were soon eclipsed and obscured by the work of Nibley and the rise of his kind of research on the Book of Mormon, exemplified in the publications of *FARMS* since 1980.[15]

During my stint in the bishopric (1957–62), I tried out my own academic wings in the teaching profession, starting in grades seven through twelve. I found an additional outlet for my religious pedagogy by agreeing to teach high school "seminary" for the LDS students in my ward. Added to my public school teaching and my bishopric services, my four years as a seminary teacher were somewhat burdensome, since the class met at 6:30 a.m. on every school day. In that era, however (1950s–1960s), early-morning seminary teachers were paid about a hundred dollars a month, as I recall, which was some incentive for taking the job.[16] I was also strongly motivated by altruism. By that time in my own academic development, I had already recognized the crucial importance of helping young people reconcile their religious heritage with the increasingly secular academic ideas encountered in the public schools. I was convinced that such reconciliations were possible if they could take place in an environment that was "safe" for inquiry and discussion of sensitive religious issues—that is, an environment where curious students did not run the risk of shocking their parents or their ecclesiastical leaders with difficult questions. Eventually, my older seminary students would graduate and go away for college, and when they returned home for the summer, some of them expressed an interest in weekly religious discussions as part of a summer program for young single adults in the ward, which I was asked to lead for a couple of summers. From those contacts, I sometimes received invitations as a speaker at similar events for young LDS adults in other parts of the San Francisco Bay Area. These encounters with bright young LDS students were very gratifying, for I sensed a special rapport with them in an informal role as adviser and confidant at times when they faced troubling issues about the church or its teachings.

However, my relationship with the Church Education System, under whose auspices I was teaching seminary, was not so gratifying. This was a transitional period in CES history.[17] Early in the twentieth century, the LDS Church had begun divesting itself of high schools (academies) and colleges and turning these over to public school systems in Utah and elsewhere. High school seminaries and college institutes for LDS youth were then gradually established to provide students with the religious component that they would no longer be receiving in public school education. Originally, the pedagogical philosophy of CES seemed to embrace intellectual reconciliation, if not always integration, between secular and religious learning, with legitimate academic standards and textbooks that would justify high school and college credit for at least some of the CES courses. To facilitate this prospect, a few of the young CES faculty were sent at church expense to major universities outside Utah for advanced academic training in religion.[18]

By midcentury, however, this pedagogical philosophy had about run its course, as certain conservative apostles became increasingly concerned about the sectarian (if not, indeed, the secular) influences on CES faculty and students.

A major initiative to reverse this trend was signaled as early as 1938 by J. Reuben Clark of the First Presidency with his well-remembered address "The Charted Course of the Church in Education," in which he defined that course as devoted strictly to indoctrinating and building the faith of LDS students.[19] Teachers unwilling to follow this course were invited to resign, but a generational turnover in faculty would be required before this new philosophy would firmly take hold across all the seminaries and institutes. That turnover was just getting a good start when I agreed to teach high school seminary in Walnut Creek. Of course, I did so with the traditional CES philosophy in mind, as exemplified in the careers of institute directors such as Lee Kenner at UC-Berkeley, George Boyd at the University of Southern California, and Lowell Bennion at the University of Utah. Yet the CES administrators sent out to supervise the seminary teachers during the 1950s and onward were trying very hard to implement the indoctrination approach, insisting on meticulous adherence to the formal curriculum materials and on the displacement of questioning and intellectualizing by a more pragmatic pedagogy—that is, an emphasis on behavior and observance, rather than on understanding scripture or theology for their own sakes. Scripture study took the form mostly of proof-texting and rote memorization (which seems still to be the general CES policy).

Various new pedagogical theories were also being bandied about in CES circles, which I considered no more valid scientifically than when I had encountered them in the School of Education at Berkeley. I certainly recognized that as a seminary teacher I was dealing in religious apologetics by definition, but I still felt that the students needed a stronger knowledge and intellectual component in their apologetics than the new pedagogy permitted. Yet intellectualizing was discouraged in favor of catechistic indoctrination. I stayed with the early-morning seminary job during four of the five years that I was also teaching in public secondary schools, but I relinquished the job in 1962 when I was hired as a community college instructor at Diablo Valley College. My seminary experience had given me a personal introduction to the conservative transformation of the CES philosophy, much to my sadness, as it was soon joined with other developments in the LDS ecclesiastical retrenchment movement during the subsequent several decades.[20] That was my first clue, of many that followed in later years, that the emerging CES culture would not welcome my approach to teaching young Mormons about their religion, no matter how authentic my LDS "passport" might be. Nevertheless, during those years of my young adulthood, I strongly embraced a self-concept as a defender of my faith, not with the weapons of zealotry but with those of the intellect that I had acquired during my mission, my discipleship under the Jesuits, and my graduate work so far at Berkeley. That graduate work was to resume with increasing intensity from 1962 through 1967, with as much time and effort as I could spare, given my family responsibilities and my new faculty position at Diablo Valley College. I knew that I could not realize my growing aspirations for a university faculty position without a PhD (or at least the so-called ABD—"all but dissertation").

STUDYING THE SAINTS FROM WITHIN THE KINGDOM

By 1964, through my graduate studies in sociology, I had learned how to do survey research, so I conceived and launched a small survey of the members of three LDS wards in eastern Contra Costa County. Its main focus was on prejudice toward Jews and blacks in relation to LDS religious beliefs. I intended this as a kind of "pilot study" for a larger survey that I would eventually do for the dissertation itself. I had been given permission by my graduate mentor, Charles Y. Glock, to replicate many of the questions he was using in a major survey on religion and prejudice, so that my data on Mormons would be comparable to his on other Christians.[21] I succeeded in getting permission from the bishops over the three local LDS wards to administer the surveys and to use their membership lists in mailing my questionnaires. Obviously, this was not a church-sponsored survey, but its relevance here is that it came to the attention of one E. Richard Wooley, a high councilor in my stake and an attorney (as I recall), who periodically accepted special assignments from the LDS Presiding Bishop's Office and was just starting a new PBO project.[22]

Aaronic Adult Study

Wooley contacted me in 1965 to solicit my participation in a review that the PBO was conducting of some of the programs for which it was especially responsible, starting with the one for "Aaronic adults."[23] Wooley was reporting to Ray L. White, who was then full-time chief of staff for the PBO. When I agreed to participate, I found myself a member of an ad hoc committee called the Bay Area Committee on the Aaronic Adult Program (or something close to that designation), which held meetings periodically at the large new multistake tabernacle (the Interstake Center) on the temple grounds in Oakland. Besides Wooley and me, this committee included several seasoned church leaders from two or three of the local stakes, and we were charged with developing a proposal to the Presiding

Bishopric for revising the Aaronic priesthood adult program. Still somewhat in my mode as "defender of the faith," I was pleased at the prospect that I might be doing something that would really help the church.

The proximate objective of the Aaronic programs was to enhance and maintain the church activity of men and boys who held the lesser or Aaronic priesthood, so that they could advance to the higher Melchizedek priesthood in due course. For all practical purposes, the program for adults entailed primarily a religious reactivation strategy that would increase incentives for the men to prepare for advancement in the lay priesthood. By 1965 I had collected survey data in the "pilot study" mentioned above of those three local LDS wards in my stake, and these data proved suggestive of what could be learned through questionnaires about the attitudes and feelings of church members toward religious teachings and programs. Wooley asked me to replicate a portion of the survey among a new sample of Aaronic adult men from the same (Walnut Creek) stake whose responses (given anonymously, of course) might be indicative of typical reasons for inactivity in the church. A kind of "qualitative analysis" of these cases could form the basis for some of our ad hoc committee's recommendations to the Presiding Bishopric in Salt Lake City. Among the unsurprising discoveries of this analysis were indications that inactivity in the church had multiple explanations. There were, in fact, several "dimensions of separation," as Wooley and I explained to the committee. During our committee's deliberations, we had also come to recognize that the existing program inadvertently stigmatized Aaronic adults by requiring them to meet as a group separate from the Melchizedek priesthood quorums during the weekly priesthood meetings. Ray White accordingly supported our idea that perhaps Aaronic adults should meet jointly with elders' quorums, at least part of the time, to minimize their sense of separateness. These and other insights from our survey informed some of the report that was eventually completed by our committee in February 1966 and submitted through Ray White to the Presiding Bishopric.[24] However, the most consequential idea that emerged from our committee was the recognition that a person tends to strive less toward fulfilling an identity that he already has than toward an identity to which he *aspires*—that is, toward what he *wishes* to become; what he wishes to become is influenced, in turn, by the expectations of others in his reference group. The process is called "anticipatory socialization" in mainstream social psychology. Informed by this understanding, Wooley and I eventually recommended to the PBO that both the program and the name for the "Aaronic adult" in the church should be replaced by "prospective elder," implying an expectation that the religiously inactive men would be working toward the office of elder in the higher priesthood. To this day, the term *prospective elder* is used to designate men in the church who are not active or who are not yet prepared to receive the higher priesthood, and when those men come to the Sunday meetings of the priesthood, they participate fully in the discussions, activities, and assignments of the Melchizedek quorums, rather than in separate groups of their own. Such is, in effect, their "reactivation" program.[25]

I cannot now recall just how or when "anticipatory socialization" and "prospective elder" emerged as ideas in our discussions, and I make no claim to sole personal credit for those discoveries, and least of all for the originality of the underlying theory, which has a long history in the social sciences.[26] What I do remember is that contemporaneously with my committee work for the PBO, I had been working with some advanced students at Diablo Valley College on a research project to discover reasons for the recurrent finding that high school students aspiring to college were more likely to be using marijuana than those not planning on college. The explanation we finally advocated was the concept of "anticipatory socialization"—namely, that high schoolers bound for college saw marijuana use as a normal (if not necessary) part of college life (somewhat in the same way that youth more generally had always seen tobacco use as part of becoming "grown-ups"). Our empirical analysis of data from high school students supported this theoretical explanation and was eventually published.[27] It has even been cited with some frequency over the years, to judge from the frequency of its appearance on Google. It might seem somewhat ironic that my thinking about reactivating Mormon men would have been informed by my research on youthful marijuana use, but I clearly recall making that connection during our committee's discussions, and reference to it does appear in the minutes of our committee meeting for January 23, 1966.[28] In any case, this episode illustrates how social science theories and research can be embraced by priesthood leaders for direct application in new church policies.

Aaronic Youth Study

Late in 1967 or early in 1968, I was called back by Ray White of the PBO to serve on a new committee for a study of LDS Aaronic youth (teenage boys).[29] This committee consisted (besides myself) of Evan T. Peterson, of the sociology faculty at BYU, and Victor B. Cline, of the Psychology Department at the University of Utah. During this period, I was in a transitional stage of my career, having left my position at Diablo Valley College in California in favor of an appointment in sociology at Utah State University (beginning in the fall of 1967). Our committee worked together intermittently for perhaps a year, communicating sometimes by mail and telephone (well before the digital age, of course), but sometimes Ray

White would summon us to a meeting with him in the Presiding Bishop's Office at church headquarters to hammer out a progress report about our work for presentation to the Presiding Bishopric. On a couple of those occasions, when he needed a special report for his Monday meeting with the bishopric, White, in effect, barricaded us inside the otherwise closed church office building (at 47 East South Temple) throughout the preceding Saturday, so that we could have access to the typewriters and other office equipment normally used by the staff.[30] I found this a rather bizarre experience, but we did get a lot of work done!

It is useful to recall that in those days, Mormon girls tended to be seen by church leaders as docile creatures who would seldom get into any trouble if their parents were sufficiently vigilant. This stereotype was shared generally in the surrounding American society, but (like most stereotypes) was only partly justified by actual experience. Still, it was the Mormon boys who seemed much more inclined to test the boundaries of religious and moral propriety, and this tendency seemed to grow all the more conspicuous with the arrival of the permissive "Age of Aquarius." Our project on Aaronic youth started with a review of the professional literature about factors implicated in the religious commitment and activity of teenage youth, followed by a proposal for a large survey of LDS boys of Aaronic priesthood age (twelve to eighteen) to assess the impact of such factors in their actual lives.[31] Our proposal was accepted by Ray White and the Presiding Bishopric, which then funded an extensive survey carried out under circumstances that most researchers can only dream about, with resulting data that were both voluminous and rich.[32] Our initial findings were quite informative; they were duly reported in both oral and written form to Ray White and to the entire Presiding Bishopric and seem to have had some influence on future policy. Unfortunately, however, the potential for a more extensive study of Mormon boys was squandered with the passage of time by neglect of the data set, and eventually the cards on which the data were stored became obsolete and inaccessible, as punched cards were replaced by electronic tapes and discs.[33]

Our first report to the PBO from these data was made in early 1969 and took the form of an oral presentation accompanied by a series of graphics on an easel at the front of the room. I do not recall now who made the presentation (it was probably either Ray White or Evan Peterson, who had actually done most of the statistical analysis to that point). It was apparently planned by the PBO as a major event, for it was held with a dinner at what was then the Temple Square Hotel (since replaced), and more than a dozen church leaders and staffers were invited, including the entire Presiding Bishopric. The outcome, however, was somewhat abortive for reasons that I never quite understood. Our presentation started right after dinner, with a promise that we would get dessert at the end of the proceedings. This first presentation was to convey an overview of what the data indicated about the attitudes of the boys toward their religious observances and obligations.

We were well into the presentation when we learned what the boys had reported about their observance of the Word of Wisdom. Mixed with some fairly optimistic findings were data showing that the boys were nevertheless using marijuana and other drugs at about the same rates as were reported by non-Mormon boys in national surveys. After a moment of seemingly stunned silence, Bishop Vandenberg himself intervened to call a halt to the presentation and ask for dessert to be served. We never returned to the rest of the report, and the bishop never explained why. We just had dessert and went home. Ray White might well have delivered the rest of the report more privately on a later occasion, but I never heard about it. Nor was this the last indication in succeeding years that Mormon boys were experimenting to a noticeable extent with controlled substances, as well as with alcohol and tobacco, but the good bishop apparently did not want to air the matter any further on that occasion.

A little later we prepared a written report, confidential and proprietary, on the apparent effectiveness of the Aaronic priesthood youth program in preparing boys for missions and for church leadership. One of our recommendations was that more responsibility should be given—and more publicly—to the boy leaders as they rotated through the positions in the leadership of their respective quorums (deacon, teacher, and priest). The major tendency in those days was for adult leaders (quorum advisers) to conduct quorum meetings and to make assignments for the boys to handle the various quorum activities and responsibilities during church services and during the coming week. Our survey had indicated that the boys identified more strongly with their respective bishops, as priesthood leaders, than with their quorum advisers, who were, after all, not their line leaders. We surmised that if local bishoprics could model the principles of good leadership, and then offer guidance to the boy leaders in the actual (and not just symbolic) implementation of quorum responsibilities, the boys' investments in their roles as leaders would increase, and they would be more likely to acquire the skill and confidence to be effective leaders as young adults. This concept has often been labeled "shadow leadership," but I am not sure whether we used that term in our recommendations to the PBO. Yet I noticed that both the concept and the term began to appear during the early 1970s in the writings of the presiding bishop and his counselors, as Aaronic priesthood activities were subsumed under the new "correlation" movement of the church.[34] I feel sure that our committee's report to the PBO contributed significantly to the eventual implementation of the shadow leadership policy that has continued to inform the Aaronic priesthood program.

Projects of the LDS Research Information Division

After years of ad hoc research projects conducted by the staff of the Presiding Bishop's Office with the help of consultants, the church in 1976 organized the Research Information Division (RID) under the Correlation Department.[35] The initial staff consisted of a handful of social scientists, most with doctoral degrees, who responded to assignments from church leaders for periodic surveys of various segments of the membership and for systematic social research to evaluate existing church programs or to assess the need for new ones.[36] For the first several years, this relatively small staff continued to make use of volunteer consultants from the universities in Utah and elsewhere, but gradually the permanent professional staff was increased enough to keep all the work essentially "in-house"—a decision made in part to protect the proprietary work and data of RID from outside appropriation. Having seen the recent fate of the Arrington regime for its candor in the production of works in Mormon history,[37] the staff at RID took very seriously its orders to keep its projects entirely confidential. Accordingly, during the thirty-five years of its existence, RID has permitted very few of its work products to enter the public domain, especially in recent years, except for passing references occasionally in the church magazines. Within a decade of its founding, RID received high praise for the professional quality of its staff and their work from Rodney Stark, a prominent non-Mormon sociologist of religion.[38]

By the time RID was organized, I was on the sociology faculty at Washington State University, in Pullman, but I responded twice to invitations to serve as a consultant on RID projects. The first of these occurred in early 1982 and involved nothing more than a "workshop"—that is, a day of discussion with staff about a new project to identify and assess the importance of various factors (temporal and spiritual) implicated in disaffection or inactivity in the church.[39] In early 1982, the RID staff had prepared a research proposal to church leaders for this project, and I was asked to critique and discuss their proposal. I had written a theoretical article on church inactivity several years earlier, which was probably the reason my services were requested.[40] I was not involved in this RID project any further after the proposal stage.[41] Though some of the work products published from this project cited my early article, I never got the impression that such "consultation" as I provided for this project played a very important part in its eventual conclusions. Yet I was pleased to see some of the work from that project appear in the public domain.[42]

My involvement in a second RID project occurred during 1982–83 and was much more extensive. Early in 1981, I had been asked to provide a critique of a large prospectus for research on the conversion process, which had been prepared by the staff of RID.[43] As this project eventually developed, it consisted of a gigantic and systematic longitudinal study of the conversion process in selected missions of the western United States, as well as a more general worldwide study of the structural determinants of missionary success in various countries.[44] Among the consultants working on this project were several BYU professors from the Departments of Sociology, Psychology, and Communications, as well as myself.[45] Some of the BYU participants actually had portions of their BYU salaries covered by RID for their work on this project. My involvement was not that extensive, so I volunteered my time.[46] Nevertheless, I got deeply involved in the planning, as well as in the construction of some of the instruments for measuring key variables. The longitudinal study drew on systematic samples of recent converts, current investigators, and unconverted former investigators in an effort to determine which variables were most and least predictive of a successful conversion process and of retention for at least a year thereafter. The missionaries and the local LDS ward leaders involved with these converts and preconverts were also studied, as researchers actually accompanied missionaries on their visits and conducted interviews both with the missionaries and with the local leaders. In design it was a very sophisticated study intended to yield actual statistical weights assessing the relative importance of key variables (personal, pedagogical, theological, and situational) in the conversion and retention processes.[47]

It would be too much to expect such a complex study to go forward without unanticipated flaws and glitches, and there were plenty. Yet certain findings emerged that strongly informed the creation of the next edition of the standard missionary training manual, *A Uniform System for Teaching the Gospel* (1986), though less so in the case of the later version, *Preach My Gospel* (2004). Among the key findings was that *what* missionaries taught (special LDS doctrines) was not as important as *how* they taught. What seemed especially important was the skill of missionaries in building *affective relationships* based on common needs and experiences and in building friendship and trust in the investigators. Another finding was that the participation of LDS members as friends of the investigators greatly increased the likelihood of conversion and retention—a recurrent theme from earlier studies—but that only 3 percent to 5 percent of members were thus participating in identifying potential investigators and collaborating with the missionaries in teaching them. A few findings from this study appeared in bits and pieces in church magazine articles and conferences, and one major PhD dissertation came out of the study, but generally its methods and findings remained proprietary and out of the public domain.[48] During the intervening years, I have continued to have cordial and collegial contacts of various kinds with the RID staff, but I have not served as a consultant to any of the projects since the ones I just described. My impression is that as the staff has grown in size and experience, the resort to "outside" consultants (even to those from BYU) has greatly diminished.

My experiences in serving on various church research projects enhanced my understanding of how LDS leaders see the relation between the social sciences (or other sciences), on the one hand, and the revelatory processes claimed by those leaders, on the other hand. A widespread and useful myth among the Mormon rank and file is that all of the policies and programs implemented by church leaders have been received through divine revelation.[49] The flock in general is totally unaware of how much the revelatory process is informed by the research of experts and consultants, both from inside and outside the church itself. It is also important, however, to understand that this does not mean priesthood leaders simply (and cynically) take the findings of research and claim them as divinely revealed—any more than a government body or a corporate board would indiscriminately adopt the findings and recommendations of hired consultants. Mormon leaders might, however, with sincerity claim divine guidance in *how they choose to use* the products of research, and the faithful flock would accept that explanation, as long as the eventual decisions about policies, programs, and doctrines are understood as *ultimately* the products of divine revelation. The ultimately revelatory basis of all church teachings and policies is an important myth in Mormonism, and all the actors in the church leadership—whether apostles, bishops, or the professional church bureaucrats and researchers—function on that premise. Indeed, ordinary Latter-day Saints and potential converts are also urged to claim the right to divine guidance in making their own important life decisions.

A person at the managerial level in RID once offered me a revealing anecdote, which might be apocryphal, at least in part, but nevertheless illustrative: During preparations for the longitudinal conversion and retention research project, described above, the in-house research team was asked for a progress report by Elder Bruce R. McConkie, one of the most conservative apostles. After he had listened to a recital of all of the variables that were to be measured as "predictors" of an investigator's ultimate conversion, McConkie responded (in effect), "Well, all this talk about variables that will predict conversion is very interesting, but where in the conversion process have you made room for the influence of the Holy Ghost, which Moroni teaches is the power that really does the converting?"[50] One of the researchers might have anticipated such a question, for he quickly replied (in effect), "Moroni instructs those who receive the teachings of the Book of Mormon to seek the confirmation of the Holy Ghost *after* they have pondered and prayed, and what we are studying as social scientists is the process that gets investigators to the point where they are *motivated to ponder and pray* for divine confirmation." This partnership between research and revelation seemed to satisfy the apostle, and it illustrates well the pragmatic Mormon approach to managing the tension between the two in church governance more generally.

Chapter 3 | TOURING ACADEMIA IN SEARCH OF NEW REALITIES

WITH FIVE YEARS' BISHOPRIC SERVICE BEHIND ME, I VENTURED BACK INTO the secular academic world to resume my graduate studies in 1962. I was, of course, expecting to be exposed to new intellectual territory, especially since I was switching my disciplinary focus from history to sociology for the doctorate.[1] I did not, however, expect to be confronted with an entirely new ontology and episte- mology. As my intellectual development continued, the sociological concept that truth or reality is *socially constructed* turned out to offer a greater challenge to my religious faith than anything else I was to encounter in my entire academic career. I gradually came to terms with that challenge, however, and eventually became quite comfortable with the "social constructionist" way of understanding reality.

REALITY AS SOCIALLY CONSTRUCTED

My upbringing as a Mormon, as well as my intellectual training under the Jesuits at Sophia University, had equipped me with an absolutist or essentialist ontology. I recognized, of course, that there could be a variety of understandings and interpretations of reality derived from different cultures, religions, and life circumstances. Yet, among all of these, or perhaps outside of them, there would be a single ontology—an absolute reality as defined by God or as given in nature or both. The search for truth was a matter of applying the empiricism, the logic, and the epistemology, well known since the ancient Greeks, to get beyond all these differing conceptions to the *real truth,* or the *true reality,* in the universe. I have observed that most people, at least in the Euro-American world, grow up with similar epistemological and ontological assumptions and rarely have reason to question them.

I am not sure exactly when my own doubts about these assumptions began, but it was sometime after I returned to sustained doctoral study in sociology in the 1960s. I recall no sudden epiphany or "breakthrough," no sense that I was leaving behind one entire intellectual paradigm for a different one. My intellec- tual transitions always seem to have been gradual and evolutionary. I simply became increasingly aware of the need to reconsider and revise earlier assumptions in light of new ideas to which I had been exposed. Perhaps I also felt more free to venture into new intellectual territory because of certain changes in my "reference groups": I was no longer preoccupied with church service in a Mormon bishopric, and now that I was teaching in a community college, I was no longer limited to issues that were primarily of interest to schoolchildren and their parents. Instead, I was increasingly exposed to models of adventurous thinking by the faculty and graduate students in a doctoral program at a major university.

Among the works assigned for my graduate courses in sociological theory was Karl Mannheim's *Ideology and Utopia,* a collection of essays published decades earlier in Germany.[2] The prose was dense and the reading slow, even in English, but its effect (perhaps after a time lag) was eventually to help me realize how different visions of reality emerge from different social circumstances and, in turn, produce different prescriptions for social change. A more direct influence on my thinking came a little later from Peter L. Berger's and Thomas Luckmann's work *The Social Construction of Reality* and Berger's book *The Sacred Canopy.*[3] These works made clear the processes by which different cultures and interest groups construct the ideas, facts, and "plausibility structures" that come to be "taken for granted" by their respective members—a process defined as the "sociology of knowledge" in academia. The major implication here is that any notion of "absolute" truth or reality, of the kind promulgated by the Judeo-Christian traditions, might ultimately exist in the mind of God, or in some other great cosmological sense, but if so, we as human beings have no access to it through any field of science.

Therefore, if we embrace any reality as "objective," existing independently of human invention, of the kind claimed in religions like Catholicism or Mormonism, then we do so on *faith,* as a matter of *choice. Operationally* speaking, the only reality we "know" is that which has been constructed by our families and passed along to us as part of our cultural heritage. In this way of looking at reality, it is easy to see how different claims to truth are embraced as ontological realities, not only in religion but also in science, in politics, and in many other fields of human knowledge. Where religion was concerned, at least in my case, it became increasingly obvious that if I were to continue as an active believer in the LDS faith, it would be mainly a matter of *choosing* to embrace a certain construction of reality, not the result of a meticulous process of testing and proving incontrovertible claims about the supernatural. Where politics was concerned, the nature of reality would be equally elusive in an ontological sense; it would always be a matter of contention and would eventually depend on whatever the most powerful interest groups in a given society or community claimed it to be.

It was with these new realizations gradually dawning on me that I confronted both the religious issues and the political issues surrounding me in the 1960s and 1970s. The implications for my religious thinking will be discussed later. Here I want to deal mainly with the intellectual and scholarly issues raised for me by the *political* ferment of this period. Nor is this the place for an elaborate analysis and rationale about my personal political affiliations and preferences and how they evolved during my lifetime. Suffice it to say here that as a young adult coming out of the 1940s and 1950s, and a military veteran, I shared a nationwide yearning for a "normal" and peaceful domestic life after the disruptions of World War II and the Korean War. Yet I was pulled in two different directions: On the one hand, as a vigilant voter, I tried to pay attention to our evolving Cold War foreign policy, and to our internal conflicts, not only over civil rights for "Negroes" (of special concern to liberals), but also over "communist infiltration" (of special concern to conservatives). On the other hand, as a young father trying to get a career started, I was impatient with all ideological interest groups demanding strenuous action for change, seemingly with little regard for the unintended consequences or side effects upon other interests beyond their immediate horizons. In appealing to ultimate values, and in constructing truth claims with selective empirical evidence, these political interest groups, whether liberal or conservative, resembled religious sects contending over different constructions of reality.

John Kennedy's election as president in 1960 did nothing to calm the Cold War, of course, but it did represent a more liberal turn in the domestic politics of the nation and growing popular support during the ensuing decade for liberal causes such as civil rights and disengagement from the hostilities in Indochina. The 1960s eventually had a tremendous demographic and cultural impact on the nation, for that was the decade in which the first postwar "baby boomers" reached college age. Theirs was an age cohort that had grown up knowing neither war nor depression and thus tended to share a youth culture imbued with idealism, impatient with seeming injustice, and holding presumptions about certain kinds of entitlements. It was also a huge and growing cohort that created an anomalous bulge in the usually symmetrical population pyramid.

Many of the institutions of the nation, furthermore, especially the educational institutions, were overwhelmed by the sheer number of youngsters that they were obliged to handle. This unusually large proportion of adolescents and postadolescents, impatient for social and political change, created a crisis in what sociologists call "social control." Young people who were inclined to test the boundaries of behavior in schools, universities, churches, and even the law were less likely than in earlier generations to face or fear the traditional sanctions and penalties. Under the pressure of such boundary testing by so many of the youth, some of the nation's institutions were substantially changed, and many of the traditional norms and restraints on personal behavior gave way to academic permissiveness and hedonistic expressions quite bewildering to people in my generation.[4]

Exactly at what juncture this cultural transformation began is hard to say, but it burst upon the national consciousness in the form of one student uprising in Michigan in 1962 and another at UC-Berkeley in 1964.[5] Soon such uprisings occurred on many of the more elite campuses of the country (and even some not-so-elite ones by the end of the decade). They originated on different pretexts and claims in different places, but eventually they all took up about the same causes, namely, civil rights for black Americans, an end to the war in Vietnam, more student participation in the governance of universities, and in general the spread of greater "participatory democracy" in the nation's major institutions. They came to be known collectively as the "New Left" as distinguished from the "Old Left" earlier in the century, which had been based mainly in the labor movement and in the smaller political parties such as the Socialist and the Farmer-Labor Parties.

What is always at stake in the confrontations of such social movements with the surrounding society is *contending constructions of truth and reality* (though this is not always obvious to activists and observers while social movements are in progress). The New and the Old Lefts differed somewhat in their social-class origins, in the average age of their constituents, and in some of their issues, but they shared a critique of American society as essentially flawed by racism, inequality, oligarchy, and militarism. Such an image of America clashed, of course, with the reality that most Americans had constructed by the time of the Eisenhower era, having just saved the world from tyranny in just and righteous wars, entered a new and dangerous Cold War with the Soviet Union and its client states, and regained a level of economic growth and prosperity not known for decades. In that environment, the claims of the Left (especially the youthful New Left) seemed not only contrived but unpatriotic to much of the American public.

Clearly, many of the participants in this student movement were idealistic young reformers with a vision of how society could be improved. It seemed to me, however, as a firsthand observer of the movement at Berkeley, that the majority of those engaged in the protests were not so high-minded. Rather, they were a leisured class of kids who discovered that the academic routine of lectures, studies, and examinations was not nearly as much fun as disrupting classes with marches and chants, vandalizing buildings, and sharing cannabis with their friends. In those days, many of them had been reared in privilege by indulgent parents and sent to the best universities at their fathers' expense (or on scholarships from various benefactors)—*and* with draft deferments—while many of their less privileged peers were being drafted for a miserable and unpopular war in Vietnam.

I was not willing to take at face value the meliorist claims of these young reformers any more than the earlier claims of right-wing reformers who were so concerned about communists everywhere that they ruined the careers of teachers who refused to sign loyalty oaths.[6] Activists in any cause are likely to have a mixture of interests and motives, only some of which will be altruistic, and still others entirely cynical. The fate of any new social movement will depend not only on the interests, motivations, and skills of its participants, but also upon what support and resources it can mobilize from the surrounding environment. All such contingencies are problematic, which explains why most new movements, political or religious, do not last long. However, like every other group with special claims, new social movements, whether religious or political, construct their own definitions of truth and reality to serve their own keenly felt needs and interests. And so it was with the New Left.

THE "CONSTRUCTIONIST" PERSPECTIVE AND MY NEW LEFT PROJECT

As Berkeley's New Left mushroomed from 1964 on, it occurred to me that I might be watching the rise of another new movement that, like so many others, would rise and fall within a fairly short time. Since I was not a movement participant, I could study these developments with a degree of detachment and from a theoretical viewpoint. Although I was still employed at Diablo Valley College (until mid-1967), I was making two or three trips a week into Berkeley for my graduate studies. In that capacity, I not only had many opportunities for firsthand observations of the emerging movement on campus, but was in regular contact with several other graduate students and faculty members who were themselves studying various aspects of the movement, some of them as participants, some of them not. However, my eventual decision to do such a study was largely a product of serendipity, as is so often the case in academic work. I responded to a general call for papers on the emerging student movement from the editor of the *Journal of Social Issues* (a long-standing publication of the Society for the Psychological Study of Social Issues). I had in mind writing a single article that would compare the larger national movement (coming to be called "the New Left"), of which the campus unrest was a part, with the older traditional leftist tradition (then coming to be called "the Old Left").

I submitted an outline of what I proposed to write, and to my surprise the editor wrote back and asked if I would instead be willing to serve as guest editor for an *entire issue* of the journal devoted to this kind of comparison. I would be responsible for rounding up a number of knowledgeable colleagues to submit papers, provide an introductory and a concluding essay of my own, and do the preliminary editing that would ensure thematic continuity for the issue as a whole. I hesitated quite a while, since I was just starting my doctoral dissertation and was planning to leave Berkeley soon. Yet I knew several of my colleagues there, current or recent graduate students, who were already working on related topics and could probably craft respectable articles for my special issue in a few months. In that naive belief, I was terribly mistaken but benefited, early in my career, by learning a reality that any guest editor needs to know—namely, that academics are notorious for making commitments that they cannot keep, especially where there is no compensation involved, and for ignoring deadlines even if they do eventually honor their commitments. At length, however, three years after taking on this project, and after some attrition in my original list of collaborators, I finally delivered to the editor a collection of papers for the promised issue on the theme "The New Left and the Old." It contained ten articles altogether, including my introductory and concluding essays. My efforts were ultimately vindicated when the collection was accepted and published as the very first 1971 issue of the *Journal of Social Issues.* As guest editor I was especially gratified when it was made required reading in a course taught by Neil J. Smelser, my main mentor in the study of social movements at Berkeley.[7]

In my concluding essay to this New Left collection, I put forward a theoretical scheme that was to influence my future thinking about many other kinds of movements besides radical political ones. It implicitly recognized that reality was socially constructed but went beyond that basic premise to focus on the more dynamic issue of *what happens to movements and their constructions of reality across time.* In reflecting on the histories of both the Old and the New Lefts (brief though the latter was by then), I saw a common underlying process of development, despite many differences in historical details. The common process is a struggle between the movement and its host society, with the movement seeking to achieve its agenda for social change through mobilizing political and material resources in defense of a certain definition of reality; and the host society seeking to defend a different definition and to eliminate the movement (if possible), or at least to co-opt it and assimilate it. The contention over differing definitions of reality can occur either at a fairly superficial empirical level or at the deeper levels of epistemology or even ontology (or all of these). If not snuffed out early, a movement tends to follow a certain "career," or to pass through certain stages in this interaction with society. Eventually, the movement is partly co-opted and assimilated and, in the process, achieves some of its goals in the form of new poli-cies and new institutions embraced by the host society. The most radical elements in the movement, however, will not be won over, and their continuing agitation will make them increasingly unpopular and isolated, so that their residue of the movement will fragment and disappear.[8] This is not the place to go into any fur-ther detail on this project; the published work is in libraries for interested readers.

CONSTRUCTIONS OF REALITY, SOCIAL PROBLEMS, AND SOCIAL MOVEMENTS

It might be important for me to review the sources of this theoretical frame-work for understanding new social movements, for the same framework appears again in my 1975 book on social problems and in my 1994 book on the Mormons, though with further elaboration and adaptation in both cases. It has been cited also in later articles by myself and by others. How did I arrive at this theoreti-cal framework? I do not think any scholar realizes fully what the sources are of his or her thinking on any particular subject. Ideas acquired from others, often accidentally, appear in our heads without any recollection of exactly where they came from. In other cases, we can distinctly recall or associate the provenance with certain other scholars, colleagues, or conversations. My studies in the his-tory of social theories gave me ample exposure to the likes of Georg Hegel, Karl Marx, Auguste Comte, Herbert Spencer, William G. Sumner, Pitirim Sorokin, Franz Boas, Leslie White, and Julian Steward, all of whom (and many others) advanced theories about how history typically unfolds. Theories of this kind see all of history in cycles or stages, each stage giving way to the next through histo-rical processes that operate independently of individual human agency. It is al-most as though societies and their components are seen as organisms that develop in nature and evolve without human intentionality, much as plant and animal life do. Of course, individual human beings can, at certain junctures, precipitate crucial events in history, but history and its processes unfold mostly without (or despite) human intention.

Such a view of history is sometimes considered a variety of "historicism," and it has been widely criticized by both historians and social scientists. I never quite subscribed to any "hard-and-fast" version of this theoretical perspective (with inevitable sequences of stages, as Marx, for example, had argued). Nor do I subscribe to any version of teleological inevitability, but I have been persuaded that "soft" versions of theories about stages or cycles help us to make sense out of historical developments that no one seems to have planned or even wished to see occur. Such theories also provide a context for one of the enduring clichés in the social sciences, namely, the "law of unintended consequences." Somewhere in my studies, I came across the term *natural history* to describe such unintentional processes.[9] I had early associated that term only with the world of nature (plant and animal life) or natural systems, but when I saw "natural history" applied also to stages of development in human institutions, it seemed immediately to make sense as a way to understand *social* change as also made up of "natural" and unintentional processes. While this theoretical outlook has its origins in the biological disciplines, it seems to converge nicely with the social theories mentioned above. Indeed, nineteenth-century social theorists like Spencer and Sumner were sometimes called "social Darwinists." Again I hasten to add, however, that I do not associate myself with any theories of inevitable "progress" in the unfolding of history.

No historical episode exemplifies *contending constructions of reality* any better than a social movement does. By the time I finished my New Left project, I had come to recognize that the same processes involved in such movements also characterize certain historical episodes *not* usually considered "social movements," as this term is commonly applied. *New religions,* for example, at least those that survive any appreciable period, typically begin as *social movements* with their own constructions of truth and reality, with which they contend against the reality taken for granted in the surrounding society. Scholars eventually recognized this likeness as many new religions burst upon the scene in the wake of the student political movements discussed above, so eventually the highly publicized new religious expressions of the 1970s, such as the "Jesus Freaks," the "Moonies," and many others, came to be understood by sociologists as new religious movements, or NRMs, understandable through many of the theories already developed to account for other social movements.[10] As another example, nearly all conventional discussions of *social problems* have failed to recognize that a "social problem" is also simply a kind of social movement. That is because a condition in society is not identified as a "problem" until enough *powerful citizens and interest groups say so* and mobilize politically to get their constructions of reality widely accepted and placed on the national agenda for change or amelioration—just as any *social or religious movement* attempts to do. In other words, a "social problem" cannot exist except as the defining focus of a social movement.

This view of social problems has proved difficult for many Americans to grasp, especially young college students. The popular conception seems to be that "problems" in society are as susceptible to identification and correction as are problems anywhere. It is as though "everyone knows" what is bad for society, so it is just a matter of getting politicians and experts to study the problems and "solve" or ameliorate them. In such thinking, there is often an implicit analogy to human physical health and illness. That is, social problems are something like diseases that can be treated and cured. In fact, old textbooks in sociology sometimes used the term *social pathology* to refer to conditions in society that are considered harmful or "unhealthy," such as poverty, alcohol and drug addiction, and "illegitimacy" (children born outside of marriage). Sociology emerged as a new discipline in America during the so-called Progressive Era (late nineteenth and early twentieth centuries), when many social movements were under way for the "improvement" of society: alcohol prohibition, child and female labor protections, elimination of prostitution, immigration restrictions against certain "undesirable" populations, and other conditions that seemed to the political and religious leaders of the time as bad for society. Out of such thinking arose new organizations such as the American Social Hygiene Society (1913), dedicated to "cleansing" society from its ills and problems. A "mental hygiene" movement started during the same general period. Such terminology signified a growing tendency, still with us, to "medicalize" all social and psychological conditions considered "undesirable"—that is, to think of them as analogous to medical problems in the human body. The analogy is false, of course, because there is no equivalent in society of the "normal" in the human body—that is (as only one example) there is no societal equivalent of the standard and universal body temperature of 98.6 degrees Fahrenheit in healthy humans. Instead, conditions considered undesirable or "unhealthy" in some societies are considered in others as normal, irrelevant, or even preferable.

In other words, the very definition of terms like *unhealthy, undesirable, pathological,* and *social problem* have depended operationally upon the *political power* of those doing the defining. Yet this political process has never seemed obvious to most citizens. Instead, the great reform movements of American history, such as women's suffrage and the abolition of slavery, have been popularly considered in retrospect as simply natural and necessary "progress" toward making American society better. It is usually only with later historical study that people recognize the political mobilization that made such movements possible. People tend also to forget that some movements, which might have looked like "progress" at the time, produced "reforms" in public policy with such pernicious consequences that they had to be overturned by later generations. This was especially true of many reforms during the Progressive Era (for example, Prohibition, "protective" legislation for women restricting their access to certain occupations, and the selective immigration restrictions of the 1920s). More recently, the homosexual orientation, once regarded as a "disorder," has been redefined in the medical literature as a normal alternative to heterosexual preferences, and new "disorders" have been "discovered" that were once considered natural and unavoidable.[11]

Clearly, the definitions of *pathological social conditions, social problems,* and similar concepts have varied from one generation to another even in the same society. So how can we tell when any given social *condition* becomes a social *problem*? The historical record is very clear that there must be significant political mobilization focused on a condition in order for it to become a "social problem." Only when a large-enough (and powerful-enough) segment of the population comes to regard a condition as needing change does it become a "social problem." Only then are resources allocated to change or ameliorate the condition, and laws are advocated to discourage or even prevent the behavior believed to contribute to the newly problematic condition. No matter how undesirable a given social condition might seem, there is simply no *objective* basis on which to define any condition as a "social problem" by its very nature. Nevertheless, for a century the standard textbooks of sociology have taught students that social scientists can objectively identify a society's social problems and prescribe solutions for them, just as physicians do for physical ailments. Such an oversimplification of the sociology of "social problems" might make teaching easier, but ultimately it does a disservice to students by confirming their own naive understanding of the political realities.

Having taught the standard "social problems" course for several years at both the community college and the university levels, I became increasingly dissatisfied with this "objectivist" definition of social problems as the conceptual framework for the course. Then, at both Utah State and Washington State Universities, I was asked to teach courses also in "deviant behavior" at the upper-division level—an easy transition, since so many forms of deviant behavior have also been considered social problems, and vice versa. The more I studied and taught about theories of deviant behavior, the more obvious it became to me that both social problems and deviant behavior were never objective realities but were always relative to culture, subculture, and generation. Only as new norms of conduct or new laws were established by the politically powerful interest groups in a society did any form of behavior come to be considered "deviant" or in some way objectionable. In that sense, one could reasonably claim that the chief cause of crime is *law*! In order, therefore, to understand where deviant behavior comes from, we need to understand the origins of laws and of other standards of conduct by which behavior is judged in a given society; ultimately, that means we need to understand the *political processes* that produce those laws and standards. Such processes are, of course, the very dynamics of *social movements* (including religious movements).

The product of all this experience and reasoning was a new graduate course that I prepared at WSU on the theories of deviant behavior and social problems. The year was 1973, and the enrollment was about a dozen graduate students. The course was organized in traditional seminar format, which meant that the class members would study a common body of professional literature, but then each would apply what he or she had studied in general to a specific and empirical case of a "social problem." The product from each student would be a seminar paper that would contribute something new to our existing knowledge about the origin and development of the "problem." The common focus of the class was on theories of deviance and social problems, culminating in the theoretical innovation I was proposing, namely, the analysis of any "social problem" as fundamentally the product of a *social movement*. I provided a comprehensive theoretical framework, and each student submitted a paper applying that framework to a different "social problem" on the national agenda at that time.

From the beginning, I held out the prospect that some or all of these papers might be published in a collection based on my theory. I had been negotiating with an editor at Lippincott to write such a book by myself, but I recognized that it could be done much faster if I enlisted some able students to function, in effect, as research assistants to collect the empirical evidence that would illustrate and vindicate my theory for many *different kinds* of social problems. In addition to regular graduate credit for the course, I offered each student two hundred dollars if his or her paper was strong enough to be included as a chapter in the forthcoming book. I offered a similar amount to a few other students and colleagues from outside my course whom I knew to be capable of following my theory and producing good chapters. I was to write two introductory chapters. The eventual outcome was *Social Problems as Social Movements,* a sixteen-chapter work of more than six hundred pages, published by Lippincott in 1975. A derivative edited collection, *This Land of Promises: The Rise and Fall of Social Problems in America,* published by the same company two years later, contained a few papers from the same project that could not be included in the 1975 book, plus a few previously published by other authors (with appropriate permissions) that also seemed to illustrate and support my underlying theory.

These projects took an enormous amount of my time, since almost all of the student drafts required extensive reworking on my part (and this was in the typewriter age, well before word processors were available!). Both books were academically successful in the sense that they provided a unifying focus for my graduate course and "converted" most of the participating graduate students to my theoretical framework on which the books were based. Some of the students later even published work of their own based on the same framework.[12] Two or three of the students, however, let it be known that they were dissatisfied with the compensation and recognition that they had received in this process (despite the course credit, the two hundred dollars each, and their names at the front of the book as contributors). It was then that I came fully to recognize that when two authors collaborate, especially when one is professionally junior to the other, they can never fully agree on who did whom the greater favor in the collaboration! For the senior author, the safest course ethically is to give the junior person top billing (first authorship), no matter who does most of the work on the project. Such became my general policy thereafter in my collaborations with students, even when the eventual written product was mine from the very first word (which was often the case).

These two books on "social problems," or at least the first one, nevertheless brought me a fair amount of professional visibility in the discipline of sociology. Yet they were not very successful commercially. Unbeknownst to me, the publisher was having financial difficulties and was not able to do the vigorous marketing required in promoting the books. A more fundamental reason for the mediocre sales of the 1975 book was my decision to produce it as a textbook for students, rather than as primarily a work of scholarship aimed at my professional peers. I was anxious for the book to make inroads into the education of college students, who were then (even as now) captive of the conventional "objectivist" theoretical orientation toward social problems with its pathology analogue and meliorist agenda. Of course, I also saw the large student market as potentially a new source of income. Yet, on the other hand, I wanted to start a theoretical and intellectual debate over the regnant "objectivist" paradigm among my academic peers in the discipline of sociology, perhaps to convince them that there ultimately was no independent theoretical basis for the study of "social problems" apart from the theoretical study of social *movements*. Although my *Social Problems as Social Movements* was quite favorably reviewed in the main review journal of the discipline,[13] it never was a great success in the marketplace. The book fell into a crack, as it were, between two markets: textbooks and academic trade books. Each market seemed to relegate it to the other category in considering its uses. It was never widely adopted for classroom use ("too theoretical"), for total sales of the book never went much beyond ten thousand copies.

On the other hand, among scholars and teachers who thought of themselves as specialists in "social problems," my thesis identifying social problems as simply a variety of social movements proved controversial and generated a certain amount of discussion in the professional literature. It was still being debated in that literature more than a decade later.[14] It seemed to me that there were two main reasons for the difficulty in recognizing the truly novel nature of my theory. First, intellectually, politically, and temperamentally, social scientists (especially sociologists) are social meliorists; that is, they are hopeful that their work can ultimately improve society, and they are reluctant to accept an argument (such as mine) that the very definition of "improvement" itself is not objective but is culturally relative and is dependent on political action for its very meaning. Second, in the social sciences (and, I suspect, in the humanities), truly innovative theories—especially paradigm shifts—are so rare that a desperate search for them constantly generates neologisms—that is, words or terms that might seem at first to refer to some new and different ideas, but under real scrutiny turn out to be only new terms for well-known concepts that earlier generations had called by some other names. I noticed this problem especially in the case of some valuable early work by John Kitsuse and Malcolm Spector, whose two 1973 essays had very much influenced my own thinking—as had the work of Fuller and Myers (noted earlier).[15]

Eventually, Spector and Kitsuse expanded their articles into a short book, *Constructing Social Problems,* which happened to appear two years after my *Social Problems as Social Movements.*[16] As I perused their new book, I expected to find that it would acknowledge the convergence between my theory and theirs, since, after all, I had embraced the general approach in their articles but had simply gone beyond it with my claim that "social problems" ultimately have to be treated as social *movements,* rather than as some separate sociological category. Instead, Spector and Kitsuse referred to my book mainly to dismiss it with the passing observation that it was actually about social *movements,* which they considered *altogether different* from social *problems,* the topic of *their* book! They never dealt with my fundamental argument that "problems" and "movements" turn out to be *operationally* the same thing. Spector and Kitsuse then went on at great length (with numerous examples) to elucidate the process they called "claims-making," complete with stages or phases in the development of "social problems," seemingly oblivious to the sociological literature treating claims-making as one (but only one) key ingredient among typical social *movement* processes. Their book was not as favorably reviewed as mine in the main review journal of sociology, but it seemed to gain greater currency in the marketplace, perhaps because it was so short (!), or perhaps because Kitsuse had been so long associated with the general social constructionist perspective on social problems.[17]

In the decade that followed, arguments continued in print and in conferences between sociologists like myself, who were "subjectivists"—believing that "social problems" were socially constructed and therefore in the eye of the beholder—

and the more orthodox "objectivists," who believed that "social problems" were objective conditions (somewhat like pathologies in the human body) that could be identified as failures in social structures or processes and therefore could be "treated" by the right kinds of social and political interventions. A few "subjectivists" shared my contention that a social problem is operationally only a kind of social movement launched by powerful interest groups, but the larger and more important division has remained between the *subjectivist* and *objectivist* camps. To all appearances, the latter camp has won the argument as far as the textbooks are concerned, virtually all of which, now even well into the twenty-first century, still make the standard presentation of social problems as objective conditions that can (and should) be changed. Rarely does one see any of these textbooks address the issue of why these "problem" conditions are *historically relative*—why, for example, homosexuality was once considered a "social problem" discussed in textbooks, but is not so considered anymore, or why traditional gender role differences that were widely considered "normal and natural" for centuries have lately become "problems."

Yet after its publication in 1975, my book was gradually recognized by many sociologists for its innovative theoretical contributions. A year after its publication, it was praised in letters from two of the most venerable scholars in the study of collective behavior and social movements, Professors Joseph Gusfield (University of California–San Diego) and Herbert Blumer (UC-Berkeley), both of whom recognized its importance. Gusfield's letter, in particular, was quite long and praised the book for (among other things) its "freshness of ideas, thoroughness of coverage, and consistent concern with basic assumptions" and went on to note that he had assigned the book as a major part of the reading for his *graduate* seminar.[18] Despite the limited marketing that the book received, it has been periodically rediscovered during succeeding decades by scholars who have found my basic conceptualization of social problems to be useful in their own work—that is, recognizing social problems as ultimately *movements,* or at least the products of movements, based on *constructions of reality* promoted by politically powerful interest groups.

During the arguments over my theory in the years that followed, some of the most prominent scholars in the study of social problems and social movements have sent me letters concurring with my theoretical position as I periodically reiterated it (for example, in my 1984 *Newsletter* article, mentioned above).[19] Even a few textbook authors selected excerpts from my 1975 book to emphasize the "social movement" aspects of social problems.[20] More gratifying yet was the occasional citation of my book by scholars in other professions, such as law and medicine. For example, a 1982 article in the *Indiana Law Journal* cited the book three times, and a 1993 article in a European medical publication "[drew] heavily upon the work of Armand Mauss (1975, 1989), who sees social problems as inseparable from social movements."[21] However, the widest professional exposure of my book and its main thesis occurred when it was cited as the basis for the general theme in two annual conferences of the Society for the Study of Social Problems.[22] Professor Rudolfo Alvarez, SSSP president for 1986, announced that the theme he had chosen for the national conference of the SSSP that year ("The Social Problem as an Enterprise") was explicitly derived from my 1975 book.[23] Three years later, for the 1989 national conference of the SSSP, President Joseph Gusfield announced, with an even more explicit reference to my book, that the conference theme that year would be "Social Problems as Social Movements," the very title of the book itself.[24]

In recognition of the work I had published in both social problems theory and in alcohol studies, I was invited in 1995 by the Society for the Study of Social Problems to apply for the editorship of its journal, *Social Problems*.[25] I would probably have made a pretty good editor, considering that I had published some rather visible work in both theoretical and applied aspects of "social problems" and that I had recently completed four years as editor of another major journal, the *Journal for the Scientific Study of Religion*. However, I declined the invitation, for by this time in my career, I was starting on a trajectory toward gradual retirement, and I no longer had the appetite for another heavy responsibility such as editor of a major academic journal. Then, in the final decade of the century, I was invited to write the sole article "Social Problems" for the authoritative *Encyclopedia of Sociology*, where I was able to advance my conception of *social problems as social movements* in a form and venue where it will prevail for some years as an authoritative definition of social problems whenever it is consulted by users of this enduring encyclopedia.[26] Thus, in sum, my theoretical framework has received a certain amount of vindication considering its use two times as the theme of national conferences of the SSSP, the invitation I received to apply for the editorship of *Social Problems*, and the adoption of my position in an important encyclopedia article. My theoretical innovation will always be encapsulated in the title of my 1975 book, *Social Problems as Social Movements*, though, alas, both the book and its author have long been forgotten in the intervening four decades!

At least as important as any contribution that I might have made to theoretical sociology through this line of work, however, was the intellectual impact on me of the *social constructionist epistemology* on which this work was based. Now rather conventional in the social sciences generally (if not in the study of social problems), this conception of epistemology is radically relativistic in its rejection of any conception of truth or reality that might unite all humans around a single understanding thereof. Certainly, it challenges both the traditional Christian and the Mormon conceptions of reality that I had embraced as a youth. As I gradually came to recognize and adopt this social constructionist understanding in my sociological work on political processes, social movements, and new religions, I could not, of course, escape its implications for my own religious commitments. I thought back to my early experiences in Japan and finally realized how my exclusive resort to a Mormon epistemology in those days had prevented me from fully understanding and appreciating the Japanese culture.

My reflections on this predicament, however, led me *not away* from faith but rather *toward* a realization that in order to engage any community of discourse, whether ethnic, religious, political, or any other kind, I would first have to understand that community's epistemology and ontology. My understanding, then, would depend on interpreting its discourse and behavior through the lens of its own shared conceptions of reality, rather than through my own or other lenses that I might bring to the examination. The same would be true, of course, for understanding the discourse and behavior in *my own* religious community. I had already learned to understand LDS reality as an insider and had taken that for granted. My new understanding, however, did not require me to abandon my religious community, ontology, or epistemology, but only to embrace them as a matter of *choice,* rather than as the only valid way of seeing reality.

Such a recognition seemed to accord also with a theological conception of *faith* as an *active personal choice,* rather than as a passive acceptance of a religious tradition. A social constructionist understanding of reality, furthermore, leaves one free also to reject any *secular* definition as the only "true" understanding of reality, since no particular epistemology can claim privileged status in the eyes of God or nature—or (still less) in Academia. Any epistemology has validity only within its own community of discourse. My "Mormon passport," then, was as valid as any other as I traveled through the various communities of discourse that I encountered. This line of reasoning, one might say, further relativizes the relativity of the social scientist's construction of reality. The scholar thus remains free to embrace the epistemology and ontology of a religious believer for ordering his or her *own* life and world, while at the same time being entirely free to venture into other epistemological worlds to understand other peoples with *their* respective discourse and behavior.

Chapter 4 | REVISITING THE MORMONS
New Perspectives Encounter
Narrower Boundaries

MUCH HAD CHANGED IN MY LIFE AND IN THE WORLD AROUND ME WHEN I resumed my graduate work in the early 1960s. Since it was no longer feasible for me to continue in Asian studies and history (as explained in the previous chapter), I accepted an offer from the director of graduate studies in the new Department of Sociology to enter the doctoral program there.[1] In the new department, I was left free to progress through the program at my own speed. That was important, since I was still a full-time teacher. Even though I was now at a community college, where I had more control over my teaching schedule and time out of class, my teaching load was still heavy, and my graduate work, though sustained, was still only at about half speed.[2] My remaining graduate school years seem, in retrospect, to have been a blur of advanced course work, with written and oral examinations in sociological theories and methods—as well as in the two required foreign languages—plus preparation of scholarly papers for advanced courses, for conferences, and for eventual publication. Still more children were born (to a total of eight), and my church work continued at a somewhat reduced level. During the next five years, I served Walnut Creek Ward first as head (then called general secretary) of the Aaronic adult program (as it was then called), and then as head of the Aaronic priesthood program for young men (teenage boys).

NEW MENTORS AND NEW INTELLECTUAL DIRECTIONS
Even though my bishopric service had necessitated a hiatus from regular graduate studies, I had made frequent trips to the Berkeley campus, as time would permit, for an occasional evening or summer course offered by the Sociology Department. My entry into that department was made easier by the hospitable and friendly attitude of the faculty and several other graduate students. Especially helpful from the faculty were Neil J. Smelser, the late Hanan C. Selvin, and Charles Y. Glock. Smelser, from Harvard, had been a student of Talcott Parsons and a leading sociologist in the study of collective behavior and social

movements, which became a major focus of my own graduate study. During those days, he was also dean of the graduate school at Berkeley, and helped to facilitate my progress through the graduate program. He was about my own age—actually two years younger—and he seemed to sympathize with my aspirations to make up for lost time in finishing my graduate education. Selvin, like Glock, had been a student at Columbia University and a disciple of survey methodologist Paul Lazarsfeld there. Selvin was thus my first teacher in survey methodology and the first of my mentors to suggest that some of my work was good enough to be published. The constant encouragement of Smelser and Selvin gave a big boost to my self-confidence and morale. In the long run, however, the most important of all my professors was Charles Y. Glock, who soon became my chief mentor and the sponsor for my doctoral studies.[3]

As another Columbia expert in survey research methods, Glock continued my education in that field, but he was my mentor mainly in the sociology of religion. He was a reserved, unpretentious, and cautious scholar with a continuing and sincere commitment to his own Lutheran upbringing. He had already done some organizational studies of churches, and he regarded the institutional church as a potential source of improvement in society. He knew nothing about Mormons, and was somewhat intrigued with what I had to say. However, he also seemed wary of students who, having acquired religious doubts, might be using sociology as a rationale and vehicle for rejecting faith or even ridiculing it. I recall once being surprised, and a little bemused, at his response when he learned that I was questioning some aspects of my own religious heritage of Mormonism. He said something to the effect that he hoped my studies would not devolve into simply debunking my religious tradition, Mormon or otherwise. I was certainly able to relieve his concerns on that score. Ironically, however, somewhere during the final decades of his own long life, Glock became increasingly jaded about the efficacy and usefulness of institutional religion and even about religious belief in general. I think that eventually he came to consider himself an atheist, or at least deeply agnostic.

Nevertheless, our teacher-student relationship in the early 1960s increasingly developed into a lifelong friendship, which continues to this very time (2012), when Glock is ninety-three. Such has been possible in part because at his early retirement (age sixty), he left Berkeley for pleasant rustic habitations in northern Idaho, very close to where I had my own thirty-year career in eastern Washington. He and his wife, Margaret (Mickey), were extraordinarily hospitable hosts, as they regularly invited Ruth and me for overnight visits to their picturesque waterfront homesteads (as they did also for many other guests every summer, well into their advanced years). Charlie has been a faithful friend—and still a mentor—for a half century, despite significant religious and political differences between us. His encouragement, sponsorship, and promotion of my work have been a constant inspiration, and I have felt highly flattered to have been kept among the few of his former students with whom he still retains regular contact.

Among Glock's other students was Rodney Stark. He too became a good friend, beginning in our graduate school days, and even now we have occasional contact. Rod was a few years younger than I but had entered the graduate program well before me, and he had quickly been handpicked by Glock as his main research assistant for an extensive new research project on the Christian sources of anti-Semitism (of which I shall have more to say in a later chapter). Glock and Stark eventually became a very visible team through joint authorship of several books, somewhat surprisingly in light of the contrast in their personal styles and belief systems. Rod was loquacious, confident, and occasionally self-aggrandizing, with but few doubts about which colleagues were his equals and which were not. He could easily monopolize a conversation, but he was always worth listening to, both because of the substance and because of the colorful, and often hyperbolic, style of his expressions.

For the first few years, I considered Rod also as a mentor, since he was close to Glock and knew the discipline and methodology of the social sciences much better than did I as a novice. He was always gracious to me during our early days, and complimentary about some of my work. He kept me apprised of the methodology and progress of his research with Glock on anti-Semitism, and on one or two occasions he even helped me a bit on my research with Richard Wooley about East Bay Mormons, which I described in chapter 2. Stark too became somewhat intrigued with Mormons, partly because of what he was learning about them from me, but also for more personal reasons: his aging parents eventually moved to Berkeley (from North Dakota), where they encountered Mormon missionaries and eventually joined the LDS Church. They apparently had considerable physical needs, which were willingly provided by the local LDS community, much to the astonishment and admiration of son Rod. He always retained an appreciation and admiration thereafter for all things Mormon, but he was never convert material, for he always insisted that he was agnostic.

I left Berkeley a few years before Rod did, but by 1971 we were both in Washington, he at the University of Washington in Seattle and I at Washington State University in Pullman. During the 1970s, whenever I had occasion to visit Seattle on research business, we would go out together, frequently to a favorite Japanese restaurant, compare notes about our current research endeavors, and share gossip about erstwhile Berkeley colleagues. Gradually, his ties to Glock frayed and left him free to turn toward other research interests.[4] By the end of that decade, he had developed those interests in the directions for which he was to become justly renowned for the rest of his career. This work began in collaboration with William S. Bainbridge, a junior colleague of Rod's on the University of Washington faculty, and soon resulted in a series of articles drawing on social exchange theory to explain religious behavior. Eventually, those essays were assembled into a substantial book that is still important.[5] During the 1980s and 1990s, he collaborated with a series of his students at the university, most notably Roger Finke, in applying his general theory to certain specific historical cases.[6] Finally, around 1990, he discovered the work of Laurence Iannaccone, resulting in a merger of their theoretical approaches into what has come to be called the "new paradigm."[7] Based on "rational choice" theory from economics, this theoretical framework has largely set the modern research agenda in the sociology of religion, both for its advocates and for its critics. My own first book on the Mormons drew heavily on this "new paradigm," so I shall have more to say about that in the next chapter.[8]

As Rod and I became more involved in building our respective careers at the two Washington universities, we acquired different professional preoccupations, and we came to have decreasing personal contact. We occasionally phoned each other about issues of mutual interest in the sociology of religion, and I continued for some time to be his main informant on Mormon matters. Quick learner that he is, he soon felt less need to consult with me, and, in fact, he became well acquainted with several other LDS scholars who could also be helpful to him. He never lost his interest in Mormons or Mormonism, even finding in the Mormon movement a number of useful analogies for his 1996 book on the success of early Christianity.[9] When I was president of the Mormon History Association, he accepted my invitation to deliver the annual Tanner Lecture at the 1998 MHA conference in Washington, DC.[10] Eventually, however, he left behind his collaborators and old friends for a remarkable series of solo-authored books on the importance of religion—especially Christianity—in the history of Western civilization. His retirement from the University of Washington was followed by a new affiliation with Baylor University in Waco, Texas, in 2004, where he established a program in the sociology of religion, the Institute for Studies of Religion, and an online academic journal. In the process, he also came to think of himself more as an "independent Christian" than as an agnostic.[11]

Perhaps rather ironically, therefore, Glock and Stark have moved in opposite directions where religious faith is concerned, the one becoming more agnostic and the other less so. Although I have had but little contact with Stark in recent years, I have always admired him for his powerful intellect and his prodigious scholarly output. I made this clear in a tribute as part of a panel commenting on his work at the annual conference of the Society for the Scientific Study of Religion in 1990—and this was before his career was to have its major impact on the above-mentioned "new paradigm"![12] For his part, Rod has always acknowledged the early orientation I gave him in all things Mormon.[13] However, for some reason he has given but little attention to my published work on Mormons, even when it was directly relevant to his own (a quandary that I mention also in the next chapter). At the end of the century, in a kind of summing up of his work in the "new paradigm," Stark reflected on the debt that he and I and many others have always had to Charles Glock, the founder and center of the "Berkeley Circle," which Stark describes as an "extraordinary collection" of dozens of graduate students and younger colleagues who gathered around Glock, and in many cases were financed by his research projects, during the 1960s and 1970s.[14] Stark was certainly one of the stars in that circle, as were few others. I never considered myself among the stars, but I benefited enormously by my identification with the Berkeley Circle, for it served as a network of colleagues who always supported my professional development and aspirations and who collectively had such an impact on the flowering of the sociology of religion in those halcyon days.[15]

In my doctoral studies at UC-Berkeley, I learned and used the latest methods in survey research, and I came increasingly to understand the alternative ideologies from which sociological theories were derived. My intellectual orientation, as well as my religious faith, were increasingly influenced during these years by three lines of thought in particular: the ultimate nature of "reality" as so many *social constructions* by interest groups with the power to enforce their definitions of truth (as explained in the previous chapter), the empirical regularities found in the operation of complex human societies and organizations, and the theories advanced to explain those regularities.[16] These new understandings did not so much undermine my Mormon apologetic tendencies as they taught me to recognize and focus on the *human element* in all religious doctrines and practices, a realization that was firmly established in my thinking by the time I finished my graduate work.

Meanwhile, the Age of Aquarius was dawning in American society and fast approaching both the campus and the church.[17] The effect of this movement was to "liberate" a whole generation of youth from the moral constraints that their parents and grandparents had regarded as the basis for responsible citizenship. On many college campuses, this liberation ended such reluctance as most students had ever felt to test all sorts of boundaries, whether academic, political, or moral.

Historians of this period will disagree on the extent to which either the youth or their academic institutions have been improved or debased by this cultural revolution, but it did unleash a political consciousness and energy among the youth that replaced the traditional political apathy on college campuses.[18] Thereafter, colleges and universities—at least some of the elite campuses—became hotbeds and recruiting grounds for various political movements, especially for the antiwar movement and for the civil rights movement (at first on behalf of African Americans but eventually extending to various minorities and to women). Most Mormons of that time, the mid-1960s, at least those living in the traditional Mormon heartland of the Mountain West, did not seem very attentive to these movements, except, of course, for a small group of liberals.[19]

However, for me as a resident of the San Francisco Bay Area, a social science instructor at community colleges there, and especially as a graduate student in sociology at UC-Berkeley, there was no escaping the turmoil. As for my own personal political inclinations of the time, I was increasingly a disciple of William F. Buckley, and I shared the national ambivalence about both the antiwar movement and the civil rights movement from the mid-1950s onward. I was doubtful about the justification for the war in Vietnam, yet I believed that the world in general, and our country in particular, was in a decisive struggle with the Soviet Union and its client states. I recognized that black people in our society had been subjected to centuries of oppression and injustice, but some of the immediate remedies proposed struck me as disruptive without proving efficacious. Furthermore, in the world of academia, where I was a self-supporting graduate student, I also felt a certain resentment (as noted in my previous chapter) about campus disruptions by youthful social reformers with the luxury of raising hell on stipends from others.

The LDS Retrenchment Response

If some college campuses, and even some religious denominations, were welcoming the emerging political and cultural changes, the leadership of the Church of Jesus Christ of Latter-day Saints was moving in the opposite direction—strengthening traditional moral and political boundaries rather than relaxing them. Indeed, a major movement was developing within the LDS Church, seemingly in direct reaction against some of these changes in the surrounding society—a movement that I eventually came to describe as "retrenchment." At first I found it hard to articulate what I was feeling in the changing ecclesiastical culture of the church. As a lifelong member in California, I had grown up with certain assumptions and expectations about how the church worked and what constituted the Mormon way of life. The church of my youth, though ultimately hierarchical in its organization, was nevertheless quite loosely controlled (even in Utah), with much autonomy for the auxiliary organizations and not much pressure on individual members for homogeneous thinking, or even for very meticulous compliance with behavioral strictures. I had always experienced the church as a *formerly* radical religious community in the process of being assimilated and "Americanized." Increasingly, it had been embracing the "normal" in America, politically, intellectually, and culturally. Of course, from a contemporary vantage point, that America now seems very conservative. At that time, however, Mormons did not feel a great cultural or political gulf between themselves and other Americans, even though that feeling was not widely reciprocated from the outside. Yet with the increasing retrenchment after midcentury, the gap between Mormon culture and the surrounding American culture began to widen, and the two seemingly began to evolve in opposite directions. The church was feeling less comfortable for me, and I sought explanations. Was it all just because of changes in me?

At first I looked to the standard sociological explanations, such as the time-honored (if somewhat simplistic) theory of *secularization*—namely, that all religious movements were dying out or being assimilated as insignificant cultural relics of a primitive age, for modern societies were all growing increasingly scientific, sophisticated, and free of traditional superstitions about an unseen world. Up to the middle of the twentieth century, it certainly seemed that Mormonism had been making a series of accommodations with modernity that were leading it in that general direction. Polygamy had been renounced, there was no more United Order, no new revelations had been formally promulgated by mid-century, Mormon preaching and proselytizing resorted much more often to the Bible than to the Book of Mormon, Mormons were all voting for the two major parties (in about equal numbers), and significant material resources of the Church were going into somewhat professionalized social welfare programs. The most senior and visible leaders were men of advanced education and worldly sophistication, whose writings defended Mormonism on scholarly and intellectual grounds, not just with faith claims. (One thinks of Roberts, Talmage, Widtsoe, and Merrill.) That had been the church of my youth, but clearly something different was happening as I became a young adult, something that could not be explained by seeing Mormonism as simply on its way toward assimilation into the American religious mainstream.

Beginning in the 1960s, I began to see changes that seemed to represent a somewhat more deliberate and assertive posture on the part of the LDS leadership. Though I now describe that era in retrospect as a period of retrenchment, at the time I did not know quite how to articulate what seemed to be happening. The first signs I noticed were extensions of new or augmented programmatic efforts to shape religious training at the grassroots. One of these was a churchwide program called Family Home Evening (FHE), which had existed as a concept throughout the twentieth century but had never been implemented as a formal church program. Starting in the early sixties, however, the church called for each family to hold regular Family Home Evenings and actually provided manuals to guide families on how to establish and conduct these meetings. Eventually, the church institutionalized the FHE as a weekly event and forbade the scheduling of any other LDS-sponsored meetings or activities on that night anywhere in the church. My wife and I became personally committed to this new program and regularly held FHEs for almost the next twenty years, until our children had all left the nest. We could not have managed such a large family otherwise.[20]

Also in the early sixties (if not a little earlier), the church began a massive expansion of its formal religious education program. A daily program of religious instruction during released time from the public school day, called "seminary," had existed in Utah and Idaho since early in the century, and a few college-level "institute" programs had been established at the University of Utah and other colleges in the region. In Utah and Idaho, seminary and institute typically even had their own buildings, usually found across the street or nearby the schools and colleges that they served. However, after midcentury, the Church Education System was charged with setting up institute programs at all the major universities of the land, eventually to include even junior colleges. Later in the century, institute and seminary programs were established also in many foreign countries. Seminary was also restructured and expanded into a non-released-time format, so that LDS students all over the country could take their seminary classes in the early morning before school, meeting either in nearby churches or in members' homes. This restructuring and expansion of CES programs, with heavy pressures on all families and students to participate, greatly intensified the church's influence over the daily religious instruction of its youth. As I mentioned in an earlier chapter, I had taught an early-morning seminary class for four years before and after 1960, for which I was paid and was expected to attend monthly training sessions held by traveling administrators.

I recall being pleased originally with the new FHE and CES initiatives of the church leaders, since they seemed likely to enhance and strengthen both family life and systematic religious instruction around the church. However, I was increasingly restive and concerned about certain other signs indicating that a new postwar generation of church leaders was moving to magnify and intensify its control not only over organizational processes, but also over the religious and intellectual lives of its members as individuals. In particular, a re-vitalized "correlation" effort (rather dilatory since the 1920s) began gradually to centralize operations of the entire ecclesiastical organization, including all the auxiliaries, under the apostles and the First Presidency, with operational authority confined to the priesthood ranks. Although not apparent during the 1960s, at least not to the rank and file, this "correlation" process was gradually to have certain consequences and implications (some no doubt unintended) during the succeeding decade: for example, reduction in the status and power of LDS women, both in their ecclesiastical and in their domestic roles; reduction in the tenure and authority of local bishops, stake presidents, and mission presi-dents; standardization and reduction in the intellectual rigor of church publi-cations and instructional materials for the auxiliaries (such as Sunday school); declining tolerance in the priesthood leadership for independent intellectual activities of members that it could not control (publications, symposia, study groups, "firesides," and so on); and the interposition of a large paid, professional civil service–like bureaucracy between the members and their lay priesthood leaders[21] in the planning and implementation of the "correlated" policies and teachings from headquarters.

As I watched all these developments occur, I was already enough of a social science buff that I began searching for a coherent general explanation that might make sense of what I was seeing. I knew in a general way what was obvious to any knowledgeable observer of the time—namely, that the membership of the church was growing rapidly (both from proselytizing and from a large birthrate) and that the growth was occurring mainly in urban areas, especially in the Far West, but also along the Eastern Seaboard. I began thinking deductively about how these processes of growth and urbanization might logically be expected to affect Mormons and their church. My general reading in the sociology of religion to that point, as well as my observations of religion in the San Francisco Bay Area, suggested that religious denominations with memberships based mainly in urban areas tended to be more modernist or liberal in their religious beliefs than their counterparts with heavily rural membership bases and that even within the same denomination, the thinking, preaching, and behavior among church members would become less traditional and less conservative as they moved from rural to urban areas. In my Mormon experience, I saw the same general tendencies in the differences between urban and rural wards, and especially in the differences be-tween the somewhat parochial culture of Utah and the more cosmopolitan cul-ture of California. Yet, at the same time, as indicated above, I was seeing trends within the LDS Church leadership that looked more conservative than liberal. What was happening?

Living and Working with a Church in Retrenchment

As my graduate studies progressed, I began thinking about making this quandary the topic of my doctoral dissertation. However, as the civil rights campaign grew in strength and intensity around the nation, so did national attention to the Mormons' anachronistic racial policies. Especially because I was living in the San Francisco Bay Area, the race issue urged itself increasingly to my attention. For a while, I thought of simply including that issue as part of a dissertation that would have a broader focus, which I described as "Mormonism and urbanism," but as the 1960s unfolded, it became obvious to me that the consequences of Mormon doctrines and practices about black people and other minorities would be the most important sociological topic for that decade or longer. It also had special interest for my new mentor, Charles Glock (for reasons explained in a later chapter). Yet I continued to nurse the idea of writing in some way on the broader topic of the impact of urbanization on Mormons.[22]

My growing awareness that any such academic treatment of Mormon matters might not be welcomed by the church leadership was suggested by a visit I made during the summer of 1966 to Elder Boyd K. Packer, who was then mission president in New England. I had attended a monthlong seminar on economic theory in upstate New York and decided to seek an interview with Elder Packer on my way home to California. I surmised that as a general authority (then an assistant to the Twelve) of about my same age, Elder Packer might have some useful information and insights about the impact of growth and urbanization on the church in recent years. I had hoped also that my own service as a missionary in New England two decades earlier might help to give me entrée for an interview. In fact, he did agree to see me, and my earlier mission experience there seemed indeed to facilitate my access.

I began the interview by explaining the nature of my interest, mentioning that I was working on a doctoral dissertation, and reciting my bona fides as a recent consultant to the PBO and active church member with benign intentions (flashing my Mormon "passport," as it were). He responded by mentioning that he too had earned a doctorate, which I thought was an encouraging sign that the interview might be conducted in a context "among us scholars," with academic openness and candor.[23] I was quickly disabused of this optimistic expectation when I took from my briefcase a writing tablet where I had recorded a number of interview questions. As I asked the first question and began to take notes on his response, he stopped and asked what I was doing. I explained that I wanted to take notes on the interview for my future reference. To that he responded, "As soon as you start writing, I quit talking." Somewhat taken aback, I proceeded by taking only such mental notes as I could. The interview thus was brief, and I departed after eliciting only a few guarded responses on his part. I suppose I had been rather naive to expect otherwise, for that experience has seemed to me in retrospect as quite congruent with Elder Packer's public persona as it has emerged since then.[24]

In any case, by 1969, I had finished collecting some rich survey data from Salt Lake City and San Francisco for my doctoral dissertation, as I shall explain in a later chapter. The topic of the resulting dissertation, however, was not "Mormonism and urbanism," as originally planned, but rather "Mormonism and minorities." Yet the former topic continued to intrigue me, especially as I conducted various additional analyses of the data and saw the stark differences between the Salt Lake City and the San Francisco Saints in social, political, and even religious beliefs. Lest my findings grow cold and dated before their introduction to the public, I prepared and published two long articles in successive issues of *Dialogue,* exploring in statistical detail the thesis that church growth was occurring disproportionately in urban areas outside of Utah and the Mountain West and that the more secular culture of those urban areas was undermining the traditional religious and social conservatism of the Mormon membership, just as predicted by traditional sociological theory.[25] My chief evidence was a simple comparison between the Salt Lake City Saints and the San Francisco Saints (with appropriate controls for differences in age, education, and other demographic variables, as necessary). To be sure, I also found evidence of resistance to secularization in church programs, but even that resistance was less effective in urban than in rural areas. Even as I was writing these articles, and analyzing the data on which they were based, I could sense the tension between the secularizing trends at the Mormon grassroots and the increasing efforts of the church leadership to resist those trends, but I could not articulate a theoretical framework that would predict an outcome of that tension. That would come to me later.

Meanwhile, an incentive to set aside temporarily my interests in religion came with my assessment of the expectations of my professional colleagues at Washington State University and of the internal politics in my academic department, all of which indicated that my prospects for career advancement at WSU would likely suffer unless I put aside my scholarly interest in the Mormons for a while and turned to research of a more "mainstream" kind in my discipline of sociology.[26] Accordingly, for the rest of the decade (1970s), I focused my efforts on seeking grants to support a research program in alcohol studies, which was becoming a resurgent topic on the national agenda. By the end of that decade, I had earned tenure and a full professorship, so my academic career seemed secure. I had also acquired a special expertise not only in the study of alcohol abuse, but also in more general theories to account for deviant behavior and social problems of *various* kinds, aside from substance abuse.[27] Such topics thus predominated in my publications during the 1970s and 1980s, and my few publications in religious studies during that period focused mainly on national religious topics more generally, much less so on the Mormons in particular.[28]

A New Ferment in the World of Religion

During the 1980s and 1990s, therefore, I gradually finished up and phased out my work on deviant behavior, social problems, and alcohol studies, so that I could turn my main scholarly attention again to the sociology of religion, and particularly to the study of the Mormons. It was a good time to resume studies of religion, since a new ferment had arisen in the religious world, which called for new theoretical perspectives. Even during the years that I had recently devoted mainly to other lines of research, I had continued to reflect on Mormon developments and to study the proliferating academic literature on religious movements, which was growing rapidly in response to the rise of various new "cults." Of course, I had also maintained at least minimal connections to the sociology of religion from graduate school days on, participating in the conferences and councils of the Society for the Scientific Study of Religion (SSSR), the Association for the Sociology of Religion (ASR), and the Religious Research Association (RRA). For Mormon studies in particular, I helped to found and lead the Mormon Social Science Association (MSSA) in 1976 and have strongly promoted its activities ever since.[29] Also, in 1980, after a hiatus during most of the 1970s, I began again to participate actively in the annual conferences of the Mormon History Association, of which I had been a charter member when it was first organized in 1965.

A refocusing of my academic career on the sociological study of religion more generally was facilitated by a sabbatical leave of two semesters from Washington State University—the first and only such leave I ever had. With all our children well out of the nest, my wife and I decided to spend the calendar year of 1985 in Santa Barbara, California, where I was able to supplement my reduced sabbatical salary with part-time teaching in both the Sociology Department and the Religious Studies Department at the University of California. My choice of Santa Barbara was the product mainly of a new relationship that I had recently formed with the late Philip E. Hammond, who was chairing the Department of Religious

Studies during that period. Phil and I had shared an interesting experience a year or so earlier, when we were both invited to attend a conference on religious freedom in Los Angeles, sponsored by the Church of Scientology and a couple of the other so-called cults of the time. During that conference, he invited me to spend my contemplated sabbatical leave at UCSB and offered to give me an office and a couple of courses to teach in his department during that year. I shall always appreciate his generosity and the friendship between us that deepened considerably during that year and afterward.[30]

It is worth digressing here to remind readers of the ferment occurring in the world of religion during the 1970s and 1980s, which provided the context for the above-mentioned conference that Hammond and I were attending. The New Left, the "hippies," and other expressions of the counterculture of the 1960s and early 1970s spun off a certain portion of disaffected youth who turned away from politics to new religions as vehicles of their quest for meaning and purpose in that somewhat chaotic Age of Aquarius. Some of them embraced various quasi-Pentecostal Christian expressions called collectively "Jesus Freaks," while others turned to Scientology, the Unification Church ("Moonies"), ISKCON ("Hare Krishnas"),[31] and various Eastern gurus. Some of these new religious movements had grown very fast in North America, Western Europe, and parts of Asia during the late 1960s and the 1970s, causing alarm especially among parents and clergy from the Christian and Jewish mainstream denominations.[32] This alarm, fed by salacious stories of "brainwashing" by such "cults," gave rise, in turn, to a new and rapidly growing industry of "cult busters" made up largely of apostates from the NRMs and entrepreneurs of various kinds from the religious and academic establishments, claiming expertise in "rescuing" these youthful converts from the clutches of the cults—sometimes by forceful kidnappings.

For social scientists in the field of religious studies, these NRMs also provided an ideal opportunity for the study of the conversion process, at the individual level, and the "natural history" of NRMs at the institutional level. The NRMs also had the effect of dividing religious studies scholars into two main "camps." One camp, represented mainly in the Society for the Scientific Study of Religion, tended to see these new youthful movements as simply alternative religious expressions, some of which might eventually gain institutional stability and last across many generations (like, say, the Mormons), but most of which would probably not survive one generation. They were considered worth studying with the same scholarly detachment that would be expected in the study of any traditional or mainstream religion.[33] The other camp, made up disproportionately of psychologists, took a more clinical and ameliorative posture, considering "cult" conversion as aberrant and probably pathological behavior in need of containment and therapy. This division into the two camps made not only NRMs themselves but the very study of them questionable as a legitimate topic for academic investigation. As a scholar acquainted with the history of the Mormon movement, I had no trouble identifying with the first of these camps, for the second seemed to me to be simply replicating the scandalmongering visited on the early Mormons, but now in clinical rhetoric. Arguments between these two camps regularly occurred at the annual conferences of the SSSR and in the pages of its journal, as well as in many other academic venues.

Our colleagues in the second camp were not reassured when some of us in the first camp began to accept invitations to attend conferences under the auspices of the Unification Church, Scientology, or other NRMs. During the heyday of these movements, they seem to have had a lot of money, which they used, in large part, in an effort to enhance their public image(s) by hosting academic conferences at which reputable scholars would present papers on the NRMs and various other religious topics with the same scholarly neutrality that would be expected in an analysis of, say, the Presbyterians. Many of these conferences yielded papers that were subsequently published in books printed by the NRM presses themselves. For the scholars, these were interesting academic jaunts, all expenses paid, sometimes to foreign countries. Those who made these trips claimed that their scholarly objectivity was no more compromised by attending a Moonie-sponsored academic conference than in attending one sponsored by a mainline Protestant or Catholic seminary or university, and my own experience was that the scholarly give-and-take at these conferences closely approximated what occurred at the annual meetings of the SSSR itself.[34] In any case, the two "camps" of social scientists in question here have continued to the present day, with the first camp criticizing the second for its biases against unconventional religions and religious freedom, and the second criticizing the first as being mainly "cult apologists."[35]

Thus, during the 1980s and 1990s, I became much more heavily involved in the business of the various professional social science organizations and publications in religion than I had ever been before, and therefore much more visible as a mainstream scholar in the sociological study of religion. I was regularly called on for peer reviews and critiques of others scholars' papers submitted for publication in the journals, and I was elected or appointed to various responsible positions in these academic organizations.[36] Of these, the most important was my four-year appointment as editor of the *Journal for the Scientific Study of Religion,* from which I gained a great deal of professional experience and growth, especially in the review and editorial process through which academic papers are eventually published. I was also in a position to influence the quality of some of the most important scholarly literature published during that period. Perhaps my most enduring contribution, however, was not intellectual so much as it was artistic: I commissioned and helped develop the current logo for the *Journal for the Scientific Study of Religion*![37] All in all, I enjoyed my close association with SSSR and the other professional societies during those years, and I felt that my "Mormon passport" was generally treated with respect among scholars of religion in the social sciences, though occasionally I detected certain muted misgivings about the Mormons in their midst.[38] In any case, having thus been reconnected more extensively to scholarship in religious studies, I turned again especially to studying the Mormons.

MORMON RELIGIOUS RETRENCHMENT AS LOCAL AND PERSONAL

My first *Dialogue* article had appeared at the end of 1967 and dealt with the burgeoning race issue in the church. Already in some of my earlier encounters while in Walnut Creek or Logan, people who were important to me tried to warn me away from association with controversial publications and ideas. My own dear father, for whom free agency was among his most sacred principles, expressed his concern that I might be going a little too far in my criticisms, though he never pressured me to stop.[39] My beloved mission president S. Dilworth Young, still a general authority, on one occasion shortly after my *Dialogue* article had appeared, complimented me on a good article, but added, "I wish you hadn't published it in *Dialogue*," thereby reflecting the growing official hostility toward this new journal that was being published outside church control.[40] Certain stake presidents or bishops of my acquaintance would periodically admonish me that I would "never get anywhere" in church leadership if I continued my association with such unauthorized topics and publications. They were right. I never regained the fast track to ecclesiastical prestige as a bishop, stake president, or other relatively high office. I did, however, continue to serve in responsible positions at the ward level: in Walnut Creek as head of the ward's program for Aaronic adults, and later of the ward's Aaronic youth; in Logan again as head of the Aaronic adult program; and in Pullman as Gospel Doctrine teacher and (during my final decade there) as group leader of my ward's high priests, a position that I found very fulfilling for its regular and important pastoral opportunities.

In reflecting later upon my rather ordinary career in ecclesiastical leadership, I have been grateful that my intellectual independence was never compromised by the restraints of a highly visible church leadership role, as I suspect was the case with some of my academic colleagues who aspired for, or accepted, high office. Yet I have known others who served in bishoprics or stake presidencies during this period despite their association with controversial issues or publications. Many considerations, besides spiritual and intellectual ones, enter into the process of calling people to important positions in the church.[41] Furthermore, in all fairness and candor, I must concede that my own feelings and posture toward the church and its strictures during the 1970s were somewhat in flux, and my boundary-testing proclivities in those days would not have been reassuring to any of my ecclesiastical superiors seeking exemplary leadership material!

Although my academic career had required me to turn mostly away from Mormon studies during the 1970s, my wife, Ruth, and I tried to keep such studies alive in our own personal intellectual interests. We participated regularly in the Sunstone Symposia, both the annual one in Salt Lake City each summer and in some of the regional ones elsewhere (especially those in California and in Seattle). I recall being surprised by the creation of the *Sunstone* enterprise, since it occurred only a few years after *Dialogue* had just gotten a good start.[42] At first I was a little concerned about a new publication that might compete for the same intellectual and material resources that were so important to *Dialogue,* so I was anxious to find out what and who were behind *Sunstone.* I got an opportunity to find out during a business trip to Berkeley in 1972 or 1973, as I recall. While I was there, I arranged to call on Peggy Fletcher, who was the "founding mother" of *Sunstone* (alongside "founding father" Scott Kenney). I learned that Peggy, Scott, and others in the founding group were students at the Graduate Theological Union in Berkeley. They had been inspired by the rise of *Dialogue* but envisioned the creation of a journal for a younger generation, with somewhat shorter articles and more emphasis on the arts and literature, in contrast to the heavier and more academic fare in *Dialogue.*

During my visit with Peggy, I was impressed by her energy, enthusiasm, and vision, so I became a charter subscriber to the *Sunstone* magazine. During much of its first decade and more, Peggy was the editor of the magazine and carried it, largely single-handedly it seemed, through some of its darkest days of financial struggle and official opposition from certain church leaders.[43] She proved very effective in rounding up help, at least on a temporary basis, from many volunteers and donors, as she waged a constant battle for the survival of *Sunstone.* My own financial contributions during those years were not unusually large, as I recall, but consistent, and so was my moral support. I did not write anything appropriate for *Sunstone* until 1990, by which time Peggy had relinquished the editorial reins to Elbert Peck as editor, while she moved on to a new career and marriage to Michael Stack.[44]

The most highly visible of Peggy's accomplishments (and most vexing to the conservative church leaders) was probably the annual Sunstone Symposium, with its first meetings at the Hotel Utah during the summer of 1979 or 1980.[45] The symposium was originally conceived mainly as a forum for theological papers and discussions, but it soon morphed into a rather wide-open opportunity for actual and aspiring intellectuals to discuss all sorts of issues and events in Mormon history, culture, and ecclesiastical practice. I participated regularly for the first twenty years or so in the annual meetings held at various hotels and other venues in Salt Lake City, often presenting papers or just enjoying the company of many like-minded friends and scholars.[46] This symposium has survived now for more than three decades, though I am not sure that Peggy's original vision for it has survived. Younger generations have transformed both the concept and the content of the Sunstone Symposium to accommodate interests that now seem less often intellectual and more often emotionally expressive and cathartic. It seems sometimes to focus disproportionately on the "issue du jour" preoccupying the currently discontented or, on the other hand, to revisit old issues without any new information or insights. In that evolutionary process, it has lost much of its appeal for old-timers like me and Ruth, although we are still supportive of both the magazine and the symposium.

In more recent years, Peggy Fletcher Stack has had a distinguished career as senior religion editor for the *Salt Lake Tribune.* In that capacity, she calls on me from time to time for my opinions and assessments of newsworthy developments in the LDS Church and leadership. Since her early salad days as a founder of *Sunstone,* we have remained close friends in regular communication, and we always enjoy encountering each other at various conferences. She has made a tremendous contribution to both the intellectual and the popular culture of Utah, walking a narrow line, but with perfect balance, between the Mormon and the non-Mormon interests in her constituency.

Aside from our interests in *Sunstone* (and, of course, in *Dialogue* and the Mormon History Association), Ruth and I also tried to keep a little intellectual stimulation going among local LDS friends in our home ward and stake in Pullman, where we had moved in 1969 for my new faculty position at Washington State University. This local effort involved a few stresses and strains, for it turned out that the LDS membership in that area was more conservative than we had expected, in religion as well as in politics, probably because a relatively large proportion of the ward members were connected professionally with the College of Agriculture. The college dean, Louis L. Madsen, was, in fact, our local stake president, and the stake membership was not much given to intellectualized versions of the LDS faith found in the social sciences and the humanities—to say nothing of *Sunstone* and *Dialogue*!

Nevertheless, in 1973, amid the misgivings of some ward and stake leaders, we joined with four or five other couples in our Pullman LDS ward to form the Third Sunday Study Group (TSSG), as we eventually came to call it. Virtually all participants were active members of the ward. At first we met irregularly, rather than monthly, as seemed feasible given our time, our interest in given topics, and our small numbers. All mature but youngish couples, we simply wanted a forum where we could have periodic discussions of literature and issues occurring in the LDS Church and culture. Eventually, the attendance averaged between twenty-five and forty. Each meeting would be hosted in a different home, and a different group member would be responsible for choosing the topic and leading the discussion. Topics ran the gamut of LDS history and doctrines, plus occasional reviews of books or articles from *Dialogue* and other journals. Almost all programs were produced from within the group—that is, by the members themselves—but occasionally we would learn of a celebrity who would be visiting the area under auspices of one of the local universities or otherwise, and we would try to get that person as a speaker for our TSSG.[47]

By remaining alert to such opportunities, we were able to enjoy gratis presentations from a surprising variety of well-known speakers, including historian Leonard J. Arrington (1977), feminist Sonia Johnson (1980), poet Carol Lynn Pearson (three times), sometime Mormon convert Eldredge Cleaver (by video, 1984), black author Mary Sturlaugson Eyer (1987), scholar J. Gordon Melton (1990), cartoonist Steve Benson (1990—before he disavowed Mormonism), author Orson Scott Card (1991—by teleconference), organist James Welch (1991), author Avraham Gileadi (1992—by teleconference), scholar F. Ross Peterson (1997), and young historian Matthew Godfrey (1998). Besides myself, the most frequent speakers from within the TSSG itself were Brian McNeal (in the early years), Terence Day, Robert Wilson, and Clare Wiser (who specialized in great book reviews), all of whom were on the university faculty and long-term residents of Pullman. Several other periodic speakers lived there for only a few years as students or mobile faculty (for example, Randy Day, Hal and Ardell Kerr, Rob and Dynette Reynolds, Tom and Martie Mumford, and Dean and Ann Fletcher).

We discussed a tremendous range of Mormon-related topics in these meetings, and there were even a couple of visits by the group to a local Islamic mosque and a Hutterite community. All of the programs were open to the public and well advertised, and virtually all those who attended were faithful church members—

though more adventurous intellectually than most. This TSSG lasted longer than twenty years, until nearly the end of the decade, though with declining frequency during its final years. I was a little disappointed to see how much the continuation of the group seemed to depend on my personal participation. When I left Pullman for a sabbatical leave during the calendar year 1985, few meetings of the TSSG, if any, were held that year—or at least there is no record of any. Then again, after 1994, when I began to phase into retirement by spending spring semester each year in California, very few meetings were held. By the time we left Pullman permanently in early 1999, the group was pretty much defunct, partly, of course, because so many of the founders and "regulars," besides Ruth and me, had retired, moved away, or died.[48]

During the group's twenty-year life span, a great many Pullman Saints and church leaders participated in our TSSG, some thirty-five or forty with great regularity and perhaps another twenty or so on an occasional basis. We count several of the couples from that group among our dear friends, even to this day. Our very earliest meetings, though, starting in 1973, had been met with reactions ranging from a certain wariness to outright alarm in the responses of the local LDS leadership and the most orthodox members. Predictable rumors circulated about the dangers of an apostate group in the making. We had not felt it necessary to ask anyone's permission; we just got together privately whenever we could, but always very openly with regular public announcements in the mail to a growing list of interested ward members. However, unbeknownst to any of us instigators, our stake leaders, especially the stake president, were very concerned about the development, fearing that a subversive apostate group was emerging. No public comments, warnings, or even acknowledgments about our group were ever given by local church leaders, but they did take certain subtle steps behind the scenes to deal with this perceived threat to orthodoxy.

President Madsen even sent his first counselor, John L. Schwendiman, to investigate the situation by attending some of our meetings. Schwendiman's reports back to the presidency characterized our group and its meetings as interesting, constructive, and harmless, so there were no grounds for any action against us. Nevertheless, the president and others remained concerned, and our group was a topic on the agenda of several meetings of the stake presidency and high council during that period.[49] No overt action was taken by the leaders to close the group down, but some of the tactics were almost comical: for three or four months, the ward leadership started its own "cottage meetings" to compete with the TSSG meetings on the same nights. In response, the TSSG members happily joined the rest of the ward in attending these "cottage meetings" but then held our own monthly study group meetings besides, but on a different night. The ward-sponsored cottage meetings soon disappeared.

Early on, as we had learned of the concerns of ward and stake leaders, we offered to bring our little study group under the auspices of the LDS Institute program as a special advanced course at the graduate level. The seminary teacher in our ward, already "cleared" for service in the Church Education System, had joined our group and offered to be our "instructor" on the CES records. We thought that such auspices might relieve concerns about our intentions in the minds of some local priesthood leaders, while also enhancing local institute enrollment figures (which would help to justify a new institute building that had been proposed). We applied both to the stake presidency and (at their direction) to "V. Dan Roberts" (as I shall refer to him here),[50] who was the local institute director, as well as our resident high councilor, and we prepared an outline of the nature and purposes of the course, with a clear indication of the kinds of literature and topics that we would be discussing.[51] We were assured that Roberts would take our proposal to one or more meetings of the presidency and high council and that he would report back to us on their decision about extending institute auspices to our group. We submitted the proposal, as instructed, to Roberts, and after several weeks he reported back to me that the stake leaders had decided against our proposal, adding the condescending observation that "the kinds of members likely to attend such a group would do better to concentrate on the gospel basics"! John Schwendiman, in his 1991 interview with me, claimed that Roberts never did submit our proposal to the stake leaders for discussion but simply contacted a few of them individually with his own negative assessment of our proposal.

The issue became a little more personal for our family a couple of years later, when our eldest son married a local student and became active in the Pullman student branch. They began to attend our TSSG as a young couple, and gradually some of their friends from the branch did the same. This development so alarmed their branch president, "Virgil L. Spicer" (as I shall refer to him here), that he summarily forbade any of the young people in his flock to attend the TSSG meetings. Spicer, like Roberts, was an institute teacher and CES employee of modest and narrow education. Both of them seemed threatened by alternative sources of authoritative LDS ideas, and they used their ecclesiastical positions to try to insulate their students (and others) against ideas that might challenge their own intellectual authority.[52] I urged John Schwendiman, who by then was the stake president, to countermand this exercise of "unrighteous dominion" by Spicer, but Schwendiman was reluctant to intervene in Spicer's "stewardship." Later, in my

1991 interview with Schwendiman, he deplored the practice of calling full-time CES employees as bishops and stake presidents, which, he recognized, created conflicts of interest for them. In any case, our experience with the TSSG indicated that retrenchment was fully operational in Pullman, as elsewhere, in the 1970s and 1980s.

Yet such informal study groups as the TSSG had been going on for decades among Mormons in more cosmopolitan settings—even in Salt Lake City.[53] No one felt the need to seek the permission of church leaders for these informal gatherings held outside church auspices, and church leaders had no authority to forbid them; they did, however, sometimes express their displeasure over such unauthorized meetings held outside the control of the formal leadership—in line with the emerging retrenchment and correlation processes abroad in the church more generally. In 1990 I heard of some such groups in Utah that had been in existence for years but voluntarily disbanded in the belief that they would otherwise be in disobedience to church leaders after hearing the 1989 general conference address of Elder Dallin Oaks on "alternative voices."[54] In any case, with the passage of time, our local TSSG eventually lost its fearsome image, as it was increasingly attended by a variety of active ward members, including the sister of an apostle, the new local institute director, various ward and stake leaders, and eventually even by President Schwendiman himself.

Chapter 5 | TRAVELING BACK AND FORTH WITH A NEW THEORY ABOUT MORMON HISTORY

SHAPING A NEW THEORY ABOUT RELIGIOUS RETRENCHMENT
RATHER SUDDENLY IT SEEMED, IN 1982, ON THE INITIATIVE ESPECIALLY, I believe, of Leonard J. Arrington, I was invited to deliver a lecture under the auspices of the Charles Redd Center for Western Studies at BYU.[1] In November of that year, I delivered a lecture entitled "The Angel and the Beehive," which I was then invited to repeat the next January at a meeting of the B. H. Roberts Society held at the University of Utah.[2] This lecture proved to be the juncture at which my career finally took its turn strongly back into Mormon studies, and I shall always be deeply grateful to Arrington, Tom Alexander, and the Redd Center for this opportunity.[3] In those days the Redd Center did not routinely publish its lectures, but some of them were picked up by one or more of the BYU publications. My lecture, for example, was solicited for publication by the BYU alumni magazine (then in tabloid format).[4] I submitted the lecture in print exactly as I had delivered it, and the editor who had requested it was prepared to publish it pretty much intact.

However, important parts of the lecture made the editorial board and certain BYU administrators rather uncomfortable, so an eight-month process ensued in which various versions of the lecture were negotiated between me and the editor, and between the editor and the administration, all the way up to BYU president Rex Lee, who had to approve the final version. The offending passages in the lecture were apparently those that detailed one of my main arguments, namely, that the retrenchment process during the 1970s and 1980s had made the LDS Church resemble Protestant fundamentalists culturally and ideologically. When it finally appeared in print, those passages had been removed, so that the lecture appeared to celebrate the retrenchment process without acknowledging any of its unintended consequences! The editor in question did not remain long on the job, and my subsequent conversations with him indicated that the controversy over publishing my lecture had been importantly implicated in his decision to leave.

Yet the most important consequence to me of the lecture invitation from the Redd Center was that it presented me with both the opportunity and the necessity for making a coherent argument that would draw upon sociological theory to explain the paradox that I had been pondering ever since my earliest thinking about Mormonism and urbanism—namely, how could the Mormon Church be headed down the path toward secularization and assimilation into the general urban culture of America for the last half century, while at the same time resisting that assimilation and striving to maintain its distinctive and peculiar traits? My research convinced me that the answer, in short, was that although the Saints at the grassroots were being assimilated and somewhat secularized, a new generation of leaders was undertaking to steer the church back in the opposite direction—a process that I dubbed "retrenchment" in my lecture, in two derivative articles, and eventually in the book-length treatment of my full argument.[5] *Finally,* I had been able to synthesize a theoretical explanation for the anomaly that had been bothering me: Mormons and Mormonism had been affected by the increasingly urban environments in which they were operating, as conventional sociological theories predicted, but their most distinctive ecclesiastical and cultural traits seemed to be resurgent rather than disappearing. Not only that, but by the 1980s, as discussed in the previous chapter, it was clear that in America generally—and in certain other countries as well—a new religious ferment was producing a variety of new religious movements, especially among the youth, and a return to more fundamentalist thinking even in some of the traditional religions. I was not the only one who was noticing this new ferment, of course, and finally the accumulating evidence for it was presented in a skillful and insightful literature review by R. Stephen Warner.[6]

That review was not published in time to inform my own emerging perspective directly, but it definitely converged with and confirmed my eventual theoretical synthesis. I had created that synthesis by combining the "natural history" model used in my earlier work on social movements with the newly developing work of Stark and Bainbridge from exchange theory and that of Laurence Iannaccone drawn from "rational choice" theory in economics. My argument was basically that the LDS Church represented an anomaly to the conventional *sect-to-church* theory, which predicted that normal secularization of new religions would gradually reduce their emphasis on their own distinctiveness in the process of seeking greater acceptance in the surrounding society. The Mormon Church had exemplified that process until about the middle of the twentieth century, when it had deliberately reversed course and begun to reemphasize its diminishing peculiarities and recover its eroding distinctiveness—moving, in other words, back in a *sect-*

like direction and away from the churchlike path it had recently followed. In doing so, the church was seeking greater *tension* with the surrounding society and clearer *boundaries* between itself and the rapidly secularizing modern world. This process of retrenchment not only increased that tension with the *outside* but also strengthened the boundaries defining the identity of the membership on the *inside*.

As I have reflected on the origins of my theoretical synthesis, I can identify certain key sources.[7] In general, I drew upon my earlier doctoral studies, which had included the classical and more recent literature in social organization and social change, as well as in the sociology of religion. I found the succinct overview of the social change literature by Wilbert Moore especially helpful with its description of all societies and organizations as "tension-management" systems.[8] That seemed to me an apt description of the LDS Church, especially in the 1960s and 1970s. Two of my Berkeley mentors had used the tension theme in a collection of essays on emerging developments in American religion more generally.[9] The *idea* of tension as a dynamic element in the history and evolution of social movements and organizations (with or without the specific term) goes back at least as far as the work of Max Weber, and I recall being intrigued by its use also in the little-remembered work of Pitirim Sorokin, founder of the Harvard Department of Sociology.[10] Early on (as explained in chapter 3), I had used the same general idea to account for the evolution of radical social movements and of important movements surrounding "social problems": that is, the idea that tension between emerging social movements or organizations and their surrounding "host" societies would, in turn, inevitably produce tensions within the movement itself, requiring it to modify and adapt in certain ways in order to survive.[11] Such was the general theoretical perspective that I finally adapted to twentieth-century Mormon history.[12]

Meanwhile, Rodney Stark, in collaboration with coauthor William S. Bainbridge, had developed a new theoretical paradigm that was to constitute the chief challenge to the traditional assumptions about the inevitable secularization of religious movements and their concomitant transformation from sects to churches.[13] The first of a series of articles in this new direction appeared in 1979 and in the early 1980s, eventually coming together as chapters in a large new 1985 book.[14] The theoretical roots of this new paradigm were traceable to well-known earlier works on social exchange (George C. Homans, Richard Emerson, Karen Cook, Rosabeth Moss Kanter) and on cognitive dissonance (Leon Festinger, among others), even though such roots might not always have been explicitly acknowledged by Stark and Bainbridge. More directly, this new work constituted an important modification and adaptation of the classical ideas of Max Weber,

Ernst Troeltsch, Richard Niebuhr, and Benton Johnson about the differences between sects and churches in relation to their host societies.[15] The Stark and Bainbridge challenge to the "secularization" tradition could be found in the claim that secularization would never succeed in eliminating religious devotion altogether, because (to oversimplify) a constant human need for otherworldly meaning would always generate new religious claims and movements. As older religions become secularized, worldly, and moribund, schisms will always be creating new sects and cults in "a never-ending cycle of schism, secularization, and schism."[16] Secularization, then, is ultimately "a self-limiting process."[17] Here again, tension was seen as the main dynamic: the tension created in secular societies by the social and cultural deviance of new sects and cults would lead to their repression and eventually to either their destruction or their assimilation (secularization), leading again to the schism of the less secularized, and so on.

During the 1980s and 1990s, sociologists—apparently with the help of economists—began to discover that tension was not necessarily a handicap for a religious movement's prospects, especially if that tension arises from the *costs* that the movement imposes upon the faithful, for the *costs* demanded of members by high-tension religious organizations would only *increase the value* they placed upon their membership. This had already been a theme in two 1972 studies that were, for some reason, slow to be noticed by sociologists of religion: Kanter's study of the "commitment mechanisms" in religious and other utopian movements and Kelley's provocatively titled (for its time) *Why Conservative Churches Are Growing.*[18] This theme then emerged in a series of articles and eventually in a book by Finke and Stark, which attributed the success of the newer denominations in early American history (for example, Methodists) to the enterprise of traveling preachers who offered their followers otherworldly rewards requiring real commitment. In other words, *stricter demands* (that is, costs) were placed upon adherents by comparison with the older denominations (for example, Congregationalists, Episcopalians), which had accumulated a lot of "free riders" and had become "lazy monopolies," increasingly assimilated into the American social and political establishments.[19] The use of terms such as *religious economy, monopoly,* and the like suggests a convergence of the original sociological theory of Stark and Bainbridge with economic theory, which (as I observed earlier) can probably be attributed to the influence of Laurence R. Iannaccone, a student of Chicago microeconomist and Nobel laureate Gary S. Becker. At some point during the 1990s, Stark and Iannaccone discovered each other's work and apparently recognized the conceptual affinity between the exchange-theory tradition in sociology and microeconomic theory in economics. Thereafter, the "new paradigm," as R.

Stephen Warner had called it, emerged as the joint effort, in large part, of Stark, Bainbridge, Finke, and Iannaccone, singly or in various combinations.[20]

THE RETRENCHMENT BOOK AND SUBSEQUENT DEVELOPMENTS

Such was the emerging intellectual and theoretical context in which I offered my 1994 book, *The Angel and the Beehive,* the major argument for which had already been outlined in my 1982, 1983, 1989, and 1991 articles, as noted earlier. My debt to the "new paradigm" was made explicit in the opening chapter of this book, but I thought I had discovered also a new element that should be added, namely, the notion of retrenchment. Up to 1982, when I first introduced this idea in my BYU Redd Center lecture, I had not seen any recognition in sociological theories that the classical sect-to-church process in the history of religious denominations might be *reversed.* That possibility seemed to have been mentioned in passing by Benton Johnson in his 1963 reformulation of so-called sect-church theory, and it certainly would seem to have been one implication of the argument by Dean Kelley about increasing "strictness" as conducive to church growth. Yet I had never seen an analysis arguing that a *reversal from churchlike to sectlike* developments (or retrenchment, as I was calling it) had actually occurred in the history of any religious denomination or church, so I began my book by referring to the Mormon case as an "anomaly" in the usual sect-to-church theoretical formulation.[21]

Eventually, this reversal idea was discovered by Rodney Stark and Roger Finke and integrated into their new paradigm. Stark and Finke made much of their discovery by devoting an entire chapter to it in an important book they published in 2000. They pointed to signs of this reversal process as far back as the Catholic Counter-Reformation, as well as in some more recent Protestant and Reform Jewish examples. Yet I was astonished to see their declaration that they had been "unable to find even a hint in the theoretical literature that [entire] *denominations* can become more conservative."[22] Of course, my 1994 *Angel and Beehive* book had been all about *precisely* such a theory in the case of the Mormon denomination, supported with a variety of empirical evidence. The same theory had been exemplified also in some of my earlier articles about the Mormons, all of which would have been easily accessible to such a longtime Mormon watcher as Rodney Stark and to his coauthor.[23] Through formal theory, they made a convincing case for the church-to-sect reversal process, but without an entire denomination as a specific example, they were forced to support their case empirically with an unsystematic miscellany of developments from a variety of denominational settings. Citing the Mormon Church as a case of an *entire denomination* would have made their reversal argument much stronger. I have long been mystified about how two such accomplished scholars, in any responsible review of the extant literature, could have overlooked my publications on the Mormons, which were so highly relevant to their own work. Maybe they were so anxious to claim new intellectual territory that they did not notice the modest Mormon pioneer cabin marking my earlier arrival in that territory!

In any case, *The Angel and the Beehive* was my first book-length entry into the scholarship on Mormon history and culture, and it had been germinating ever since my thinking on "Mormonism and urbanism" in the 1960s, as explained earlier. It represented an important milestone in my aspirations to became a major contributor to Mormon studies during the second half of my academic career. The book was the focus of an "author meets critics" session at the 1994 annual conference of the Society for the Scientific Study of Religion, held in Albuquerque, New Mexico, and my publisher, the University of Illinois Press, was by then the most prominent of all those that were producing books on the Mormons.[24] Reviews of the book in academic journals ranged from good to glowing, and it won a "best book" prize from the MHA.[25] In 1999 it was highlighted in the *Religious Studies Review* as among the half dozen of the (then) most recent books in the burgeoning field of "Mormon studies," where it was described as "the best study to date" on the modern Mormon Church.[26]

Yet it has always seemed to me that the book was rather slow to achieve significant notice, either in the world of Mormon studies or in academia more generally. Sales, especially after the first thousand copies, could certainly not be considered brisk. Of course, by now, in this new Google age, a search of references to the book in connection with my name will turn up numerous entries, but most of these are (somewhat ironically) either marketing references or passing citations and comments on other topics. Perhaps my originally high hopes were just unrealistic. I am pleased to see that the book seems to have been rediscovered during the past few years, in large part by a new and younger generation of scholars who have started to cite it on various Mormon-related Internet sites. A particularly up-and-coming young author of a new (2012) book on Mormons even acknowledged the usefulness of my book in framing one of his chapters on modern Mormonism.[27]

Indeed, I have been gratified in later years to see my work on Mormons more generally receive favorable attention in the academic settings that have been the most important to my career. At the 2002 SSSR conference, meeting in Salt Lake City,[28] Session G-9 was devoted entirely to a review of my work by a panel consisting of C. Y. Glock, my own early mentor, plus Mormon studies colleagues

Gary Shepherd, O. Kendall White, and Thomas Murphy.[29] It was attended by both my first graduate student at Washington State (Reginald Bibby, 1974) and my last one (Stacy A. Hammons, 2000). Then a few years later, some younger colleagues organized two more sessions focusing at least partly on my work at the 2008 annual conference of the SSSR, meeting that year in Louisville, Kentucky. Session E-8 was titled "Mormonism and Theory: Critical Reflections on Armand Mauss's Work and a Change of Generation in Mormon Studies." Session H-4 was titled "The Rise of the LDS Church Considered as a Successful Revitalization Movement" and contained two papers intended partly as critiques of my work. I was the designated commentator at these sessions, both of which occurred on October 18, 2008. Conveners and contributors to these two sessions included both junior and senior scholars: Jordan Haug, Aaron Parry, Ryan Cragun, David Knowlton, and Melvin Hammarberg, plus a couple of others scheduled but finally unable to attend.

NEWER THOUGHTS ABOUT RETRENCHMENT AND THE LDS FUTURE

As I have discussed *The Angel and the Beehive* with various readers and academic colleagues over the years, and have watched history unfold in the LDS Church, certain new ideas and information have occurred to me that could be used in updating the book. Two or three important colleagues have, in fact, urged me to put out a new and revised edition.[30] However, I doubt that I have the energy or enthusiasm to do the thorough kind of revision that would be required. Yet I did write a follow-up article that takes into account some of my new thinking.[31] At this stage, I can think of at least three points that should be developed if I were to do a wholesale revision. First, I need to make clear, as apparently I did not do originally, that the LDS "retrenchment" after around 1960 was primarily an *internal* process, affecting the ways in which the church and religion were experienced by its *members.* The *external* posture of the church has remained essentially assimilationist, driven by a public relations strategy aimed at convincing the world that the Mormon Church is fundamentally a respectable *Christian* denomination in the United States and that its members are just normal citizens, pretty much like those in America or in any other country.

Of course, since the internal and external strategies are implemented by different bureaucracies, they sometimes run afoul of each other. For example, in the early years of the "correlation" policy, the standardization of curriculum in Sunday-school and CES classes, influenced by the theologically conservative senior apostles then in power, took a somewhat fundamentalist turn in favor of scriptural literalism, along with a pointed rejection of "modernist" theories about the age of the earth and about human origins. Also, the church's program to re-furbish family life led it to resist the resurgent feminism in the surrounding soci-ety and eventually to oppose the national Equal Rights Amendment for women. Both these developments were dictated by the *internal* retrenchment motif, but the *external effect* was to make Mormonism resemble evangelical Protestantism much more so than in the past. Certain LDS leaders and academics, furthermore, began to explore rapprochement with evangelicals politically and even across the "wide divide" theologically. In light of such developments, some of my friendly critics have suggested in book reviews that despite retrenchment, assimilation ef-forts were still under way in Mormonism through its convergences with evan-gelical Protestantism. My responses would be that an unintended convergence of Mormon ecclesiastical culture with that of another *high-cost* religious tradition does not constitute "assimilation" in the larger societal sense, for this convergence was actually a limited and indirect consequence of the dominant *retrenchment* strategy, not a continuation of the assimilationist strategy of the early twentieth century, and it complicated, not reinforced, the external public relations strategy of Mormons as normal, everyday Americans. It remains the case that while the *external* message is "We're just patriotic Christians like most other Americans," the *internal* message continues to be, "There is only one true church, and ours is it; don't forget that!"

The *second* element required in any updating of my 1994 book is the ac-knowledgment that the most recent retrenchment phase of Mormon history seems to be receding, as a new assimilationist posture is emerging with a new generation of leaders. Such changes in phases of the cycle do not, of course, occur suddenly or discretely, but only in gradual and overlapping ways. By 1994 conser-vative president Ezra Taft Benson, and most of his like-minded senior apostles, had passed from the scene, as new leaders, sharing quite a different orientation, came to power. Although I would trace the beginning of this course correction to President Howard W. Hunter, he did not survive long enough to lead very far in the new direction. That was to be the main accomplishment of his successors, Gordon B. Hinckley and then Thomas S. Monson. Whatever might have been the origin of the change, I see signs now that retrenchment in the church is slow-ing down, perhaps even rolling back somewhat, and is gradually giving way again to a more assimilative posture toward American society and the rest of the world. A new posture of diplomatic outreach by the church leadership can be seen in many ways, perhaps most concretely in the greatly enhanced resources devoted to humanitarian service in different parts of the world. However, this new posture is at least a concomitant, if not a direct, consequence of the greater role and sophistication of the church's public relations program in the leadership's strategy at all levels of ecclesiastical organization.[32]

Yet the formal public affairs program of the church, in both its professional and its volunteer expressions, is far more pervasive than humanitarian outreach. It bespeaks a strategy aimed at persuading the world, but Americans first and foremost, that the Church of Jesus Christ of Latter-day Saints is an authentic, respectable Christian religion entitled to a place in the ongoing civic conversations about the world's future. The expansion of the role of public affairs has been necessitated in part by outside scandals and events over which the church has had little control (for example, the unexpected resistance to the 2008 and 2012 Romney campaigns from both secular and religious sources, the resurgence of the dormant "polygamy" issue both in the news and in popular entertainment, and the blowback from its energetic political opposition to same-sex marriage).[33] The new public affairs strategy has been necessitated also, however, by traditional public images of the church as "cultlike" in its secrecy about temples and about its own history, in its "control" over members' lives and votes, and in its "oppression" of women—images that all arose, ironically, from the church's own *internal* retrenchment efforts in temple building and worship, from its emphasis on obedience to ecclesiastical authorities, from its constant counsel against extradomestic careers for married women (or at least for mothers), and from its attempts to control the "unauthorized" publications of certain intellectuals. All of these developments, and others that could be cited, have combined to create an unpopular image for the church and to require the renewed efforts by LDS leaders to reconstruct its public image in more positive directions.[34]

A certain return to an assimilative direction inevitably follows from this new public relations emphasis. I have mentioned several examples in this and other chapters. Examples I would cite: first, the growing *rapprochement* with the Catholic Church and increased outreach to Jews, Muslims, and others, with a corresponding decline in the special—and seemingly exclusive—overtures toward Protestant evangelicals with whom LDS interests seemed more convergent during the retrenchment of recent decades; and second, the public muting of certain traditional (but not essential) doctrines and literature that were once considered by the faithful and critics alike as indispensable marks of Mormon identity. Examples of such "muting" would be removing key doctrines of the *King Follett Discourse* from lesson manuals; identification of only *some* (not all) American aborigines as Lamanite descendants in the introduction to the Book of Mormon; the 2010 rewriting of certain introductions to chapters in the Book of Mormon, in order to eliminate their racist connotations; the decision to end publication of

McConkie's classic *Mormon Doctrine;* efforts to neutralize the "secrecy" charge by bringing key opinion leaders from various religions to visit new temples before dedication and by giving greater access to church archives for non-Mormon (and even some ex-Mormon) researchers; and finally, a *rapprochement* with Mormon scholars themselves (though not ever publicly announced, of course), including many who are independent of church employment or sponsorship. These scholars are now once again writing books and articles on delicate and controversial subjects and participating in forums like *Sunstone, Dialogue,* and the Mormon History Association, without reprisals from conservative church leaders.[35] The appreciative acknowledgments, and even some tacit support, by church leaders for new academic initiatives, conferences, and endowed chairs in Mormon studies would also be part of this new accommodation of independent scholarly work on the LDS religion, history, and culture.[36]

I see other developments, at least among American Mormons, that are also likely to attenuate the retrenchment efforts of recent decades and to push the church toward acceptance of greater diversity in the ways in which Mormonism is understood and lived. These developments are relatively recent and likely to continue. One of them is the emergence of what might be called different "cultural constituencies." Here I am not referring to the different institutional "branches" of the movement founded by Joseph Smith, for that is another and quite different subject. By "cultural constituencies," I mean the amorphous and somewhat overlapping segments of membership within the LDS Church itself that find, respectively, the principal *meaning* of their church membership in different forms and degrees of participation. For some members, frequent temple participation provides that special meaning; for others, it is found in ordinary ward activities that provide social support for families and individuals. (This distinction is roughly parallel to Douglas J. Davies's contrast between "ward Mormonism" and "temple Mormonism.") These are not mutually exclusive constituencies, but the temple and related activities occupy far more of the time and energy of the one than of the other.

Yet another constituency would be the intellectuals for whom the main meaning of their LDS association is the production and consumption of sophisticated literature (whether apologetic or critical) on LDS theology, history, or culture. Again, these intellectuals also participate somewhat in either ward or temple Mormonism (or both), or they might be virtual nonparticipants in both, but they are intensely involved intellectually with the LDS heritage. Furthermore, the extent and diversity of this intellectual constituency is readily apparent from the publications, websites, and blogsites that they continue to produce. Also, the rise of a segment of LDS membership focused especially on the African American experience is another example.[37] Finally, this typology might also include those who think of themselves candidly as only "cultural Mormons," who acknowledge the influence of Mormonism in their upbringing but no longer find that it provides meaning in their lives. No doubt other such "constituencies" could be identified as well, including those in international Mormonism that are ethnic or nation based. The emergence of all these various constituencies is but a consequence and reflection of the growth and spread of Mormonism into diverse populations (American and otherwise) since 1950, thereby breaking down the social and cultural homogeneity that analysts such as O'Dea saw in their time. Indeed, it was the growing official concern over this emerging cultural *heterogeneity* that partly gave rise, in my opinion, to the institutional retrenchment motif that accompanied it after 1960, particularly the "correlation" aspect.

The correlation process has had some ironic outcomes. One of the consequences of the heavy-handed standardization of catechistic and proselytizing literature has been to displace much of the traditional doctrinal uniqueness of Mormonism with bland Christian and Mormon platitudes. For example, in *Gospel Principles,* the lesson manual for the adult priesthood and Relief Society course during 2010 and 2011, all of the unique teachings of Joseph Smith from the Nauvoo period, found in earlier editions of this manual, have been omitted or watered down in favor of a more discreet phrasing of key doctrines (even though the original version of the manual itself had *already* been watered down for investigators and new members!).[38] An ironic side effect of this reduction of doctrine to the lowest or simplest "common denominator" is to make Mormon teaching appear less "peculiar" and more generically "Christian," and therefore more "assimilated."

In general organizational terms, too, if I am right about the recent move of the cyclical pendulum away from retrenchment and once again toward assimilation and accommodation, then I would expect the "correlation" process to be loosened somewhat and adapted to the predicament, which the church increasingly faces, of trying to retain a rapidly growing membership, in which perhaps half of all new converts are lost to defection within the first year. The success of the church in this effort, between now and the middle of this new century, will depend in large part on whether and how this adaptation takes place, as well as upon the ability of the church to enhance its public image. Much will depend also on *national American* developments over which the church has little or no control, including both domestic and international policies and events. For better or for worse, the church can never substantially separate itself from its American origins and geopolitical location, so it is fated to "work out its salvation" in the context of that patrimony, both at home and abroad.

The *third* element that I would include in any updating of my 1994 book would be a recognition that the cyclical pattern I have traced (assimilation > retrenchment > assimilation, and so on) does not necessarily protect a religious tradition from a more or less complete assimilation eventually, just as predicted by the conventional "secularization" theory. While the function of retrenchment (intentionally or not) might be to restore an assimilating religion to "optimum" (rather than minimal) tension with the surrounding society, each new retrenchment campaign seems to start from a more advanced stage of assimilation than the last one did, so the ecclesiastical culture is never pulled all the way back to the tension level from which it started. The actual pattern, then, seems to be two steps toward assimilation and only one back toward retrenchment. The end result is still a well-assimilated religious community in the long term.[39] The LDS retrenchment since 1950 has not taken Mormonism all the way back to its nineteenth-century peculiarities and cannot do so. The signs of returning assimilation are already apparent and have been traced above. To the extent that the public relations strategies continue to have a high priority for LDS leaders, and the public relations bureaucracy continues to thrive, we might yet find a much less "peculiar" version of Mormonism by the end of the present century.[40]

Such, then, is the story of how I came to write *The Angel and the Beehive* and how my thinking has evolved through that project—and since. Having thus studied the retrenchment process, as well as having lived through it, I could both see and feel how that process had narrowed the intellectual boundaries of the kingdom within which Mormon scholars were able to "renew their passports," so to say, as approved emissaries to the outside world. Particularly in the world of race relations, I became a traveler somewhat embattled from both inside and outside the kingdom, as will become apparent in the next chapter.

Chapter 6 | RECURRENT VISITS WITH THE RACE ISSUE

GROWING UP BEFORE THE RISE OF THE NATIONAL CIVIL RIGHTS MOVEment, I internalized the demeaning notions about black people that were common in my Oakland, California, surroundings. The few encounters I had with them at school, or at my summer job in a downtown shoe store, seemed friendly enough, but I generally stayed out of the "Negro" part of town, and the "Negroes" rarely ventured above a certain street (about Fourteenth Street, as I recall). I understood clearly that these people were "the Other." Yet my boyhood experiences included some confusing anomalies. An elderly black couple named Graves regularly attended worship services in my ward, but no one could explain why they were there or why they did not participate much in the proceedings. One of my pals was a boy named Richard from a recently converted family. During the teen years, we never understood why he did not receive the Aaronic priesthood along with the rest of us, but we learned that the matter had something to do with supposed African ancestry in his family, even though they were all blue eyed and light skinned. Not surprisingly, Richard's church participation did not survive his teen years. His older sister married into a devout Utah Mormon family, but their marriage could not be sealed in a temple for another quarter of a century, after several children had been born. Certain other experiences of mine with the race issue inside the church are reprised in a *Sunstone* article.[1] In one way or another, the issue remains with me, for even now many Latter-day Saints and their leaders are still struggling to find a satisfactory "explanation" for the racialist thinking throughout the history of the church.[2] There is space here only to highlight briefly my most important experiences with the race issue during my career as an academic scholar and a Mormon.

The race issue burst upon the Mormons a little later than upon most of America, partly because of the relative remoteness of most of the Mormon population in the Mountain West. Even the well-informed non-Mormon sociologist Thomas F. O'Dea, in his insightful study *The Mormons* as late as 1957, had not mentioned the race issue as one of the "sources of strain and conflict" that he saw among Mormons.³ However, during the 1960s, as the retrenchment process was starting in the LDS Church, the controversy over Mormons and race was ramping up in the nation more generally, and in the San Francisco Bay area I encountered it constantly. We had not yet gotten the benefit of Lester Bush's research on the dubious origins of the church's race policies, so I was as mystified as anyone about those origins. Yet my own search of the LDS scriptural canon convinced me that neither the origin nor the doctrinal rationale could be found in the scriptures unless they were read through the prism of accumulated post hoc folklore in the writings of nineteenth-century LDS leaders. After my 1964 pilot study, mentioned in chapter 2, I had evidence for *two* arguments, one that I addressed to Mormons and the other one to non-Mormon observers and critics outside the church. *Inside* the church, my appeal was: we can't yet see a change in church policy on the horizon, but meanwhile *we must get rid of all the racist folklore* that passes for "doctrine." My arguments to this effect convinced but few of my LDS friends or leaders and infuriated others. Most Mormons were inclined just to circle the apologetic wagons against the onslaught of the growing national criticism.

However, *outside* the church, among my non-Mormon friends at the university and on the college faculty where I taught, my argument was different, for it was based on the data from the pilot study, which I had conducted among three wards in the Walnut Creek Stake (more about this pilot study shortly). Here my argument was: however one might feel about the traditional teachings and policies of the LDS Church, where is the evidence that Mormons treat black people differently in *secular, civil society*? My evidence indicated that Mormons did not have especially high levels of prejudice against "Negroes." To be sure, it was small comfort for me to be able to claim that Mormons were no worse than other Americans, but my main argument to *outsiders* was that as long as Mormons could not be shown as more prejudiced or discriminatory than others in *secular, civil matters,* the church should be left alone to solve its own internal ecclesiastical problems. Religious peculiarities with no demonstrable civil consequences were not the business of the state. Alas, however, my argument to non-Mormons was no more persuasive than had been my other appeal to Mormons! Nevertheless, I made both of these arguments in an article appearing in one of the earliest issues of *Dialogue.*⁴

Meanwhile, however, in 1967 a public attack on the LDS Church occurred on a major local radio station, KCBS, in San Francisco. The Reverend Lester Kinsolving, a Sunday talk-show host, devoted at least two of his broadcasts to excoriating the Mormon Church for its unfashionable race policies. While Kinsolving's career eventually proved highly mobile, both geographically and intellectually, he was apparently anxious, during this particular period, to burnish his liberal credentials for a Bay Area audience, so the Mormons became his target du jour.[5] Kinsolving's radio show featured special guests, as well as call-in commentators, and I listened with dismay to the one-sided anti-Mormon diatribes, punctuated by occasional well-meaning Mormon callers who sounded ridiculous in their efforts to "explain" the church's race restriction by citing all the old folklore that they had read in books by popular Mormon authors. Kinsolving was so glib that he soon had his Mormon callers tongue-tied, few callers though there were, so he called for a leader in the church to appear on his program and offer a more coherent explanation of the church's policy. He got no takers from the Mormon leadership, so at length I phoned in, cited my academic credentials, and challenged him to let me appear on his next program to offer the explanation he sought. The program in question was scheduled for Sunday evening, July 2, 1967. A small advance announcement appeared on the front page of the June 1967 issue of the *Messenger,* a local LDS newspaper published in the Oakland Stake.[6] The animated radio encounter with Kinsolving is recounted (from my viewpoint) in the above-mentioned *Dialogue* article.[7]

Reactions of local Mormons to my confrontation with Kinsolving were mixed, some expressed directly to me, others through my parents, then living in the same area. Although I had not attacked the church's policy on priesthood restriction, or even called for it to be changed, I did feel free to attack the folklore that was either borrowed or contrived to justify the policy. Such an attack carried a certain amount of risk for me, since the same folklore had been explicitly promoted by prominent general authorities of the church who were still very much alive, especially Joseph Fielding Smith (then the senior-most apostle), his son-in-law Bruce R. McConkie (then of the Seventy), Harold B. Lee, and Mark E. Petersen, among others. In the radio broadcast, I maintained respectful tones in questioning the scriptural interpretations and folklore associated with these leaders, and I never mentioned them by name. My comments, both in such public settings and in print, were actually very conservative, since I never made any demands on church leaders but only questioned the doctrinal folklore used to support church policy. Nor did I ever drop out of church activity over the race issue, as many other critics did. Nevertheless, both before and after the broadcast, many of my more conservative Mormon friends were unhappy with my public entry into this controversy and with my efforts as any kind of commentator on church issues.

LDS RACE RELATIONS AS DOCTORAL DISSERTATION TOPIC

With my return to sustained graduate studies in 1962, I had embraced the discipline of sociology and had decided to enter seriously into the study and production of scholarly literature on the Mormon experience. The two developments came together naturally: no sociologist interested in Mormons could have avoided facing the growing tension between the church and the surrounding American society over the race issue, least of all in places such as the San Francisco Bay Area. The pressing salience of this issue was all the greater because the mentor I had chosen for my graduate studies at Berkeley was Charles Y. Glock, a major methodologist in the sociology of religion, who had just received (in 1963) a large grant from the Anti-Defamation League of B'nai B'rith to study the Christian roots of anti-Semitism.[8] The study of the relation between religion and prejudice toward Jews had been an important focus in sociology ever since World War II but was soon to be overshadowed by a new focus on religion and prejudice toward black people. Glock (born and reared in New York City) knew nothing about Mormons, but during my consultations with him he became interested in my suggestion that Mormons would provide an interesting "test case" to complement his research on how religious teachings might affect prejudice among Christians generally, since traditional Mormon teachings were favorable toward Jews but unfavorable toward people of black African origin.

The project that we finally agreed should be my doctoral dissertation was to consist partly of a replication, with data from Mormons, of Glock's research on the Christian sources of prejudice against Jews, followed by an analysis of Mormon attitudes and beliefs about blacks (then called "Negroes"). Glock's Christian sample contained no Mormons, so my intention was to provide a Mormon sample that would enable me to see, as the first question, how Mormons compared with other Christians in their rates of anti-Semitism. Since prejudice against Jews is often associated with prejudice of other kinds, Glock's data also included indicators of prejudice and discrimination against "Negroes," so my second question was how Mormons compared with others in religious and secular attitudes toward blacks, based on indicators in Glock's own questionnaire. Lacking both money and time for an extensive survey, I decided to test my ideas and measures first with the small 1964 "pilot study" based on questionnaires sent to the adult members of three demographically varied wards in what was then the Walnut Creek Stake.

I designed an extensive questionnaire, derived from Glock's (with his permission), and mailed it out to household adults in those three wards. My access to those wards and their membership lists was possible only because in those days before "correlation" and retrenchment had set in, bishops felt much more free to accommodate such initiatives from people whom they knew and trusted, and because my father and family had long been prominent members of that area. All three bishops of my sample wards, in fact, supported my survey from the pulpit. The questionnaires were sent anonymously, of course, and an equally anonymous follow-up system allowed me to prod the slower respondents. I succeeded in getting back about 250 questionnaires, roughly half of the number that had been mailed out, with enough information from the ward membership records to assess nonresponse biases in my data.[9]

In those preelectronic days, such data had to be recorded on punch cards, a service to which I fortunately had access as a graduate student at UC-Berkeley. For tabulating my data, I used card counter-sorters both at the university and at the community college where I was teaching. The tabulations from this small pilot study confirmed my expectation that anti-Semitism occurred among Mormons at a much lower rate than among other Christians. My expectation that Mormons would have higher rates of anti-Negro prejudice, however, were only partially confirmed. Compared against the whole range of denominations in Glock's data, the Mormon rates were higher than those of some (such as Congregationalists) but lower than others (such as those we would now call "evangelicals"). The Mormon rates of anti-Negro prejudice, in fact, were about the same as the *averages* for Protestants and Catholics. I took this as "good news," comparatively speaking, for I had expected worse. Yet I should have remembered that other American Christians had been absorbing essentially the same racist notions from their historical environments as had the Mormons. This was not yet my dissertation, of course, but even as a pilot study, the research and its findings were good enough for publication in the principal regional journal of sociology, which became my very first academic publication.[10]

The process of getting that first publication involved a degree of serendipity, and it reflected a certain naïveté on my part that I find somewhat embarrassing in retrospect. Let me digress briefly to explain. At that stage in my career, I had no idea how one would go about getting any of one's work into print. I had attended one or two small academic conferences locally, and I knew that they were forums where scholars would present their work orally. However, I was focused on getting my dissertation done, and I regarded a conference report as a good first step in sharing the results of my research on Mormons and race. I had not thought ahead to possible publication. Accordingly, I succeeded in getting a paper on this topic accepted for presentation as part of the 1965 conference of the Pacific Sociological Association, which was scheduled, coincidentally enough, to meet that year in Salt Lake City. My wife and I made a hurried drive from our home in Walnut Creek to this conference, which was to be my very first one as a program participant. As it turned out, my paper on that occasion also offered the very first systematic survey of any population of Mormons in secular, civic attitudes toward "Negroes," and since it was being presented in the Mormon heartland, it attracted some attention from the local press.

The session where I presented the paper had a large attendance, as might have been expected. In my enthusiasm and inexperience, I proved insensitive to time constraints and therefore impinged greatly on the time available for other papers in the same session. This breach of academic etiquette (though quite common) brought me a well-deserved public rebuke from C. Wilson Record, a professor at Sacramento State University, who was chairing the session. That diminished somewhat the glow of success I was feeling as I finished my presentation. At the end of the session, I was walking out into the foyer of the hotel and was accosted by Stanford M. Lyman, who had finished his PhD at Berkeley several years earlier and was then chairing the Department of Sociology at Sonoma State University. Stan, a rather loquacious person himself, had been present for my session and proceeded to offer an unsolicited critique of my paper. I became a little defensive and began to rebut some of his criticisms, but he cut me off with an interjection that went something like this: "Hey! I'm not running down your paper. I think it's publishable pretty much as it is. I'm just suggesting a few refinements."

I was astonished. That was the second time a seasoned academic had surprised me by suggesting that my work might be publishable.[11] This time, however, I had the presence of mind to respond to Lyman by asking where I might get it published and how I would go about doing so. He pointed to an old gentleman across the foyer and suggested, "There's John Foskett. He's the editor of the *Pacific Sociological Review*. Go and ask him." I did so. Foskett directed me to cut the paper in half and submit to him only the part dealing with Mormon versus non-Mormon attitudes toward Negroes, leaving a second section about anti-Semitism for a later paper. The advice that day from Lyman and Foskett proved a career-changing experience, for I never again doubted that I could publish my work, and I have never tired of seeing my work in print. My second conference presentation occurred in August 1967, at the annual conference of the American Sociological Association in San Francisco. This one dealt with Mormons and anti-Semitism. Glock and Stark were both present and warmly endorsed the paper when called upon by the chairperson of the session, so I had little trouble publishing that paper, too.[12] Between these two "Mormon" papers, I published the above-mentioned seminar paper. So I was off and running with my first three academic publications in three successive years, one from a graduate course and two from my own private survey of East Bay Mormons (plus my 1967 *Dialogue* paper mentioned earlier).

Meanwhile, I still had to finish the doctoral dissertation, for which my earlier research had been only a "pilot project." My hopes for church support of the dissertation project were raised by Ray L. White at the Presiding Bishop's Office, for whom I had worked on the various projects described in chapter 2. White undertook to persuade his ecclesiastical superiors that it would be in the interest of the church to finance my dissertation, which was to be based on a very comprehensive questionnaire about LDS beliefs and attitudes on a whole range of questions, not just those on race issues. I had requested a fairly small grant to cover only the printing and mailing of questionnaires to a systematic sample of Salt Lake City and San Francisco Mormons, and White encouraged me (sincerely, I think) to believe I could get it.

He was as disappointed as I was when his recommendation was rejected. I do not know (and maybe he did not) what all the reasons were for that rejection, given the obvious benefit that a dissertation with such data would have provided the church, but White left me the impression that some of the reason was attributable to political intervention from an ecclesiastical leader. The main reason that White passed on to me was that a survey of that kind had "already been done" by a well-connected sociologist at BYU, who was the son of this leader. I knew pretty well that there had been no such survey, so I was wondering what this mysterious BYU study might have been. Upon investigation, I learned that the only BYU product bearing any resemblance to such a description was a small survey of LDS people in central Utah, based on interviews conducted by local church leaders—obviously not comparable to the broad and anonymous survey I envisioned.[13] I never learned the "back story" to any of this, beyond the fact that the church was not going to finance my own large survey of Mormons.

This outcome left me with the predicament of raising all the money to pay for the constructing and mailing of my questionnaires, which I was able to do partly through equity realized from selling our home in Walnut Creek when we moved to Logan, Utah, for my faculty position at USU. Accordingly, I left California in the summer of 1967 for a two-year sojourn on the faculty at Utah State University, still with my doctoral dissertation unfinished. My lack of access there to modern equipment for data tabulation and analysis was not remedied until my final career move to Washington State University in 1969, where the facilities were comparable to those at Berkeley.[14] Though self-financed, my project still benefited enormously from my friendship with Ray White at the PBO, who used his access to LDS membership data to help me pick a random sample of Salt Lake City wards (weighted by membership sizes) and the two San Francisco wards that were the most highly urbanized. White also gave me permission to contact the bishops in each of my sample wards, let them know that I had PBO permission to do the survey, and urge them to telephone White if they had any questions. With that kind of support from inside the church bureaucracy, and a months-long follow-up of slow respondents, I succeeded in getting a response rate of 60 percent for that survey, along with the necessary data about nonrespondents that permitted me to assess certain nonresponse biases in my data. Serendipity or Providence or both were with me, not only in the indispensable support I got from Ray White, but also (as I later realized) even in the decision made by ecclesiastical authorities *not* to finance my study! As I watched the growing tension between those authorities and LDS scholars grow during the next decade, I realized that if I had gotten church financing, I would almost certainly have faced attempts by church leaders to impose constraints on the publication of my research findings. In any case, my dissertation on the race issue was finished during my first year on the faculty at WSU and duly filed with the University of California in 1970.[15]

CAMPUS DISRUPTIONS AND THE MORMON SCAPEGOAT

Though my dissertation had been conceived and developed in the context of the racial tensions of Berkeley and its environs, I had hoped that the actual writing of it might benefit by the peace and quiet found in my moves to the more politically placid settings of Logan, Utah, and then Pullman, Washington. This expectation was exploded when the student movement that had been disrupting some of the elite university campuses belatedly made its way to the remoteness of WSU in eastern Washington just as I joined the faculty there. Gradually picking up steam during the 1969–70 school year, a campus campaign against "institutional racism" finally reached its apex with the return of warm weather and final examinations late in the spring. WSU had never had more than a handful of black students, but it had joined the movement developing elsewhere in the nation by establishing a Black Studies Department in 1967 under an up-and-coming young anthropologist named Johnnetta Cole, who was later to become the first black woman to head Spelman College, among other distinctions.[16] This department became the center of a somewhat amorphous campaign to identify and correct instances of racism on the WSU campus. The few black students were joined by many white student and faculty sympathizers in highlighting their objectives through sit-ins, teach-ins, and the rest of the repertory of protest made fashionable on other campuses, including occasional instances of malicious mischief, such as jamming locks to faculty offices. I found it difficult to work on campus, and I had no work space at home, so my writing was slowed down somewhat until summer arrived, when the protesting disappeared with the students—and with Professor Cole—never to return to the WSU campus.

The spring semester of 1970 was, however, a hectic one that left many ruptured relationships in its wake. A few administrative and academic changes, mostly cosmetic, were made by intimidated faculty and administrators, but the university lost some goodwill and support from the conservative wheat farmers among whom the campus had always been located and supported. More important was the damage done by the loose and unfair charges of "racism" against any student, faculty, or administrator who resisted any of the protesters' demands. I found myself the unhappy object of such charges when, as a new faculty member in the Department of Sociology, I proved unsympathetic to the "strike" that our teaching and research assistants called in support of their campaign against "institutional racism." In operational terms, this "strike" meant that the TAs and RAs would cease teaching their (mostly lower-division) classes, grading papers, or working on faculty research projects. My response was that those who joined such a strike should be taken off the departmental payroll immediately—as in any other industry. The TAs and RAs had apparently not considered that as a possible consequence, and when our faculty adopted that policy, word got out about which faculty members had voted for and against the policy. Those of us who voted against the student demands were, of course, labeled "racists."

My image with students—and even with a few faculty colleagues—was further tarnished by my appearance at a campus "teach-in" where a certain black student was the featured speaker on religion and racism. He focused most of his criticism on Mormons and the Mormon Church, but some of his charges were false or unsupported, so I arose to rebut those and to share the results of my own comparative research on Mormons versus others. My efforts were not, of course, appreciated by the crowd on that occasion, and my image as a "racist" was confirmed. For a few years thereafter, black graduate students—and some of their sympathizers—would not work with me or take my courses. Nor were my efforts to defend my religious community (and my own reputation) supported by other LDS faculty members, even those in my own department. My Pullman LDS ward community also seemed generally to have preferred that I had not "added fuel to the fire" by joining the controversy over the LDS race policy then still in effect. The general LDS posture in Pullman (as elsewhere) was to "circle the wagons" and ignore the issue. That was still very much the posture among LDS audiences there even a few years later, in 1973, for when I was asked by student leaders in the Pullman LDS institute and young adult program to address them on the race issue, their leaders first tried (unsuccessfully) to cancel my appearance—but then showed up in force to monitor and "correct" my comments.[17]

FROM DISSERTATION TO BOOK PROJECTS

When I finally finished my dissertation in 1970, my original intention was to publish it as my first book, an idea strongly endorsed by my doctoral mentor, Charles Glock, who even brokered a contract for me with the University of California Press. My failure to produce a publishable manuscript in this instance has remained a source of some embarrassment and disappointment for me ever since. One of the reasons for the failure might have been sheer fatigue, after a decade of intermittent doctoral studies, career building, and increased family responsibilities. I also allowed too many distractions from the book project to enter my life as I settled in for a new career at Washington State University. There, for the first time, I encountered strong expectations for doing research that would attract extramural grants to help support graduate assistants and would result in nationally visible publications (which, in those days, rarely included anything to do with religion). I thus spent the next fifteen years focusing on research and graduate teaching on topics such as social movements, deviant behavior, and alcohol abuse.[18] I was still able to teach occasional courses in the sociology of religion and to publish articles on religious topics in appropriate journals, but I felt constrained to give these endeavors a lower priority until I had earned tenure and full-professor rank at WSU. Yet along the way, I was able to publish a few articles out of my dissertation data, and in the late 1970s, I eventually completed a preliminary draft for the long-postponed book manuscript, but one that still seemed to me entirely unsatisfactory.[19]

The book manuscript was a frustrating experience for me as an endeavor in polished academic writing. I did well enough with works of article length, but I could not seem to escape the dissertation format in doing the book. The rough draft contained all sorts of statistical tables with very convincing data, but it needed more of a narrative format based on a focused theoretical perspective, in which the empirical data could be used selectively to illustrate important themes, with perhaps fuller statistical presentations relegated to an appendix. I recognized too that while I had plenty of data on LDS attitudes toward Jews and black people, I had only a very thin treatment of the Mormon outlook on Native American peoples, known to Mormons as "Lamanites," which was the third of the three ethnic groups for which Mormons had traditional doctrines and definitions. It is clear now in retrospect that I just lacked the theoretical and historical framework that I needed to produce a book that would provide meaning and understanding, not just quantitative data. I was not to succeed in such an enterprise until I published my 2003 book, which is what a revised version of my dissertation *should* have been, and would have been, if I had had sufficient skill and material in the 1970s.[20]

Although I was not able to produce a book manuscript to my satisfaction in the 1970s, I did continue to gather data of various kinds on the changing LDS posture toward black people, both before and after the dramatic policy change was announced in 1978. Meanwhile, Lester Bush had published his groundbreaking and definitive articles on the historical rise and development of the LDS race policies, so it seemed appropriate for me to trace their decline and fall and to assess the various factors that finally brought them to an end. My 1981 article offered just such a treatment.[21] By the 1980s, it was apparent also that the time had come for the whole history of the LDS relationship with black people to be reviewed, and its consequences assessed, as the church faced the necessity for building relationships with peoples of African ancestry everywhere. Such was the origin of our decision, Lester's and mine, to combine the *Dialogue* articles we had written into a book, with a new introductory chapter, a new conclusion, and a complete bibliography.[22]

The result was our book, *Neither White nor Black.*[23] This publication was not welcomed by the church leadership of the time, which was dominated by a segment of very conservative senior apostles, who had recently succeeded in quashing the Arrington era at the Church Historical Department and were starting to discipline LDS scholars whose work discussed any embarrassing episodes in the history of the church. That most of the chapters in our book had already been published as articles elsewhere did not mitigate our offense, since their original source had been *Dialogue,* itself considered an "apostate" publication among some of the brethren.[24]

While I continued thereafter producing occasional articles on Mormon topics among my other academic publications, I did not again engage the issue of Mormons and race for more than a decade. During that hiatus I gathered a lot more material on LDS relationships with the "Lamanites," as well as on relations with Jews and with those of African ancestry, new congregations of which were then burgeoning in Africa itself. I continued to talk with knowledgeable and interested colleagues, including Newell Bringhurst and Edward Kimball, who was working slowly on a biography of his father that would include an account of the background against which President Kimball had announced the revelation of 1978 ending the racial restrictions.[25] Equally important, I had gained more skill and experience for creating and narrating a theoretical context for the analysis that became *All Abraham's Children.*

Even before turning again to that book, however, I continued to speak out, both orally and in print, about a vexing irony in the whole ongoing story of Mormons and race: the 1978 revelation on priesthood had ended the traditional policy of withholding the priesthood from black people, but Mormons still felt the need to "explain" why such a policy had existed in the first place. Despite the meticulously documented historical record provided by Lester Bush, the official church position about the origins of the policy was a nonexplanation, namely, "We don't know, but that's all in the past, so let's look to the future." The stark inadequacy of such an official position for African Americans would seem obvious enough. However, it has also proved unsatisfying to the Mormon rank and file itself, which has apparently felt the need for even more contrived "explanations." Always uncomfortable with ambiguity in religious issues, some local LDS leaders, teachers, missionaries, and members have resorted, as usual, to the rich heritage of Mormon folklore to "explain" why the church once denied the priesthood to black people.

This "explanation" simply reaffirms the old scriptural folklore but invokes the doctrines of continuous revelation and divine mercy as the reasons for reversing the policy itself. The updated folklore explains that people who had been born with African ancestry had indeed come through a cursed lineage, as the early leaders had always taught, but that a merciful God, through a modern prophet, has nevertheless finally removed the curse and opened the priesthood and its privileges to them. This is not the *official* church position, but it has seemed to satisfy many of the members, who are reluctant to believe that all those early leaders could have been so wrong about divine intentions. It certainly has not satisfied many African Americans, however, for such an "explanation" comes across, in effect, as "Well, you folks were born under a curse because of something that happened in the preexistence, but God, in his mercy, has relented in these last days and offered you the priesthood after all! Shouldn't we all just be grateful?!"

An Abortive Campaign against the Folklore

All during this post-1978 period, I remained in periodic personal contact with many black LDS friends, especially those in the Genesis Group.[26] As conversations with my black LDS friends made clear, the circulation of this repackaged folklore greatly hindered the conversion and retention of new black members. I became well acquainted personally with one case, in particular, that produced a major national news story in 1998. This was the case of a middle-aged black couple named Jackson, who lived in Orange County, California. Betty Jackson happened to be a coworker with one of my sons at the Mazda Corporation, and through friendly conversation, each discovered that the other was a member of the LDS Church. The Jacksons had only very recently been converted along with one or two of their children. Upon learning of the traditional LDS racial teachings and policies only after joining the church, the Jacksons were having considerable trouble in accommodating the new information. My son gave Betty a copy of the Bush and Mauss book, *Neither White nor Black*, in hopes that it might help them understand and deal with the matter, which it did to some extent.

Meanwhile, however, the home teacher working with the Jacksons in their ward (who had also been instrumental in their conversion) continued to cultivate their friendship through a series of couple-to-couple visits in each other's homes. When the erstwhile racial restrictions came up during their visits, the home teacher, one Dennis Gladwell, proceeded to "explain" the issue to them with the warmed-over folklore described just above. Not only were the Jacksons unpersuaded, but David was angry enough to do some research of his own in attempting to convince Gladwell that his understanding of history and the scriptures was erroneous. After several encounters, Gladwell was convinced, and in an emotional breakthrough one evening, he broke down in tears, conceded that he had been wrong, and asked forgiveness.[27] From that point on, he and the Jacksons became allies in a campaign to disabuse the LDS Church and its members of their continuing reliance on such racist folklore.[28]

To initiate their campaign, Gladwell shared his story with an old friend in the church leadership, Elder Marlin K. Jensen, of the First Quorum of Seventy, and sought his assistance in approaching President Hinckley, and other general authorities, in seeking a formal and public repudiation of all the folklore that had once been used to "explain" the church's racial policies. Elder Jensen realized that any such repudiation would have to be approved and issued jointly by his colleagues in the leadership, particularly the Quorum of Twelve Apostles and ultimately the First Presidency. In an effort to craft a proposal to that effect for their consideration, Elder Jensen put together an ad hoc advisory committee consisting of Gladwell, the two Jacksons, William Evans from public affairs, and myself.[29] In mid-1997, we all met as a committee with Elder Jensen and formulated a collection of ideas and arguments that might serve as the equivalent of a lawyer's "brief" to be forwarded with Elder Jensen's proposal through the various channels of the general church leadership. I was delegated to write the first draft of such a document in the form of a report from the committee. Elder Jensen (himself an attorney before entering church service) then rendered my report into final form (presumably more like a real legal brief) and sent it through the appropriate channels with his proposal for a formal and public repudiation by the church president of the accumulated racist doctrines and folklore once used to justify denial of full privileges to members of African ancestry.[30]

All of us on the ad hoc committee, including Elder Jensen, were cautiously hopeful that the church president could be persuaded to issue the proposed repudiation by June 1998, which would mark the twentieth anniversary of the revelation ending the priesthood restriction. David Jackson, perhaps not fully appreciating the glacial speed at which bureaucracies like the LDS Church deal with sensitive issues, began asking me at regular intervals for reports on the progress of Elder Jensen's proposal. I tried to explain that none of us, except perhaps Elder Jensen himself, would be likely to learn what was developing within the councils of church leadership as the proposal worked its way up the channels. All we could do would be to hope and pray that divine guidance or good public relations sensitivity, or both, would lead to an issuance of the desired repudiation in time for the 1998 anniversary.

This was not enough to satisfy Jackson, who apparently got the idea that he could accelerate the process by a leak to the press about our quiet campaign behind the scenes, presumably in hopes that such a leak would exert pressure on the church leaders for an early public response. I warned him that the result would be the opposite of what he was hoping—that such a leak would simply derail the whole campaign. Nevertheless, he contacted Larry Stammer, then of the *Los Angeles Times,* with his leak. An article about the expected statement from the LDS Church appeared in late May 1998, while I happened, in fact, to be participating as president of the Mormon History Association at its annual meeting in Washington, DC. During that conference, I was tracked down several times by reporters, including Richard Ostling (then a senior correspondent and religion writer for *Time*), for my comments on Stammer's story. My comment was always to the effect that Jackson and Stammer had killed any chance for such a formal statement of repudiation to occur. I turned out to be quite right about that, of course, as President Hinckley, himself badgered by the Utah press, finally declared that he had heard nothing about plans for such a repudiation, and none such would be forthcoming, nor did he regard it as necessary.[31]

I never thought that our efforts had more than a fifty-fifty chance of getting the desired public repudiation, so I have no idea whether President Hinckley, after having eventually received our proposal, would have acted on it in 1998. He seemed entirely sincere in believing that the 1978 change in actual policy had automatically rendered moot all the traditional supportive folklore. The public relations line of the church tacitly took essentially the same position by claiming that the folklore was never official doctrine and that we simply did not know why the church had once had racially restrictive policies. Many of the church's leaders, and even some of its erstwhile critics, have sometimes cited, as an implicit repudiation, Elder McConkie's call to "forget everything that I . . . and whomsoever has said in the past," apparently not recognizing from the context of his speech that McConkie was referring *not* to the doctrinal folklore, but *only* to the traditional prophecy that blacks would never "receive the priesthood in mortality."[32] Another decade was to elapse before President Hinckley seemed fully aware of the extent to which the church and its members had been damaged by the continuing circulation of the racist folklore, and he finally issued a strong but rather oblique criticism of it in the priesthood session of the April 2006 General Conference.[33] Meanwhile, the urgent plea of David Jackson, years earlier, that the church should cease distributing McConkie's popular *Mormon Doctrine* (with its many racist teachings) was finally realized only in 2010.[34] Thus have the pain and anguish of the original race policy been allowed to live on through the doctrinal echoes that have survived the policy itself, quite unnecessarily, for decades.[35]

FINALLY, MY MAGNUM OPUS

Meanwhile, I had been continuing to collect ideas and material for what I hoped would become the kind of definitive treatment of Mormons and race that I had aspired to derive from my dissertation project thirty years earlier. In those early days, when writing my dissertation, I had been preoccupied with a critique of Mormon teachings about blacks (as an embarrassment), and secondarily with the pro-Semitic Mormon outlook on Jews (as a redeeming feature of LDS teachings). Accordingly, I failed to see the larger picture of the *entire* Mormon worldview about the divinely determined identities and destinies of certain biblical lineages. I had earlier resisted a suggestion by Newell Bringhurst that the doctrines about blacks might best be understood within the larger context of LDS teachings about the importance of *lineages in general.*[36] Indeed, as I began my research into early official and quasi-official Mormon literature, it became obvious that a preoccupation with the divine plan for *several* lineages was indeed a theme that recurred with increasing frequency in that literature from the mid-1830s onward.[37] Indeed, this preoccupation included, as part of that larger context, an increasing glorification of the Anglo-Saxon and Teutonic peoples as modern descendants of the ancient Israelite tribe of Ephraim. This retroactive construction of the Mormons themselves as a chosen lineage or "race" was the focus of my MHA presidential address in 1998.[38] My research in LDS literature across time also revealed the changing construction by church leaders of the meaning and significance of the "Lamanite" lineage. Gradually, I was able to formulate a comprehensive and unifying theme through which to interpret the part played in Mormon history more generally by the *social construction of identity* around lineage and the changes in such constructions as an important dynamic in Mormon history. Equipped with new information and insights, I was ready finally to finish *All Abraham's Children,* which has provided the culmination, and a certain sense of closure, to my decades of grappling with the racialist heritage of Mormonism.

This book was described by the publisher as my "magnum opus," which is, I suppose, an apt-enough description for a book that was three decades in the making. It had started out as a doctoral dissertation project, produced a number of derivative articles, and had one unsatisfactory iteration as a rough book manuscript. Now I had finally succeeded in synthesizing a persuasive theoretical narrative that tied together the traditional Mormons' constructions of identity for themselves, for the American aborigines (Lamanites), for the Jews, and for the black Africans. Since much had already been written, by myself and by others, on the identity and destiny of Jews and African Americans in LDS lore, I concentrated on building up the narrative on the Lamanites and on the claims to literal Israelite lineage by Euro-American Mormons themselves, both of which had been only superficially treated in my dissertation and in earlier attempts at a book manuscript.

All Abraham's Children was generously reviewed in all the most important journals inside and outside the Mormon scholarly community, and it won the "best book" award from the Mormon History Association in 2004.[39] Yet (like my earlier *Angel and Beehive*) it has enjoyed only the most modest sales, so my work on the Mormons has not broken out of the Mormon orbit to gain the greater exposure that I think it deserves in the scholarly world more generally.[40]

Fortunately, I no longer have any career contingencies at stake in my work. I still continue to write the occasional article on racial or other issues in the Mormon world, usually by special request,[41] but my principal remaining interest in the race issue since publishing the book is my desire that I shall live to see the formal, official, complete, and unequivocal repudiation by the LDS Church of all the doctrinal folklore about people of African lineage that has poisoned the Mormon tradition for a century and a half. Given my age, my hopes for this development are not high. Yet my studies and experiences with the LDS Church and its leaders make me somewhat optimistic about the future in general, for during my lifetime the church has often shown a capacity for rather fundamental changes in response to internal or external challenges. It will also eventually purge itself of the last vestiges of racism and racialism, not only where black Africans are concerned, but also more generally—a process already under way, as my 2003 book indicates.

Reflections on the Race Issue in Recent Mormon History

Meanwhile, however, a lot of unnecessary damage has been done to the church's public image, to its appeal among African Americans, and to the feelings among some white members as well. More than an entire generation has now passed since 1978, when the church finally rescinded its policy of denying the priesthood to people of African ancestry. The intervening historical distance might provide some perspective through which we can consider various implications of this issue in the LDS experience. The more I have studied the history of interracial and interethnic relations among the Latter-day Saints, the more convinced I have become that the policy of denying the priesthood to people of African ancestry was an unnecessary and completely avoidable burden upon the fundamental mission of the church. There is no evidence in the sacred scriptures, either in the general Christian canon or in the more extensive LDS canon, that the policy originated in divine revelation. The founding prophet, Joseph Smith himself, never instituted such a policy and, in fact, approved at least two ordinations of an African American during his lifetime—indeed, probably performing one of them himself. If an explanation ever is to be found for the origin of the racial restriction, we will need to look not for revelations but for developments in the political, social, and cultural world in which the LDS Church evolved after the prophet's death.

We know a lot about nineteenth-century race relations in that larger American world, but we need to learn much more about the emergence of the LDS race policy itself, and particularly what lay behind Brigham Young's decision to articulate such a policy in 1852 before the first meeting of the Utah Territorial Legislature. That event has always seemed a rather peculiar development to me, for the setting was a political one, not an ecclesiastical one, and while Young cited his prophetic calling, nothing is known about any prior deliberations among his apostolic colleagues that might have created a consensus for a formal revelatory pronouncement. If any such deliberations were ever recorded, they will have to be found by searching a variety of church archives, some of them not easily accessible, such as minutes of the meetings of the First Presidency during the period 1845–52. In the absence of information from such primary sources, we are left to wonder whether Young's 1852 declaration was the product of spontaneous theologizing (as was his wont), inspired policy improvisation, political calculation, or something else.[42] The question would be a marvelous one for a doctoral dissertation.

As the Bush historical account makes clear, the church's racial restriction simply remained the policy of Brigham Young's administration until his demise in 1877, as the Jim Crow era was just starting. Each of his successors, at least until the middle of the twentieth century, apparently assumed that the policy must have had a revelatory origin, since seemingly it had always existed and rarely was questioned. In other words, it was simply a case of organizational inertia. There was never any motivation for church leaders to wonder about a policy that was so well ensconced and so similar to policies in the surrounding states and in the nation as a whole. President McKay once joined in a 1949 letter from the First Presidency confirming the legitimacy of the restriction, but after he became president he always considered the racial restriction a "policy, not a doctrine." He continued to seek, though unsuccessfully, a revelation of his own on the matter.[43] We will never know why he felt no such divine promptings during his lifetime, but one of his successors, Spencer W. Kimball, demonstrated how important personal initiative and motivation were in eventually getting the necessary revelation.[44] Had the policy been changed under President McKay in the 1950s, before the national civil rights movement gained such momentum, there never would have been any public relations problem over such a conspicuously enduring "Mormon race issue," and with such an early change in policy, the church would never have faced the cynical suspicion since 1978 that it had merely succumbed to political expediency in finally making the change.

As things have turned out, however, the race issue has continued to tarnish the church's public image, to a greater or a lesser degree, for nearly fifty years. The irony is that this predicament has been, in large part, an unintended derivative of the traditional LDS belief in continuing revelation. Had this tradition been invoked in the 1950s, it could have provided the means for an end to the racial restriction before that became a national scandal. However, the doctrine of continuous revelation is *operationally* dependent on achieving a *consensus* among the "prophets, seers, and revelators" of the church collectively (that is, the First Presidency and the Twelve Apostles). The resulting process for obtaining new revelations is thus inherently conservative, and the more controversial the question, the slower the revelatory process is likely to be, resulting sometimes in the prolonged "organizational inertia" that I mentioned above. No matter how much President McKay might personally have favored a policy change in the 1950s, several of his most senior colleagues in the leadership, including his two most immediate successors, were on record with beliefs about black people that today would be regarded as outrageously racist in nature. That is, they were much like other white Americans of their generation. Even when the revelation came to President Kimball twenty years later, the process was long and slow, as his biography clearly indicates.

The irony arises when the doctrine of continuous revelation is complemented (as it often is) by a prevailing organizational myth that is the Mormon counterpart of papal infallibility—namely, that the prophets (collectively, at least) do not make serious mistakes—that is, they do not "lead the Church astray."[45] It would be especially difficult to acknowledge that such a "mistake" as the LDS racial restriction could have continued for more than a century. Such an acknowledgment would inevitably lead to questions about other possible "mistakes" of similar gravity. It is thus not difficult to understand why the official position of the church today is simply that "we don't know" what the origin of the earlier racial restriction was, for such a demurral is not likely to evoke any difficult follow-up questions. That is also the most likely reason that even after all this time, there has been no formal, public repudiation of the long-standing racial folklore that was used (in the absence of revelation) to "explain" and justify the restriction on priesthood ordination. After all, the most ardent apostolic promulgators of such folklore have not been so long gone, many of whom were also beloved by grassroots Latter-day Saints and their current leaders, resulting in a kind of "vested collective interest" in resisting such a repudiation. Be all that as it may, when the doctrine of continuous revelation is paired with the tradition of prophetic near infallibility, timely change in long-standing church policies will always be difficult. Thus the irony created by the countervailing effects of two important Mormon traditions.

Thus also the residual tarnish on the Mormon image, which has been unnecessary to the extent that it could have been avoided by a simple change in administrative policy, if only successive generations of church leaders had not assumed that it had had a revelatory origin in the first place.[46] The tarnish has also been somewhat unfair, of course, since the LDS Church was never any more "racist" than the rest of America, but only relatively late in dropping its restrictions. Furthermore, it has made truly strenuous efforts since then to redress the resulting grievances and to reach out sincerely to the African American community, both in the church itself and in the nation as a whole. Yet there still seems to be no disposition in high places to confront the actual origins of the erstwhile racial restriction through research in the primary archival sources, as the church recently has done, for example, with the Mountain Meadows Massacre. Only thereby can any real explanation be found, if there is one, for the historical racial restrictions, so that no longer will we have to be satisfied with the official but vapid "we don't know." Otherwise, in the future as in the past, we shall continue to see the issue raised against the church from time to time, and the racist folklore that once justified it will continue to pop up among the well-meaning but uninformed faithful.[47] So far, as a public relations posture, the church leadership seems to be counting on its racist past to disappear as time gradually filters out the popular recollection of such harmful episodes.[48] Time might thus bring the required forgetting, but forthrightness would likely bring also a measure of forgiveness.

Chapter 7 | My Journey with Dialogue

The Christmas holiday season of 1965 brought more than the usual good cheer to me and, I am sure, to other aspiring scholars in the LDS intellectual community. I received not one but *two* notifications that filled me with excitement. One was an invitation to the organizational meeting of the Mormon History Association, which was to be held in the Sir Francis Drake Hotel in San Francisco during the annual conference of the American Historical Association. The other was a brochure announcing the publication of a new scholarly journal to be called *Dialogue: A Journal of Mormon Thought.* I had nothing to do with either development, but I responded eagerly to both as a charter subscriber. I attended the meeting in San Francisco where the MHA was organized, and I sent in a subscription to *Dialogue* as quickly as I could. These two organizations had quite independent origins, the one being the product mainly of LDS historians in Utah, and the other of a more varied collection of LDS scholars based at Stanford University. Leonard J. Arrington, then a professor of economics and history at Utah State University, provided great encouragement to both enterprises, but otherwise they were totally separate. Yet, especially during its first decade, the MHA and its historians relied heavily on *Dialogue* as an outlet for their publications, until their own *Journal of Mormon History* began as an annual in 1974.[1] I participated in the conferences of the MHA during the remainder of the 1960s, and with great regularity starting again in 1980, but career imperatives, regrettably, caused a hiatus in my participation at MHA conferences during most of the 1970s.[2] By contrast, my *Dialogue* connections have been maintained with great frequency as author, board member, and correspondent throughout my career (even to the present). Although I was never editor of *Dialogue,* my investment in its survival and success has been substantial throughout the near half century of its existence.

A Struggle for Existence from the Beginning

At the beginning, many of us *Dialogue*-ers wondered how the new publication would be seen by the LDS general authorities, all of whom were sent gift subscriptions for several years. The founders of the new publication, as a matter of courtesy (and perhaps to try to preempt criticism), sent letters to the First Presidency assuring them of the editors' constructive intentions—but did not feel it necessary to ask for permission or approval. As the account (cited above) in part 1 of Devery Anderson's *Dialogue* history makes clear, there were dire warnings from many influential leaders *below* the general authorities, but no direct response from any of the latter, except S. Dilworth Young, of the First Council of Seventy, who expressed some wariness.[3] Ernest Wilkinson, president of BYU, sought to have the new publication banned from the campus, a development that was prevented by the intervention of Hugh B. Brown of the First Presidency. *BYU Studies,* which had been founded in 1959 but had usually been too bland to attract much of a following, suddenly sprang to life when faced with competition from *Dialogue* and began to become a more interesting publication itself—though, of course, carefully avoiding controversial content. *Dialogue,* by contrast, soon found itself (in articles and letters) dealing with such topics as the race issue, the Book of Abraham papyri, the church and politics, anti-intellectualism, prominent Christian theologians, and other topics likely to have given "the brethren" cause for concern. Whether from direct or indirect official criticism, or just from an abundance of caution, some of the founding group soon reduced or severed their ties to *Dialogue* and devoted their energies elsewhere.[4] Yet a diminishing few on the BYU faculty, or otherwise in church employment, continued for some years to serve *Dialogue* in various capacities, including author, until formal or informal pressures from the church leadership made it too uncomfortable for them to be publicly associated with it.[5]

The earliest crises in the history of Dialogue—that is, those that threatened its very existence—were always financial and logistical.[6] The first two editorial teams were constantly trying to raise money and were operating from hand to mouth. They not only took no salary or stipends for themselves (at least for about the first decade), but they periodically used their own funds to keep the enterprise going. In later decades, some sizable donations (in the thousands of dollars) were occasionally obtained from a very few benefactors. Apparently, during the early 1980s (I have no personal knowledge of exactly when), one major donor in particular began to take the main responsibility for financing the publication of *Dialogue,* and the editors were able to build up a small reserve fund.[7] This fund itself has had its ups and downs, but the careful stewardship of the board of directors in recent years has permitted donations and investments to accumulate toward a strong endowment that might eventually permit *Dialogue* to be self-supporting.

During and since the 1980s, therefore, the main threats to the journal's existence have come less from financial exigencies than from the serious clashes between editorial philosophy (as reflected in the journal's content) and the hostile reactions of church leaders, especially the most conservative general authorities. As Devery Anderson's installments of his "History of *Dialogue*" indicate, the tensions between this publication and the church leadership have waxed and waned across the years, depending not only upon the issues explored in its pages but also upon its editors' discretion—and especially upon the sensitivity of successive church leaders about some of those issues. In general, the leaders have taken special umbrage at discussions and publications that seem to question church teachings or policies about race, women's roles, temple rituals, polygamy, historicity of the Book of Mormon, and a few other sensitive issues in Mormon history. Such topics have appeared often enough in the pages of *Dialogue* to elicit various kinds of formal and informal ecclesiastical sanctions against various editors and authors, even when the treatments of these topics would have been considered balanced and reasonable by normal academic standards. The diverging perspectives between LDS scholars and leaders—over what constituted legitimate and appropriate commentary on church-related matters in independent journals and conferences—were increasingly accompanied by diverging mutual images: *Dialogue,* and certain cognate publications, came increasingly to be seen by LDS leaders, at both general and local levels, as hostile to the church and as questionable, if not dangerous, for faithful LDS scholars and members to be associated with. Reciprocally, to those of us who continued such associations, the church leadership came increasingly to be seen and felt as unfair and heavy-handed in its formal and informal responses to independent and well-intentioned scholarship.

The history of Dialogue has seen several serious clashes with church leaders. Every time they occurred, *Dialogue* suffered another round of abandonment by its most cautious or intimidated subscribers, authors, editorial board members, or staffers, with the usual damage to the journal's image from the constant circulation of rumors about dire consequences for any who continued their associations with it. I have felt those episodes keenly and personally, partly because I have been among those scholars periodically called in by stake presidents for discussions about my own work, but also because I have been close to nearly all of *Dialogue*'s editors and have shared in their anguish vicariously. Not that I have always approved of whatever they published, for in a few cases (mainly during the 1990s), I thought some of the articles lacked adequate balance and therefore invited ecclesiastical censure unnecessarily. On the other hand, I also felt that often the reactions of conservative apostles, and especially their personal interventions in relationships between scholars and local stake presidents, were not only overreactions but counterproductive in their effects, both upon the church's public image and upon the individuals who were harassed and disciplined—and derivatively upon their families.

Getting Up Close and Personal with Dialogue

Starting as a member of the editorial board in 1979, I have lived through many of *Dialogue*'s trials and tribulations revealed in Devery Anderson's four historical installments. My files contain copies of regular correspondence especially between me and the Newells, during their editorial term, and again with the Petersons during their term.[8] I was also among a score of persons appointed to the search committee in early 1987 to find successors to the Newells. Since the activities of that committee took place entirely in Utah, I was not able to travel there from Washington for any of the meetings. Although I offered a few suggestions about important considerations in the selection process, especially in a letter dated March 30, 1987, I saw little or no evidence of any influence from me in that search process. I was, however, pleased at the outcome, which resulted in the appointment of Ross and Mary Kay Peterson as coeditors succeeding the Newells, and I was tremendously impressed with the systematic and thorough nature of the search process. The communications to and from the search committee touched on many of the editorial concerns and issues that had vexed the *Dialogue* community from the beginning, including relationships with the church and its leaders, what topics and tone are appropriate for the content of the journal, the time and compensation connected with the editorship, and the constant need for fund-raising, among others.[9]

Then, in 1992, I found myself drawn into more direct participation in the operation of *Dialogue* than I had ever expected to have. During that year, Ross and Mary Kay Peterson, after editing the journal since 1987, were succeeded by the team of Allen D. Roberts and Martha "Marti" Sonntag Bradley. Once again a rational and orderly process of succession began in 1991 with the establishment of a formal search committee and a call for proposals from various aspirants to the role of editor.[10] I was one such aspirant, and Lorie Winder Stromberg was another, along with Roberts and Bradley, but I do not remember the others. As I recall, four of us applicants finally made the "short list" prepared by the search committee. In any case, the Roberts-Bradley team (or Bradley-Roberts) was chosen to succeed the Petersons. I recall having had somewhat mixed feelings at this outcome: I certainly approved of the final choice, since both Allen and Marti were esteemed friends and colleagues of many years standing, yet, on the other hand, I felt ready, willing, and able to take the editorial helm myself, since I was just completing a four-year term as editor of the *Journal for the Scientific Study of Religion,* so my editorial skills were well honed, and I actually had some available office space at my university, along with a well-trained LDS assistant editor who would have been able to continue on with me for a while, had I been named editor of *Dialogue.* However, that was not to be.

The new editorial team was announced in April 1992, and I remember a phone call from Lavina Fielding Anderson (as chairperson for the search committee) in which she informed me of the selection, along with the thanks of the committee for my having applied. She mentioned further that the new editors were planning to keep me on as a special adviser during their term and that I should contact Allen Roberts to see what that role might entail. I concluded (correctly, I think) that such a designation was being offered me, in courtesy and sincerity, as a kind of consolation prize for failing to gain the editorship. It soon became apparent that Allen and Marti would be installing an "advisory committee" of seven, at least some of whom had been unsuccessful applicants for the same position (see inside front cover of the Spring 1993 issue). Our advisory committee was originally informed that it would be called together for quarterly meetings with the editorial team.[11] As things turned out, however, only three or four such meetings were ever held (starting in May 1992), and the editors (capable though they were) increasingly made the production of *Dialogue* primarily an internal process, with a relatively small editorial team doing everything, including most peer reviews of manuscripts, and even all the business operations—or so it seemed from my vantage point.[12]

The Bradley-Roberts editorial term lasted six years (volume 26 in 1993 through volume 31 in 1998). The installments of the *Dialogue* history completed by Devery Anderson so far do not yet include this editorial term. Like any other period in *Dialogue's* history, this six-year term must be understood and evaluated in the larger context of LDS ecclesiastical history, with particular reference to the retrenchment regime that began in the 1960s and lasted the rest of the century (which I have discussed in other chapters). Part of that regime was an official policy of increasing repression against independent LDS scholars who were writing or speaking on certain topics in Mormon history and doctrine. That repressive policy was made especially conspicuous beginning in the mid-1970s with the termination of the Arrington program in the new Mormon history.[13] The growing tension between scholars and church leaders reached its climax with a series of well-publicized excommunications in 1993, just as the new Roberts-Bradley team was taking the editorial helm at *Dialogue.* One of those excommunicated, in fact, was Lavina Fielding Anderson, who had been active on the editorial staff of *Dialogue* for some years.[14]

As new editors, Bradley and Roberts, for their part, did nothing to disabuse the church leaders of such hostility toward independent scholarship. Their very first issue of *Dialogue* represented an obvious break with the more restrained editorial philosophy of the previous editorial regimes, featuring, as it did, male nudes on the cover (and elsewhere) by famed homosexual LDS artist Trevor Southey, plus a lead article by Lavina that was highly critical of recent ecclesiastical treatment of dissent, both at the local and at the general levels.[15] A couple of other articles critical of the church also appeared in this same issue. Surprising as this new editorial posture might have seemed to old-timers like me, it should have been anticipated by the editorial search committee that appointed the Roberts-Bradley team, for Allen Roberts, in his application portfolio for the editorship, included a determination "to be courageous and take a stand on current issues such as the recent church discouragement of participation in independent symposia . . . [and] to advocate reform, progressive change, a pointing of the way to a more ideal Mormonism."[16]

The new editors, furthermore, announced their new regime in their inaugural issue of the journal with an introduction titled "The Times—They Are a'Changin'," portending more of the same.[17] They looked forward to a new "spring of hope," in which the work of scholars might come to be welcomed by LDS leaders in somewhat the same way that the pope had belatedly accepted Galileo's truth about the solar system. Several years later, in a concluding essay reflecting back on his rather tumultuous editorial years ("A *Dialogue* Retrospective"), Allen expressed satisfaction that *Dialogue* had been both a "watchdog" and a "soul mate" of the LDS Church, somewhat akin to the relationship of *Commonweal* to the Catholic Church.[18] However, the issues of *Dialogue* produced by these editors during their years did little to make the journal seem much like a "soul mate" to the institutional LDS Church, for nearly every issue contained at least one article that, for example, questioned the historicity of the Book of Mormon, or advocated constructing a theology of the divine feminine, or debunked favorite historical myths, or vindicated the disillusionment and the apostasy of individuals (contemporary or historical), or other topics that would have raised the ire of church leaders and troubled many of the traditional subscribers.

Rarely were such controversial articles balanced by alternative arguments or viewpoints that might have given *Dialogue* a claim to intellectual diversity.[19] Such editorial imbalance was doubtless one of the reasons for a loss of more than a third of the journal's subscribers during the Roberts-Bradley editorial term.[20] At the same time, I would insist that these editors (ably assisted by managing editor Gary Bergera) published some of the most substantial scholarship and wonderful art to appear in *Dialogue* by that time, even if much of it was controversial. As especially important, I would list the regular features on scriptural history and interpretation; several articles on the history of the RLDS Church (otherwise little known among LDS readers); special issues devoted to national and ethnic diversity among LDS members; a special issue on women, including not only issues of special importance to women but also important female authors; several articles on the historiography of Mormons; and a pair of articles on the environment, probably the first in *Dialogue* to address that topic in any depth.[21]

As substantial as the contents of *Dialogue* were during this editorial term, I personally grew concerned about what seemed to me an editorial imbalance in the journal that I had not seen in previous years. I was not sure what I could do about it, if anything. I considered the editors good friends, and I assumed that I could consult with them if I wished to—for after all, they had installed me on their committee of advisers! Yet I was not sure what role an adviser had, except, of course, to advise, so I began to look for junctures at which I might raise some questions about editorial plans and policies. The opportunity came in 1994 or early 1995, when the editors invited me to serve as guest editor for an issue to be devoted to international Mormonism. As I gathered together some fellow authors and their manuscripts to produce this issue, I had occasion periodically to consult with one or both editors about the project, and both seemed pleased with the way that the issue finally turned out.[22]

With channels of communication thus opened, I initiated discussions of other matters with the editors, both in writing and during special visits that I made to Salt Lake City during the mid- and late 1990s, sometimes inviting the editors to discuss my concerns over lunch.[23] I did not keep notes on our discussions, but I recall that the lack of editorial balance in articles on controversial topics was among my concerns. I recall also that during the fifth year of this editorial term (which would have been 1997), I began to consider whether I might again apply to become a *Dialogue* editor—maybe even the next one—especially since the special 1996 issue (for which I had been guest editor) seemed so successful. Since the traditional editorial term at *Dialogue* had been five or six years, I began to press Allen and Marti on their plans about a search for their successor(s). I recall being surprised that they seemed in no hurry to turn over the editorial reins, since they understood (correctly) that the five- or six-year limit on editorial terms was nowhere stipulated but was only customary.

Yet I was bothered by the prospect that these editors—or any *Dialogue* editors—might hold the position indefinitely. I strongly approved of the tradition of short-term service in the editorial role, just as I preferred the same in church service. I had noticed (in myself as in others) a tendency to grow weary and complacent in such voluntary roles after four or five years. Creativity always seemed to give way to routine. In the case of these particular editors, I worried also about a continuation of the editorial imbalance to which I have referred, for I knew that it would mean increasing tension with church leaders, rather than the opposite, which *Dialogue* sorely needed. Another of my concerns was the de facto merger of the editorial and the governance functions when the same persons were both the editors and the officers of the foundation (as had become traditional at Dialogue).[24] Accordingly, I began remonstrating with Allen and Marti, urging them to consult with their predecessors about the wisdom of retaining the editorship longer than the traditional term, as well as certain other matters. Most pointedly, I recommended reorganizing the leadership of Dialogue to restore a board of trustees separate from the editorial staff, in place of the dual roles then obtaining for the editorial team.[25]

Meanwhile, during 1997, the editors (who were also trustees) began casting about for likely successors as editor(s). I finally decided against offering my own services again as an editor, since I was soon to retire from my university position, which had been providing me the logistical support that I would need to take on the editorship of another journal.[26] I do not know how systematic the search was—not very wide, I believe—but I recall being asked for recommendations. I was somewhat surprised, but quite pleased, when I was informed that Neal and Rebecca Chandler had been selected and had agreed to serve, for they were among the potential successors whom I and others had recommended.[27] The plan was for the Chandlers to join the board and the editorial team in the summer of 1997 and work with the existing team during 1998, gradually taking over full responsibility for the journal by the beginning of 1999.[28]

To integrate the new editors and discuss the reorganization process more generally, Allen and Marti called a meeting at Marti's home in Salt Lake City on August 4, 1997. The agenda called for a discussion of how to expand the board of trustees and whom to include in the expansion. Among those considered, besides the new editors, were Eugene England, Michael Homer, George Smith, and myself, with either Allen or Marti to remain on the board after the editorial transition.[29] The discussions at this meeting ranged far and wide beyond the initial agenda and included some comments that were apparently taken as critical by at least one of the retiring editors (Marti), who expressed to Eugene England the feeling of being somewhat unappreciated for her service. Gene had apparently written earlier to Marti (long before the meeting) with certain remonstrances (perhaps similar to mine), and he had been opposed to a prolonging of their editorial term beyond the "normal" period (roughly five years). Marti had written to Gene after the meeting to express her feelings, and in a solicitous response (with copies to me, Roberts, and Bergera), Gene did his best to allay her hurt feelings, to apologize for leaving the impression that he did not appreciate her service, and to compliment her and her colleagues on the work they had done, including a major step toward reorganizing the governance of Dialogue.[30] I bring up this exchange here only to make the point that I was not the only one who had been feeling the tension between these editors and Dialogue old-timers about some of the developments during their editorial term, despite a general appreciation for the talents and products of the retiring editorial team.

Thus it was that I found myself, for the first time, drawn into the inner workings of Dialogue—both the journal and the foundation—as I agreed to serve on the board of trustees (later directors), then newly developing out of the advisory committee. The original 1965 articles of incorporation (under Utah law) had established such a board to handle the legal and financial responsibilities of the Dialogue Foundation, but almost since the beginning, the same people who constituted the editorial team had typically served also as trustees and officers of the foundation. The obvious difference in function between the editors and the trustees always carried the potential for a conflict of interest when the same persons served in both capacities; furthermore, the demands of producing the journal on schedule always left the editors with little time or energy to handle such business functions as marketing, fund-raising, hiring, and paying the persons involved in the editorial process. Over the years, different editors had tried to hand over the various business tasks to others while still heading the board of trustees themselves, but usually both the editorial and the business operations had suffered, especially the latter. The hazards in this kind of organizational overlap were not fully recognized until the new and expanded board of trustees—then still including the editors—actually began to operate the foundation during 1998 and 1999. Indeed, since no separate board had yet been formally organized, the outgoing editors (Roberts and Bradley) simply turned over the entire operation, including the funds and other material assets, to the incoming editors (the Chandlers), who thus began by holding both editorial and board positions simultaneously, just as all their predecessors had done.[31]

TEN YEARS ON THE BOARD OF DIRECTORS

The new board of trustees, as originally conceived by Allen and Marti in 1997, was modified during 1998 to consist of themselves, the Chandlers, Eugene England (Dialogue's founder), Molly Bennion, Greg Prince, Marian Smith, and myself. Allen was made chairman of the board by common consent, and periodic meetings were held in his architect office in Salt Lake City. Marti and Marian were actually never able to serve, so it became important to add new members. Allen soon succeeded in getting John Ashton, Ross Peterson, and Hardy Redd to join the board, and thereafter changes in membership continued at a somewhat slower rate.[32] Toward the end of the first year (1999), Allen, facing a sudden increase in his responsibilities at work, recommended me to replace him as chairman, in which the rest of the board concurred. One important item of unfinished business left over from the recent organizational transition was the crafting of a revision to the articles of incorporation that had provided the legal basis for Dialogue's existence since 1965. The board formed by Allen and Marti in 1997 had charged Mike Homer with producing the first draft of a new document, which we began discussing in 1998. However, in the process finally of getting a new set of articles and bylaws, we had to bring in other legal help as well, and it was 2002 before we eventually approved and registered the new documents with the state of Utah.[33]

Starting late in 1999, then, my chairmanship lasted through 2003, which proved to be a very stressful and difficult period of transition from an operation run by the editors to one run by the board of trustees, from one based on a 1965 document of incorporation to one governed by the revised 2002 articles of incorporation with new bylaws, and eventually from one editorial team (the Chandlers) to the next one (of which more will be said later). Many other changes, including serious losses, occurred during this period. These losses included yet more subscribers, as the editorial transition to the Chandlers proved slower than had been expected, and their first issue was several months late in coming out. We also lost two founders: Leonard Arrington, who might be considered the "godfather" of *Dialogue,* died in 1999, and Eugene England, the cofounder of *Dialogue* (with Wes Johnson), was diagnosed with a brain tumor in 2000 and died the next year, leaving a large hole in the board of trustees. By the end of 2002, Allen had decided to leave the board altogether, but meanwhile several new members had been added to the board, and Lori Levinson had been hired as the business manager, responsible to the board (which, by a change in Utah law, was thereafter called the board of directors). Allen's contribution to the board had been enormous in several respects, one of which was in finding some of the new board members, and particularly in finding Lori, who turned out to be a very able and strongly committed business manager (energetically serving Dialogue to this day—2012, but now called managing director). By 2003 the Chandlers were in the final year of their editorial term, so it was time to start another search to replace them.

The Chandlers had been appointed in 1998; their first issues of the journal were scheduled to appear in 1999 and their final issues in 2003. This five-year period proved to be another crucial one in the history of Dialogue, and it fell my lot to be chairing the board of directors during four of those years. As Eugene England lay dying in 2001, the historic enterprise that he founded was itself on the verge of demise from rapidly declining subscriptions, years of dubious financial management, an unreliable publication schedule, and several years of increasing tension with LDS Church leaders. I shall always remember a poignant visit I had with Gene at his bedside in Provo during the summer of 2001, within days of his passing. He was not capable of sustained conversation, but we exchanged a few words about Dialogue, and I was anxious to reassure him that that part of his legacy would live on. Running through my mind was a jumble of ambivalent feelings, as I considered simultaneously the many struggles the board was having during this transitional period, but yet the plans and prospects that also offered us a favorable prognosis. Finally, in a burst of emotion, born of a mixture of determination and hope, I took Gene's hand and assured him that we had "saved Dialogue"! As I later pondered my optimistic outburst, I promised myself that even if my declaration had been premature, I would not rest until it was a reality—which I believe it has now become, thanks to the untiring efforts of many subsequent board members, editors, and one donor in particular.

Yet I recall that nearly the entire five years of the Chandlers' editorial term was a struggle, partly because the transfer of responsibilities to them in 1998 had occurred in a context of great organizational ambiguity and fluidity, in which their editorial operations would soon be taking place under a reconstituted board of trustees with ultimate responsibility for the foundation. I came to realize, in retrospect, that neither the Chandlers nor all of the board members had understood the full implications of the decision to create a separately functioning board of trustees. Only gradually, from 1999 through 2002, was a fairly stable new board finally in place and new articles of incorporation filed. Meanwhile, both the fiscal management and the bank account stayed with the Chandlers as the new board increasingly organized itself and began to assert its prerogatives. Gradually, during 2001 and 2002, the Chandlers finally relinquished to the board the financial resources and the full fiscal responsibility for the foundation and the journal, so that the board was able to hire Lori Levinson as the part-time business manager.

During the first years of the Chandlers' editorial term, a certain amount of tension between editors and the board was palpable and perhaps understandable. The Chandlers had moved the Dialogue operation to Ohio, with but little to sustain them, except their own considerable personal and intellectual resources and (of course) the Dialogue bank account. Subscriptions were down and declining, and there was no system in place for soliciting new or renewed ones. They had but few manuscripts in the pipeline, if any, and no existing network of colleagues on whom to call, either as an internal editorial team or as external peer reviewers. They had no office with the needed equipment, utilities, and storage space. They had no existing relationship with a local printing company (and printing that was both affordable and reliable was a problem during much of their tenure). Both Chandlers had full-time jobs, and it took them some time to find local volunteers (including at times some of their own grown children) to staff the office and carry on the operations.

Finally, a serious additional complication was Neal's decision to accept a Fulbright scholarship to Germany for a year or more, just as he and Becky were taking over their Dialogue responsibilities. Neal had applied for the fellowship some months earlier, and perhaps he accepted the Dialogue appointment without really expecting to get the fellowship. I do not know whether he even mentioned it to his predecessors or to the search committee; certainly, I did not know about it. In any case, Neal was understandably reluctant to turn down the fellowship, so he and Becky worked out an arrangement whereby he would do his Dialogue work with and through her by long distance, and each of them would travel back and forth to Europe on occasion for fuller communication and consultation. However, the net result of all these complications was that their first issue of the journal (the Spring 1999 issue) did not appear until the fall of that year, and they never did succeed in achieving the ostensible publication schedule—although they came close a couple of times by combining issues. Their final issue (Winter 2003) appeared only in early 2004, after the term of their successors had already started. Despite the high quality of many of the articles published under the Chandlers, the lagging publication schedule was something for which subscribers have always proved quite unforgiving, so subscriptions eventually dropped below two thousand and have never regained even that level.

A Chairman without Charm

In early 2000, as I became chairman of the Dialogue Board of Directors, I had the disadvantage of lacking access either to the records or to the funds of the foundation, all of which had gone to Cleveland with the Chandlers. As I began to seek the information I needed to assess Dialogue's situation and viability, I found the Chandlers as cooperative as the sudden change in their circumstances would permit. During a visit to a relative in Toledo, Ohio, during 1999, my wife and I made a side visit to Shaker Heights (in the Cleveland area), where the Chandlers had established an office, and I consulted at some length with Becky, offering advice and suggestions and looking through some of the records that had been transferred to them by their predecessors. (As I recall, Neal was in Europe at the time.) I could see that these records left a lot to be desired with respect to completeness and currency and that the Chandlers had much work to do in getting them updated. Thereafter, I contacted Becky or Neal or both regularly with questions and suggestions. Among the things I discovered were that subscription records were obsolescent and included at least a hundred complimentary subscriptions for reasons that no one could recall; although large annual donations during the previous several years from the one major donor had been far more than enough to cover all the costs of publishing the journal, the Dialogue bank account had but little reserve beyond funds needed for immediate expenses; and some sixty thousand dollars a year had been going to editors' salaries in the previous editorial term (divided in some way among Allen, Marti, and the managing editor, Gary Bergera). Although I felt sure that this figure was far more than previous editors—even recent ones—had taken as salaries, it was understandably regarded as a legitimate precedent by the Chandlers.

Given these and other important realities of the business and fiscal side of the Dialogue operation, the board of directors faced the delicate but necessary task of getting the Chandlers to cooperate in turning over to the new board all the funds and managerial prerogatives that had been left in the hands of previous editorial teams. This proved to be a long and difficult process, which must have seemed very disruptive to the Chandlers: they were just settling into their new situation and were suddenly being asked to turn over key records, funds, and managerial responsibilities to the board—including the control over their own salaries and other local expenses.[34] For my part, and the board members serving with me, we had thought (perhaps erroneously) that the new division of labor and responsibilities was clear to the Chandlers, so we could not understand why they were not more expeditious in their response to our requests for the records and the funds. Meanwhile, as Neal began spending time in Europe on his Fulbright, and as the publications continued to lag behind schedule, I became quite impatient, constantly making recommendations and pressing the editors for explanations, which I thought befitted my role as board chairman.[35] Recognizing that the Chandlers also lacked adequate help in many of the basic editorial tasks, I put together most of a special issue for them (Fall–Winter 2001) and devoted a lot of time and effort to helping them round up new manuscripts, rewriting some of these and evaluating several for publication—practices I continued for later editors, too, as long as I served on the board of directors.

Drawing on my earlier experience as editor of the *Journal for the Scientific Study of Religion,* I had thus hoped to play the role of l'éminence grise for them, but instead I seemed to become their bête noire. I realized that I had taken on the latter image when I noticed the reactions to me from a couple of their family members, one of whom referred to me as "Mr. High Maintenance" in an internal e-mail message on which I was inadvertently copied. Yet they all endured my endless pressuring with good grace and never responded with irritation. I do not know if the Chandlers ever realized that at one time the board had a long conference call in which we seriously discussed the costs and benefits of terminating their editorship, finally deciding against it. All things considered, it was a credit to all of us that discussions between the Chandlers and the board members during this period remained civil and collegial despite the pressures that we all were feeling about the lagging production schedule and in negotiating the process for transferring the funds and business affairs to the board.

During their final year or so (perhaps mid-2002 through 2003), the stress seemed to relax a little as this transfer was completed and the production schedule began to improve. I always deeply regretted that most of the Chandlers' editorial term was so fraught with stress between them and me in particular, but also with the rest of the board. I think that sometimes they took it personally, or at least some of their protective family members did, but for me it was just a matter of trying to do my job as board chairman and to save Dialogue, a beloved enterprise that was clearly in danger of disappearing. Even more regrettable was that the stress from *Dialogue,* as things turned out, was matched or exceeded by the stress Neal suffered from political turmoil surrounding his job at Cleveland State University during his final year or so with *Dialogue.* The combined stress produced a serious threat to his health for a while. Despite the stresses and strains during the Chandlers' editorial term, both with the board and in their own personal lives, they produced some of the most substantial and important articles (and special issues) in *Dialogue*'s history. Meanwhile, the tension we all felt between *Dialogue* and the church leaders relaxed noticeably, partly because a new cadre of leaders (starting in 1994) began to assume a posture of "benign neglect," in general, toward independent scholarship and partly because the stridency characteristic of the prior editorial regime had been greatly reduced under the Chandlers.[36]

The final year of the Chandlers' editorial term (2003) was also my final year as chairman of the Dialogue Board of Directors. It was a tremendously eventful year: we had completed a new version of the articles of incorporation (with bylaws) in 2002, so that all operations of the foundation, including the selection of a new editor, were now clearly under the board of directors; we had begun to accumulate a substantial financial reserve toward an eventual endowment, thanks to the investment skills of Molly Bennion; the business office was functioning efficiently with up-to-date records, thanks to the stewardship of Lori Levinson and the supervision of board treasurer John Ashton; the attrition in subscriptions had stopped; and the board now had the opportunity, for the first time, to select and appoint a new editorial team under our new rules of operation.

The board sent out a widely distributed call for applications and proposals from aspiring editors to succeed the Chandlers, and as a search committee we selected Neal Chandler (current editor), Allen Roberts (previous editor), Molly Bennion, and me with the responsibility for interviewing finalists among the applicants. As things turned out, the applicant pool was not large—only five or six cases, as I recall—and most of those were not credible candidates for one reason or another. We selected three teams as finalists, and one of those withdrew before we could start the interviewing. Both from the résumés and from the interviews, one of the two remaining teams emerged as clearly better prepared than the other for editing scholarly material, so eventually, in the spring of 2003, the board selected the team of Karen M. Moloney (as editor) and Levi S. Peterson (as associate editor) for further negotiations. Both had had careers as professors of English at Weber State University, although Levi had recently retired.

A New Storm and Then the Welcome Calm

From the beginning, our negotiations with the new team were cordial but a little difficult in certain respects. The main concern of the board of directors (and derivatively of the search committee) was to maintain the hard-won restructuring of Dialogue, such that the board would always retain ultimate authority over all operations, whether business, marketing, or staff, under our revised articles of incorporation and bylaws.[37] The board was also committed to complete intellectual freedom for the editorial team, with no interference except perhaps in a rare extremity, where editorial irresponsibility might threaten the brand of the journal or even the existence of the foundation—something that had never happened in *Dialogue*'s history and could not be envisioned except hypothetically. More than anyone else on the board, I was also hopeful that we might roll back the editorial salary of forty thousand dollars, which had eventually become the figure during the Chandler years, to perhaps half that figure. In that aspiration, I was concerned not only with the publication budget, but also with refurbishing the *ethic of voluntary service,* as the *main* motivation for taking the role of editor, as had been the case with earlier editors. That ethic seemed to me to be eroding as the large subsidy from a single donor in recent years had encouraged a tendency instead to think of editorial compensation at *Dialogue* in the same terms as in the wider publishing world. I knew it would be difficult for my view to prevail in this regard, especially since both the current editor and the previous editor, who were also two of my colleagues on the search committee, had come to think of forty thousand dollars as at least normal, if not minimal.

Aside from compensation issues, Karen seemed uncomfortable with the ultimate authority and fiduciary responsibility of the board, apparently because of fears of board constraints over editorial autonomy, at least indirectly. In this view, she might have been comparing the newly restructured Dialogue arrangements with what she had experienced in the late 1970s and 1980s, when she had worked on the editorial team with then editor Mary Bradford. In those days, the business affairs and the editorial operations of Dialogue had been merged, since the foundation officers and the editors were the same people (a situation that had continued to prevail all the way up to the Chandlers' editorial term). Karen had been used to these earlier arrangements and perhaps had not had much experience in the interim with the world of publishing (either academic or commercial), where editors are always responsible ultimately to a governing board of some kind.[38] It seemed to me that either she did not really understand how the new organizational arrangements at Dialogue had changed since her earlier experiences with it, or else she was just distrustful of these changes. Levi, meanwhile, who played an important part in all the negotiations, had been an editor of academic journals earlier in his career, so none of this was new to him. In any case, after a few weeks, the search committee and the new editorial team of Moloney and Peterson came to terms, so on March 27, 2003, I wrote a letter on behalf of the search committee to the board, recommending that an offer be extended to the new team, which swiftly occurred.[39] Karen accepted the offer for her team on April 13, 2003.

What ensued thereafter was one of the most perplexing experiences in my professional life. Since a number of financial details remained to be worked out in the transition from one editorial team to another, the board asked Karen to prepare and propose to the board two different budgets: one covering expenses connected with moving the editorial office and files from the Chandlers (in Ohio) to her home in Utah and another covering her anticipated operating expenses as editor for the coming year (2004). For help with the first kind of budget, she would have access to the Chandlers, whom she visited at their home in Ohio during May (at board expense). For help with the second (operating) budget, she would have access to previous budgets and general guidance from our treasurer and business manager. In accordance with our established business practices, these two new budgets were to be submitted for negotiation and eventual approval by the board (through the board's executive and finance committees). For more than three months, we waited for these budgets to no avail. Inquiries usually brought the explanation that since Karen was so busy preparing her first issue of *Dialogue* (for Spring 2004), she did not have time to work on budgets. Meanwhile, however, she began running up ad hoc financial charges and commitments in Dialogue's name without the approval of the board or any of its officers.

In preparation for a meeting with the board during the Sunstone Symposium in August 2003, Karen was asked to meet in advance with me (as board chairman) and with John Ashton (board treasurer) in hopes that we could discuss some of the expenses she had charged and work out some tentative budget figures with her before the board meeting. She met with us only long enough to say that she knew what we were up to and would not cooperate. We had no idea what she meant, unless it was that she suspected that we were trying to keep her from having direct access to the board. When she finally got access to the board at its formal meeting the next day, she still did not propose any budget but simply requested board approval for a series of ad hoc expenses in connection with the move from Ohio and the production of her first issue of *Dialogue* the next spring. Since the board continued to hold out for a more formal procedure, including comprehensive budget proposals, the wrangling that ensued simply brought the board meeting to an impasse until a couple of the more affluent board members offered to cover some of her ad hoc expenses temporarily out of their own funds. Despairing of getting the formal budgets that would be necessary to identify and regulate Karen's recent and ongoing expenditures, the board directed me and the executive committee to draw up a more formal memorandum of agreement specifying exactly what compensation and other expenses the board would cover and not cover and to present that to Karen and Levi for their signatures. Eventually, they both signed it.[40]

Despite such oral and written agreements that we thought we had concluded with this editorial team, we still had no budget proposals after waiting six months. Yet Karen continued to obligate Dialogue for expenditures that were neither budgeted nor approved by the board. These included commitments for copyediting, proofreading, and expensive artwork. That prompted me to send her a letter, on behalf of the executive and finance committees, freezing all expenditures and forbidding her from making any further commitments for such in the absence of a fully negotiated and approved budget.[41] I followed that letter to Karen with a letter to the board of directors apprising them of the deteriorating relationship between Karen and the board's officers, including myself, and raising the prospect that the board might have to consider terminating that relationship and finding a new editor.[42] Clearly, matters were coming to a head. During the next few days, Karen also received remonstrances from Molly Bennion (soon to succeed me in the chair of the board) and an exchange of correspondence with Levi Peterson, her incoming associate editor, who was in separate communication with board members as he attempted to do what she had not been willing to do—namely, negotiate budgets with the board for the transition from Ohio and for operating expenses in the publication of the journal during the coming year. Karen criticized Levi for such separate communications with the business manager and demanded an explanation. In this matter, she seems finally to have alienated even her friend Levi, who had championed her claim to succeed the Chandlers as editor and had even agreed to help her as associate editor, despite his own retirement plans.

Levi's response to Karen, as a friendly witness to her deteriorating relationship with me and the board, is very revealing.[43] After explaining to Karen that he had spent many days seeking help from people knowledgeable about what should go into the budgets, he noted that "I began to see many unsolved problems, and I pursued solutions on my own initiative. That is what I was doing by sending the memo to Lori which you have asked me to explain." He pointed out further that he had tried two or three times by telephone to get Karen's ideas, so that any budget submitted would reflect their joint input, but that "each time you made it clear that you saw no need" for further discussion, and in those conversations, "I had a hard time not feeling that your cold, clipped tone was directed toward me as well as toward the Executive Committee." In one of their phone conversations, Levi reminded her, "I was deflected . . . by your immediate insistence on discussing whether we shouldn't work on getting Lori [the business manager] dismissed, a possibility so remote from the way I believed we should be relating to the Board and its designated business manager that I was stunned that you were even thinking of it. I spent some minutes persuading you that we needed to focus on the Executive Committee, not on Lori, and by the time we got onto discussing the budget, my sense of appropriate procedure had evaporated."

Finally, as an indication of the contrast between Karen's and his own assessment of my efforts to resolve the impasse between them and the board, Levi wrote, "I have also been in professionally courteous communication with Armand all along. As far as I could make out last summer, you had stopped talking to him. I felt it imperative that one of us keep up a friendly communication. I have found him consistently helpful. He has done us a particularly good service by soliciting papers and assisting authors with their preparation of papers. His conservative fiscal position is reasonable, and I believe the majority of the board will be found to support him on it." In this last prediction, Levi proved entirely correct. Accordingly, Molly Bennion, soon to succeed me in the board chair, wrote Karen a letter dated December 23, 2003, in which she spelled out once again the several issues still unresolved with the board, after months of haggling, and confronted Karen with the prospect of her dismissal as editor-elect. Karen responded with her own letter of resignation. By this time, however, she had done virtually all the work required in putting together the Spring 2004 issue of *Dialogue,* so in its pages, and on the list of editors emeriti, she is identified as the editor for that one issue only.

Karen's own (selectively) accumulated correspondence shows that all along she had been privately reaching out for advice from people whom she thought might support her efforts to break free from the "overbearing" and "unreasonable" demands of the board. Her appeals went to some of the previous editors (who, to their credit, responded with neutral and constructive advice). Some of her correspondence accuses Lori Levinson and me of trying to take total control of *Dialogue,* and other communications leave the impression that she is asking some of the board members to spy for her against us as the board's own executive committee—all of which struck me as a response bordering on the paranoid.[44] Karen had proved reluctant also to sign the memorandum of agreement that we had sent her and Levi in early October, so in an attempt to resolve Karen's concerns, Levi sought the intervention of his daughter, an attorney, as a neutral expert, to engage Karen in negotiations by phone about what kind of document would satisfy her. At Karen's request, the attorney drafted a formal contract, which appeared to the board as an attempt by Karen to renegotiate terms to which she had agreed way back in April. With my strong concurrence, the contract was thus rejected by Molly Bennion, incoming chairperson of the board. The matter soon became moot anyway, for the board had finally come to the conclusion that it would not be able to work with Karen under circumstances where mutual trust had been destroyed. Before she could be fired, however, she resigned, much to the relief of all concerned. That presented us with the predicament of finding a new editor for a term that was already beginning.

Levi Peterson proved to be the man of the hour and the hero of the entire episode up to that point. He had recently retired from a distinguished academic career at Weber State University, where he was a well-published author and former editor of two academic journals. He would not have sought the editorship of *Dialogue,* but because of his long-standing friendship with Karen Moloney on the Weber State faculty, he had agreed to support her candidacy for editor by joining her as associate editor. Having made that commitment, he provided a voice of experience, reason, and collegiality throughout the entire several months of the board's difficulties with Karen, and then finally, when she resigned, he reluctantly accepted the reins as editor. He would have been fully justified if he had used her resignation as a legitimate pretext for his own, since he had, in effect, come out of his recent retirement at Weber State only to support and assist Karen. He could have taken the position that his commitment to *Dialogue* was tied to hers and that if she were departing, he would have to do the same. Instead, however, Levi took seriously his own independent commitment and agreed to step into the vacated position as editor. He served without an associate editor, so I helped him in certain marginal ways by continuing to solicit new manuscripts and by working with a few authors to make editorial improvements as their manuscripts were submitted. Levi's five-year term as editor was characterized by a warm and collegial relationship with the board and by twenty outstanding issues of the journal, published meticulously on schedule. In the process, he even shared his stipend with a few others on his editorial team whose compensation from the board he regarded as insufficient.

The completion of Levi's term as editor in 2008 coincided with my own completion of ten years on the board of directors. This gave me an opportunity to participate one more time on a search committee to find a new editor. The search process was just as systematic this time as it had been five years earlier, but with better results. This time we gave personal interviews to several finalists, any one of whom would have been a competent and successful editor. Two of them, both young women, emerged as most favored from the search committee's deliberations. At first I favored the more experienced of these two, but I was nevertheless pleased when our search committee finally recommended Kristine Haglund to the board of directors as the new editor beginning with the 2009 issues of the journal. At this writing, late in mid-2012, Kristine has now served more than three years of her five-year term, and done so with distinction. She represents, along with her editorial team, a truly new and much younger generation of authors and editors for *Dialogue,* savvy about strategic and tactical uses of the new electronic media. She has proved proactive in securing important new material and has shown a deft sense of balance in publishing articles that are intellectually substantial and occasionally provocative without being gratuitously critical of the church or its leaders.

Not that peace and rationality will always reign supreme in the leadership of Dialogue. A certain amount of drift and indecision seemed apparent in the Dialogue Board of Directors with the arrival of 2012. Such was probably attributable mainly to (1) the sudden resignation in late 2010 of the newly incoming president of the board, with no one really prepared to take the helm in 2011 (though a relatively new board member graciously agreed to step in on short notice); (2) certain other organizational lapses in the board's functions resulting from diminishing institutional memory, especially among the more recent members of the board; and (3) enduring policy disagreements over proposed changes in organization and operation. Diminishing institutional memory is, of course, an ongoing problem in any organization with a regular turnover in membership such as occurs with Dialogue's Board of Directors and its editorial team, most of whom serve terms limited to five years or less. Certain innovations, both in technology and in organization, have proved somewhat contentious at Dialogue in recent years and will not likely yield to early resolution. Enthusiasm for innovation always raises questions of costs versus benefits, both in finances and in personal relationships. Yet, all things considered, both the directors and the editors still inspire my confidence as conscientious custodians of Dialogue's future.

Reflections on a Half Century with Dialogue

To evoke again the metaphor of travel and passports, I would say that *Dialogue* has provided the borderlands where earnest thinkers have been able to gather and to share their ideas and experiences about all things Mormon. Probably most who have joined this conversation over the years have regarded themselves as devout and faithful Latter-day Saints with a desire to explore aspects of their religion beyond the confines of the institutional church curriculum and experience. Others have brought to the conversation their struggles between faith and doubt, or even their disillusionment and anger over troubling encounters with the history, doctrines, leaders, or members of the church. Still others have made their peace with a complete loss of faith in the supernatural claims of the religion but retain a genuine appreciation for its culture and community life. A few have never been part of the LDS religion but have dropped by, as it were, to listen in, ask questions, and offer alternative perspectives. The cumulative history of this gathering of thinkers has filled the Mormon cultural heritage with a variety and richness of ideas and experiences that have not been replicated elsewhere. Yet, even as *Dialogue* approaches a half century of existence, one-fourth of the entire history of Mormonism, the overwhelming majority of Mormons, even in the United States, have never heard of it, or at most have only the vaguest idea of what it is.[45]

Disappointing as this situation might be to many Mormon intellectuals, the reasons for it are understandable. First, a great deal of religious literature, both devotional and scholarly, is produced under the auspices of the church itself, far beyond merely what is offered within the curriculum of the Sunday school and other auxiliaries, and this literature is well promoted.[46] One need only browse the extensive offerings of the church's Deseret Book Company and of the Maxwell Institute for Religious Scholarship at BYU—to say nothing of the material constantly being posted on the church's various websites—in order to understand why most Mormons would feel no need to look outside of church sources.

Second, these various media under church auspices, as well as the more official institutional magazines, manuals, and broadcasts, all meticulously avoid any references to the competing books, journals, and websites that are produced outside church control. Indeed, a *non*-Mormon author of an article about Mormons in a national magazine might occasionally be quoted over a Mormon pulpit or in the official magazine *Ensign,* but never an author of an article in *Dialogue,* no matter how favorable the reference might be to the church or its members! It is as though Mormon officialdom has a "blackout policy" where such "outside" literature is concerned, or at best a policy of "benign neglect."[47]

Yet a third reason that such literature remains little known is the trained inclination of the Mormon rank and file to be wary of articles, books, or conferences about Mormon matters that occur outside of church auspices. Scores of times in recent decades, some LDS friend or another, in my home ward or stake, having heard (or overheard) something about an article I wrote, has asked me if it was in the *Ensign,* or, if about one of my books, was it published by Deseret Book? Since my answer to such questions invariably refers my questioner to other (outside) publishing auspices, he or she is always unsure of what to say next. Of course, I cannot be sure what the person is thinking, but I am guessing that he is reticent to pursue a conversation that might raise uncomfortable questions in his mind about "unapproved" sources of Mormon history or doctrine. That guess has often been verified when my curious friend reacts to my response with the comment that he or she prefers to stay with "church literature" or else wonders why I did not publish in one of the church organs. More often, the response is just cordially noncommittal, with no further curiosity expressed. I attribute this wariness on the parts of ordinary Mormons to decades of stories about nineteenth-century persecutions and twentieth-century anti-Mormon propaganda, which have resulted in a "circle-the-wagons" mentality and a prejudicial apprehensiveness about any treatment of Mormons or Mormonism that is outside church control. This grassroots reticence has been aided and abetted by the admonitions of both local and general church leaders to be wary of "alternate voices," a term that, in its very ambiguity, would seem to carry conservative implications (that is, better safe than sorry).

Fourth, *Dialogue* and cognate publications are victims of the *ambiguous status of scholars* in institutional Mormonism, especially those LDS scholars who are independent of church employment or control, despite their legitimate claims to expertise in matters that are fundamental—and sometimes controversial—in Mormon history, doctrine, or practice. This proliferation of independent LDS scholars is a relatively recent development in the Mormon historical saga, and church leaders have not been consistent in trying to deal with it. Until the middle of the twentieth century, there were but few Mormons who might have been considered scholars or "intellectuals" by most definitions, and they tended to be recruited into the church leadership itself. One thinks here of the Pratt brothers in the earliest days and then perhaps George Q. Cannon, certainly B. H. Roberts, and later James E. Talmage, John A. Widtsoe, Joseph F. Merrill, and J. Reuben Clark, all of whom (except Roberts) were apostles. By midcentury there were a few others who served in leadership capacities (for example, Levi Edgar Young and Ephraim E. Ericksen), on the struggling BYU faculty, or in the emerging Church Education System. Of course, a few noninstitutional Mormon writers and intellectuals also gained some notoriety by midcentury, but not many, and their work was often regarded as critical of the Mormon way of life, so they tended to leave Utah or the church or both.[48]

It must be remembered that until very recent times, virtually all literature on Mormons, whether scholarly or popular in nature, was primarily polemical and either apologetic or hostile. In such a bifurcated intellectual environment, it was relatively easy for Mormons and their leaders to recognize the difference between "good intellectuals," many of whom were already in the church leadership, and "bad intellectuals," who could be dismissed as enemies. This situation changed drastically after midcentury when the most highly educated generation in Mormon history emerged, their advanced education often subsidized by veterans' benefits received for recent military service. Many of these were young men who had also served missions for the church and were quite devout, and some chose academic and professional pursuits in fields of study that cultivated a questioning and intellectual turn of mind. From their ranks came the authors mainly responsible for the large body of scholarly literature since midcentury that has filled the historical gulf in Mormon studies between apologetics and critical polemics.[49] In 1965, from the yearnings and initiatives of that same generation, emerged *Dialogue* and the Mormon History Association (and later its journal) and thereafter the plethora of independent intellectual activity that has created a new predicament for the leaders.[50] As the leaders undertook to cope with this predicament, the scholars, especially those connected with *Dialogue,* also had to cope with the leaders, and that process has run through the entire history of Dialogue.[51]

When I finally stepped down from the Dialogue Board of Directors at the end of 2008, I had devoted half a lifetime to supporting the journal and its objectives and half of that period to active service on behalf of its interests and its survival. Those several decades have brought me many treasured friendships in the amorphous "community" of Mormon intellectuals, and not only with fellow *Dialogue* authors or board members. *Dialogue* has often provided the crossroads where scholars and other intellectuals have met and shared common thoughts and experiences. Indeed, as I look back on all my associations among the LDS people across the years, few of them at the grassroots in my wards and stakes have become as close or fulfilling as those I have enjoyed among my *Dialogue* friends and others of like mind. These would include, of course, many friends I have known through my activities in both *Sunstone* and the Mormon History Association, for there has been much (but certainly not complete) overlap among my friendships in all such organizations. By contrast, my ward and stake friendships have been less enduring because they have depended on my residential locations, where friendships have tended to come and go as members (including myself and family) have come and gone. I attribute the special value of my enduring relationships with *Dialogue, Sunstone,* and MHA friends to our intellectual intimacy and to the sense of common predicament that we have all shared through the years in roaming the borderlands between the institutional church and the world of independent scholarship. Our interests and concerns have seemed somewhat mysterious, eccentric, and perhaps even dangerous to most of the ordinary Saints with whom I have served in church callings. Yet my work in the cause of Dialogue and these other organizations has felt a lot like a church calling.[52]

As I write this (mid-2012), I remain optimistic about the future of Dialogue (both the foundation and the journal), but I shall always be concerned about at least three issues that have consistently been problematic in Dialogue's history. First is a rather intangible aspect of Dialogue's traditional ethos, namely, the devotion to unpaid, *voluntary* service—that sense of a *calling* comparable to that which we feel in our church activity. Sociologists have learned that religious devotion and commitment are *enhanced* by sacrifice, not diminished by it. Religions that make demands on their members are the ones that are thriving the most. Of course, cost-benefit considerations are always present, and demands for sacrifice can reach a point of diminishing returns. To be sure, those who have served Dialogue have always made sacrifices, particularly those who have been its editors. For the first decade or so of Dialogue's history, editors received little or no compensation, and sacrifices were especially hard on the earliest editors. In more recent years, as one particular donor has been providing generous annual subsidies for the publication of *Dialogue,* editors have been able to enjoy greater compensation, and at present the annual stipend of an editor is comparable to a half-time salary for an associate professor in the humanities or social sciences. The sacrifices involved in taking the editorship have thus been correspondingly reduced in recent decades, but it is not obvious to me that the devotion to the job, or the quality of the product, is the better for it. Furthermore, various tasks involved in the production of the journal, including copyediting and proofreading, which were once handled by the editor him- or herself or by volunteers, are now also covered by hourly stipends. As compensation continues to creep upward for the editor, the associate editor, and others in the process, I cannot help wondering if *income* will replace *devotion* to the Dialogue "cause" as the main motivation for service—and thus as a major motivation in future applicants for editor. I worry about that.

Second, and not unrelated to the first, is my worry about the financial future of Dialogue, given its heavy dependence, from year to year, on the generosity of one particular donor. For at least the past ten years, the Dialogue Board of Directors has discussed and acknowledged the necessity for a capital development program to build a permanent endowment. Periodically, the board has invited knowledgeable experts to attend board meetings and offer guidance and suggestions for a development plan. Individual board members have been appointed and agreed to take charge of such a plan. Yet no such plan has ever materialized, whether in good economic times or bad. Occasionally, a capital development committee has been charged to work on the problem outside of meetings and report back at the next meeting, but nothing concrete has ever resulted from such assignments. The reasons for such a desultory approach to capital development are not entirely clear to me.

One reason might be that the board meets only two or three times a year, for about three hours in a stint, and matters of more immediate urgency have always seemed to take all the time.[53] I suspect that a second reason is the substantial financial support of the one major donor, whose contributions have more than covered the annual costs of publishing *Dialogue,* even permitting some surplus to be set aside toward an endowment. Given enough time, and the continued willingness of the donor, perhaps the requisite endowment might eventually be accumulated. Maybe that is what some board members are assuming—or at least hoping. However, at current and likely future yields of interest, an endowment of at least three million dollars would be necessary for Dialogue (the foundation and journal) to become financially independent. Without a capital development program, separate from annual donations, not many of the current board members will live to see an endowment of that size. If the one major donor should decide, for whatever reasons, that he can no longer contribute to Dialogue, publication of the journal could not be continued for many years on the existing funds in reserve. I worry about that, too.

Third is my concern for constructing and maintaining a public image or "brand" for *Dialogue* as a scholarly journal that is independent of the church, scholarly rather than polemical, and neither critic nor apologist—or, in the words of the mission statement in the front of each issue, a journal that "encourages a variety of viewpoints" based on "accurate scholarship and responsible judgment." Such was the vision of the founders, and such, I believe, has remained the aspiration of *Dialogue* throughout most of its history. Indeed, two different surveys of subscribers have indicated a certain stability in the *Dialogue* brand across time.[54] These surveys, twenty years apart, both found large majorities characterizing the journal as "objective and independent" and as contributing to their "spiritual and religious growth." The same surveys, furthermore, indicated that the "typical" (actually "modal") readers were regular churchgoers who believed the Book of Mormon to be divinely inspired. Yet fewer than half in each survey were willing to follow a church policy with which they disagree, indicating an independent turn of mind. In other words, the traditional *Dialogue* reader and the traditional *Dialogue* brand seem generally congruent. Few of the responses in these surveys were affected by age, so although the younger readers have been a decreasing proportion across time, they have not been very different in their attachment to the *Dialogue* brand. I see no reason to believe that maintaining that brand essentially unchanged would be a deterrent to recruiting a lot more readers from the younger demographic levels.

To be sure, there have been articles and issues of the journal across the years that have seemed to some readers as intellectually bland or gratuitously faith promoting, but more often, in my opinion, articles—or even entire issues—have seemed aggressively tendentious and lacked scholarly balance. I mentioned earlier an entire period (the 1990s) when the latter condition seemed to me especially noticeable. There have always been readers (whether or not subscribers) who have accused *Dialogue* of having been "baptized" (or not critical enough of the church and its leaders), while others have objected to *Dialogue* authors and editors who have seemed bent on "counseling the brethren," trying to reform the church, or revealing embarrassing history to no obvious scholarly purpose. Any editor knows how difficult it is to make editorial decisions that will fulfill *Dialogue*'s mission without eliciting complaints of these and many other kinds. Furthermore, few readers appreciate how dependent the editors of *Dialogue* are upon the nature and frequency of *author submissions*—a very different situation from the stiff competition and high rejection rates that professional academic journals can impose on their authors. When a particularly provocative or controversial submission is judged as publishable in *Dialogue,* it is often very difficult for the editor to find a competent counterpiece to provide balance. Conservative authors have been especially reluctant to offer their viewpoints in such situations—probably because of their perceptions that church leaders do not approve of *Dialogue.*

Dialogue has recently been entering a period of rapid change, and it is increasingly in the hands of a younger generation representing not only the children but even the grandchildren of the founding generation. Many of these will never have known any of the founders. How these younger people deal with the three "concerns" I have described above will make a crucial difference in the future of the journal. They will be dealing also with technological changes that are increasingly rapid and drastic, particularly in electronic publishing and other forms of communication. Subscriptions to print versions of *Dialogue* have remained at an all-time low for at least a decade, and it is doubtful whether or how these can be regained to any substantial degree. At the same time, electronic versions, not only of entire issues but also of selected articles of special value, can be produced and marketed for revenue that could eventually exceed anything achieved with the traditional print versions. These and other changes will present the journal and its editors with both opportunities and challenges as the *Dialogue* "brand" competes with the many other products in the rapidly emerging Mormon studies market. Indeed, the LDS Church itself will increasingly be a competitor in that market, rather than a restraint, as in the past, for the church has apparently started to turn away from its earlier posture of trying to control or restrict scholars and commentators who offer their contributions to that market—which now seems open to all comers.[55]

In some ways, therefore, the possibilities for *Dialogue* have never been greater. Yet those in the younger generation(s) now taking the responsibility for the future of this fifty-year-old institution will first need to be secure in their own relationship to the Mormon heritage that has produced Dialogue. No earlier generations have faced such a plethora and variety of theological, political, social, and other human quandaries and controversies as are now emerging from the study of Mormon history, culture, and governance. Many Mormons, especially the younger ones, have not found the intellectual and emotional resiliency to integrate and assimilate some of the startling and controversial discoveries of human failings in the Mormon religious heritage, clinging instead to the dichotomized mentality they were taught in their youth—namely, that claims made in the name of religion must all be either "true" or "false," in a concrete sense. Finding that much in their church and religion, as elsewhere in life, does not readily yield to so simple an analysis has for many been accompanied by anger, disillusionment, and defection. Understandable as such an outlook might be, it will be poisonous for the future of Dialogue if it is brought into either the editorial or the governing board of that enterprise. Only those, devout or otherwise, who have achieved an attitude of equanimity and stability toward their religious heritage can strengthen Dialogue, nourish its readers, and ensure its future.[56]

Even the most solid and talented future leaders of Dialogue, however, will still have to find ways to attract more readers from the younger age groups—especially from those below age forty, where attrition in the *Dialogue* readership has been the greatest. This need not require a change in brand or editorial philosophy, since, as indicated in the surveys, reader preferences in such matters have not differed by age. My own assessment of the task facing current and future editors is that they must find a way to persuade their younger peers to spend less time in the blogosphere and more time in reading and writing in-depth, peer-reviewed literature on the Mormon scene. Blogging has its place, and it is a quick and easy way to get one's opinions and observations broadcast to a certain constituency.

One drawback, though, is the tendency I have noticed for many who frequent the blogosphere to ask questions, or express opinions, in seeming ignorance of the rich literature found in journals and books that would bear importantly upon the very topics they wish to discuss. I realize that there is an immediate gratification in seeing one's ideas disseminated to a large audience simply by hitting the "send" key, but in a couple of days one's treasured thoughts disappear into the archives (or into cyberspace), where their future visibility will be limited. Far better, it seems to me, to collect one's ideas (even if from one's own blogs), document them, refine them, and submit them for publication in journals that are peer reviewed, indexed, and readily available for scholarly research. I hope that many more bloggers can be converted in that way into *Dialogue* authors, for this and many other journals in Mormon studies will be heavily dependent on their talent in the future.

Chapter 8 | Bridging the Chasm between Academics and Apologetics
The Claremont Experiment

Prelude: The Chicago Experiment

Starting about a century ago, the LDS Church gradually divested itself of the responsibility for public education in the towns that Mormons had settled around the Mountain West and turned over most of its schools and academies to state or local governments. Since religious education had always been an integral part of public education in the church schools, the Mormon leaders felt the need to supplement the secular education at the new state schools and colleges with a series of courses in scripture and doctrine that students could take during the school day on a "released-time" basis. At the secondary level, this religious education was called "seminary" and was typically provided at or near the public school buildings. The first seminary classes started in 1912 in the southern part of Salt Lake City and rapidly spread throughout Utah, as well as into parts of Idaho, Arizona, and Wyoming. In the late 1920s, the church decided to extend its supplemental religious education to the college level through an "institute" program, opening the first institute classes at the University of Idaho in 1929.

This was a period in which the church was committed to a process called "Americanization," or assimilation to national institutions, in contrast to its own unique and controversial political, economic, and family institutions of the nineteenth century. The order of the day was modernization and a quest for respectability as normal Americans.[1] A new generation of Mormon leaders, a few of whom had been educated outside of Utah, were quite aware of the new developments in science and religion that had occurred in recent decades and the potential that some of these new developments had to challenge the religious faith of the Latter-day Saints—indeed, of traditional Christianity more generally. Accordingly, the original vision of the church leaders for a new LDS program in religious education, as exemplified by its first commissioner of education, Joseph F. Merrill, was one that would help Mormon students, even at the high school level, to reconcile the new knowledge from the outside world, whether secular or religious, with the traditional faith claims of Mormonism. Yet except for one or two adventurous teachers who had gone outside of Utah for their advanced education in religion, hardly any of the LDS faculty appointed to service in seminaries or institutes had sufficient education of their own to prepare them for shepherding their students through this process of reconciliation.

Led by education commissioner Merrill, church educators decided that if LDS students were to receive respectable academic instruction in religion, their teachers would first have to obtain formal training in religion, which would mean looking outside of the church itself, for Mormons had never had a tradition of formal theology or academically trained theologians. As a first step in this process, Professor Edgar J. Goodspeed, of the University of Chicago Divinity School, was invited to BYU for a few summers to offer classes for seminary teachers. Considerably impressed by these classes, Merrill began to encourage some of the more promising young Mormon teachers to seek advanced degrees at the Chicago Divinity School. This policy was continued by some of Merrill's successors, and eventually about a dozen young scholars went to this divinity school (or elsewhere in a couple of cases), some at church expense. When they returned to Utah, they were expected to take the leadership in curriculum development and teaching throughout the new Church Education System.

Some of these cases worked out well, both for the CES and for the newly educated teachers, but others found their own faith compromised somewhat by the secular influences of this graduate education outside the Mormon orbit. Eventually, some important church leaders became alarmed at the prospect that they had inadvertently admitted a Trojan horse into the CES program, and when J. Reuben Clark arrived as a new member of the First Presidency in 1933, he put a stop to this "Chicago Experiment," as it came to be called, and in a new policy document during 1938, he called for replacing the earlier CES pedagogy of intellectual reconciliation with one of strict indoctrination for LDS students in the teachings and history of their own religion.[2] An account of the "Chicago Experiment" has not often been told in Mormon circles since then, but a personal reminiscence of the experience "from the inside," as it were, was offered in 1972 by one of the retired scholars who had participated in it, and more recently a contemporary LDS scholar in the CES published a general historical assessment of the experiment.[3]

The Claremont Experiment
and the LDS Scholarly Renaissance

The "Chicago Experiment" probably would not have survived long in any case, given the economic and other problems in the LDS Church during that period, but it ultimately foundered primarily on the shoals of a deep-seated wariness in the Mormon tradition about the potentially corrosive effects of certain kinds of "worldly" learning, particularly the "worldly" approach to religion found in the divinity schools of the world's major denominations. In many respects, the same epistemological discomfort between Mormonism and modern religious scholarship experienced in the Chicago Experiment now lives on in what I shall call here the "Claremont Experiment." Meanwhile, however, a recent evolution has occurred in the LDS relationship with the academic world. With the administration of LDS president Howard W. Hunter (1994), and especially since that of Gordon B. Hinckley (1994–2005), a new friendliness toward unsponsored commentary on Mormon matters has occurred in the public relations posture of the church. Traditionally, the LDS Public Affairs Department seems to have been charged mainly with resisting transparency and defending the church against criticism, whether from the outside or from the inside.[4]

However, especially since the appointment of Michael Otterson to head the Department of Public Affairs, the church seems to favor far more transparency and proactive outreach in its relationships with the outside, and it has fostered the uses of the Internet on a very large scale, both in official and in unofficial ways. This new posture carries certain risks, of course, but the church in recent years is apparently expecting more benefits than costs from such an overt engagement with the world's mass media.[5] This engagement, furthermore, extends increasingly into academia, as well as into journalism and other opinion-making institutions. It can be seen also in a seemingly sudden proliferation of lectures, college courses, conferences, and even blogsites, under various auspices, in which LDS scholars from various universities have been involved. At some of these conferences, even high-ranking LDS leaders have appeared—not simply as authority figures, but rather as equal participants.[6]

Academia has reciprocated: a few universities have begun to consider raising the funds to endow special professorial chairs in Mormon studies. Two universities, both of them secular institutions, have actually done so. In 2007 Utah State University created the Leonard J. Arrington Chair of Mormon History and Culture, the first occupant of which is Philip L. Barlow, with a Mormon studies program primarily at the undergraduate level. In the following year, Richard L. Bushman accepted a three-year appointment to the recently created Howard W. Hunter Chair in Mormon Studies at the Claremont Graduate University. So far no other colleges or universities have yet established chairs, but several have created partial Mormon studies programs with limited course work and periodic public lectures. The first of these was Utah Valley University (formerly Utah Valley College), a relatively new campus of the Utah public university system, which has embedded a Mormon studies program of courses and public lectures within its Religious Studies Department.[7] In 2006 the University of Wyoming launched a lecture series, "Latter-day Saints and Their World," as part of its religious studies program and contemplated an endowment to establish an eventual chair in Mormon studies. Inquiries about the CGU program have been received by me and others from Arizona State University and (somewhat surprisingly) from the University of Virginia. Having been consulted for advice and information at various stages in the development of some of these programs, I have remained very interested in their progress.[8]

CLAREMONT GRADUATE UNIVERSITY ENCOUNTERS MORMON STUDIES

However, my chief involvement with the emerging Mormon studies focus in academia started at the Claremont Graduate University, while the Howard W. Hunter Chair was in the process of being established in the School of Religion there.[9] That such could occur in an elite, private, secular university is in itself a unique, not to say idiosyncratic, development.[10] In 2000 a small but energetic School of Religion was created out of a Department of Religion that had been part of the School of Arts and Humanities at the university.[11] Dr. Karen Torjesen, who had recently arrived to chair this department, became the first dean of the new School. Drawing on the remarkable religious diversity of Southern California, she devised an innovative strategy expected to bring early prominence and resources to this new school: influential leaders in the various local religious communities were invited to form special councils that would provide a conduit for advice and communication between the school and each religious community and would raise funds for endowments that might support an academic chair for each such community. Advisory councils were eventually created for Catholic studies, Protestant studies, Mormon studies, Jewish studies, Coptic studies, Islamic studies, Indic studies, and even Zoroastrian studies.[12]

The inclusion of a council and program for Mormon studies did not originally occur to Dean Torjesen but was the product of some initiative on the part of her LDS graduate assistant, Amy Hoyt, who (perhaps somewhat naively) asked why no such council had been envisioned for Mormon studies. The rest is history. Torjesen, who had come from the Lutheran Midwest, knew little or nothing about the Mormons but was intrigued to learn more about any religious community that was so prominent in California. Her interest was vastly enhanced as a result of a trip to Utah with Amy late in 2002, where she received red-carpet treatment at BYU and at LDS headquarters. Amy persuaded her father, Blair Hoyt, a prominent California leader in the LDS Church, to head the first LDS Council on Mormon Studies, starting in 2002. The Hoyts, along with another advanced student in the School of Religion, set about recruiting prominent local Mormons to the LDS Council, including Keith Atkinson, who was then the main public affairs professional for the LDS Church in California. He, in turn, helped recruit others. And so it went.[13]

Dean Torjesen had been persuaded that Mormon studies was entitled to a place among the councils that she was creating in the School of Religion, mainly because of the large LDS membership in California, and she was favorably impressed by the prominent LDS Church leaders and academics whom she had met both in Utah and in California. Yet much work and much negotiation between the LDS Council and the School of Religion were necessary before the disparate interests of the two parties could be reconciled to permit the establishment of a chair in Mormon studies. For its part, the LDS Council sought recognition that the study of the Mormon heritage and experience would be considered academically legitimate on the same basis as would the study of the ancient religions of the world (for example, Christianity, Judaism, Islam, and so on) and that any person appointed to a chair in Mormon studies would be a scholar with a proven record of respectful and balanced treatment of Mormon-related topics in his or her teaching, research, and publications (but not necessarily a member of the LDS Church).

The CGU School of Religion, for its part, sought to add to its faculty a distinguished scholar who could teach some of the courses in its regular curriculum, as well as a limited number of courses focused on the Mormon religion itself—and all this without requiring any additional financial or other resources from CGU or the School of Religion. For such to occur, all the resources would have to be provided by the Howard W. Hunter Foundation through endowing a chair in Mormon studies. The endowment was expected to cover the salary and all expenses of the professor occupying the chair, including the costs of research, travel, and any conferences, lectures, or other special events under the auspices of the chair. Funding for student scholarships was to be an especially important objective of the endowment. Furthermore, the faculty of the school would need to be satisfied that whoever was selected for the chair would not be simply a devout Mormon apologist but would have an established record as a teacher in legitimate academic institutions and as a scholar whose work was appearing regularly in recognized, peer-reviewed academic publications. There was some skepticism from the beginning about whether any candidates with such qualifications would be available and, if so, how many.[14] Whatever else the religion faculty might have

known about Mormons, it certainly knew far more about their proselytizing proclivities than about their academic achievements. To assure itself in such matters,
the School of Religion would insist on conducting both the search and the ultimate selection of the occupant for the chair.

Even if the LDS Council and the School of Religion could reconcile their
respective interests in this matter, a very large question remained about the level
of support, whether financial or moral, that could be expected from either the
LDS Church or its membership. After all, the church had its own religious education system and its own university, both of which had widespread loyal support
from the general membership. Why should the Mormon membership or leadership welcome an alternative "Mormon studies" program that would be controlled
by non-Mormons? Here, of course, we come to the tremendous gulf between
believing Mormons and academic scholars in the way that "religious studies" is
understood. For Mormons, as for many other religious traditions with exclusiv-
ist claims, the purpose of studying religion is to find *truth,* and especially the *one*
religion that is true and authentic above all others. Conversely, the object of an
academic or scholarly study of religion is not truth, but *understanding,* in which
the truth claims of any religion are simply acknowledged and taken into account,
along with ritual, scripture, and all other aspects of a given religious culture or tradition. The purpose is not to support or refute such claims, or any other aspects
of a religion, but rather to *understand* them, insofar as possible, both internally
(that is, as they are understood by adherents) and externally (that is, within the
appropriate historical and comparative contexts).

Given this difference in the meaning of "religious studies," the Mormon rank
and file tends to regard the *academic* study of their religion as irrelevant at best
and at worst as fundamentally secular in nature—and therefore potentially subversive of faith. On the other hand, academic scholars tend to regard devout believers (even if they are academics) as essentially apologists at best and as narrow-
minded or bigoted at worse. I realize that these characterizations are somewhat
stereotypic and that I have polarized ways of thinking that are more nuanced and
complex in actual people. However, I think I have fairly characterized at least the
two basic *tendencies,* even if the lines between them are sometimes a bit blurred.
Clearly, the LDS Council at Claremont would need to find Mormon leaders willing to cross the gulf between these two perspectives long enough to lend at least
legitimacy, if not moral or financial support, to the Mormon studies project at
Claremont.

Perhaps even more important, the council could not expect any funding from
the church per se, but would have to identify wealthy individual Mormon donors

willing to help endow the proposed chair and program. Garnering the *moral* support proved easier than one might have thought.[15] In early 2004, through some of its more influential members, the council sought and received a formal letter from the LDS First Presidency declaring that it would have "no objection" to the use of the name of Howard W. Hunter (a former church president) in connection with the proposed chair and program. Not only did the Hunter family concur in the use of the name, but the two Hunter sons (John and Richard) agreed to serve on the first board of directors for the Hunter Foundation.[16] In addition, a couple of apostles, in their private capacities, agreed to help the council chairman gain access to potential donors. One apostle in particular, Elder Jeffrey R. Holland, who had been especially close to President Howard Hunter, appeared with a strong endorsement of the project on a DVD used in soliciting funds for the Hunter Chair.[17]

By 2004 more than a dozen members had joined the council from various walks of life, including several prominent Mormon attorneys, four of whom have since succeeded Blair Hoyt as chairman seriatim. Until 2010 one member of the council was always an Area Authority Seventy in the Church (a regional representative of the general hierarchy). One of these was John Dalton IV, from a prominent local LDS family, who was a major figure on the council from 2003 until he left for another church assignment in 2010. Short-term members included two different BYU religion professors, the local LDS institute director, and Professor Ann Taves, of the School of Religion, who helped gain moral and material support from CGU until she left to take a chair of her own at UC–Santa Barbara. There was a certain amount of turnover in the LDS Council generally throughout those years, of course, but the membership became quite stable by 2010. My own invitation to join the council occurred in 2004 as a result of contact with council member Joseph I. Bentley at a meeting of the Mormon History Association that year. Presumably because of my own academic background, I then became deeply involved as liaison for the council in its relationships with both the School of Religion and the highly active student association.[18] I was also charged from time to time with keeping track of the operating budget that the council provides for the Mormon studies program at CGU.

During four school years, starting in 2005, I taught (as adjunct faculty) the only course in Mormon studies offered by the School of Religion.[19] Beyond my role on the LDS Council (which serves primarily an advisory and fund-raising function), my academic participation in the Claremont Mormon studies program will be apparent from various CGU and Claremont Mormon Studies Student Association (CMSSA) publications.[20] Given both my academic and my council roles, Dean Torjesen appointed me during 2006–7 to the search committee responsible for selecting the first occupant of the Howard W. Hunter Chair in Mormon Studies.[21] This turned out to be Richard Lyman Bushman, who served in that role energetically during a three-year inaugural period (2008–11). His wife, Claudia, served with him, teaching several courses in an adjunct faculty role. But how did the Bushmans find themselves at Claremont? Thereby hangs a tale that is still unfolding in 2012.

FUNDING AND FILLING THE HOWARD W. HUNTER CHAIR

Having received the tacit approval of the LDS Church and the Hunter family for the use of the family name, the LDS Council moved to establish a formal relationship with CGU and its School of Religion. In February 2006, a group of five principals organized themselves as the board of directors for the Howard W. Hunter Foundation, filed articles of incorporation as a nonprofit religious corporation with the State of California, and applied to the federal government for 501(c)(3) status as a tax-exempt organization.[22] A month later, the foundation concluded an agreement with Robert Klitgaard, president of CGU, for the Hunter Endowment to be established and administered at CGU.[23] The formal signing of this agreement launched the fund-raising effort, but a ceremonial signing and a public launching of the program also occurred, along with a banquet at the president's home, in April 2006.[24] It was attended by CGU officers, the LDS Council, the board of the foundation, representatives of LDS Public Affairs, the LDS *Church News,* and other media representatives.[25] By that time, the LDS Council and Hunter Foundation had made a good start on funding the Hunter endowment, but progress was already proving disappointingly slow. Furthermore, unbeknownst to any of us, even our partial endowment was about to be seriously undermined by a national recession.[26]

I was somewhat surprised that the implicit endorsements from the Hunter family, and from certain LDS Church leaders, did not seem to help much in the crucial matter of fund-raising for the Hunter endowment.[27] Joseph I. Bentley of Newport Beach, one of the officers of the foundation, also chaired the council with remarkable effectiveness from 2005 to mid-2010, during which time the sum of three million dollars was raised, more than enough to establish the Hunter Chair permanently. Yet the LDS Council had declared from the beginning its intention to raise at least five million, half of which would go to salary and benefits for the holder of the chair and the other half for student scholarships, outreach activities, and such programs as conferences and lectures. Although more than a hundred donors contributed to the Hunter endowment, most of the first three million dollars, perhaps three-quarters, came from only two donors, both in Southern California. Potential donors elsewhere—even in Northern California—seemed to regard the Hunter Chair as a particularly Southern California project, perhaps understandably so.[28] Wealthy and high-profile Utah Mormons seemed especially impervious to Bentley's efforts. Their commitment and sense of "ownership" for such capital campaigns seemed pretty much limited to Utah institutions, mainly BYU. Even Bentley's special forays with Bushman to campaign for funds among wealthy East Coast Mormons brought very little response. There could be more than one explanation for the limited interest in the Claremont project among Mormons in these other places, but anecdotal feedback suggests two in particular: first, a certain amount of geographic parochialism, in which worthy local causes took precedence over a Southern California project, however worthy—especially given "all the wealthy Mormons" supposedly living there!—and second, an implicit skepticism among donors, of the kind found generally in the Mormon rank and file, about the usefulness of a Mormon studies program outside of BYU or other LDS Church auspices.

Beyond the financial requirements for a new chair, a favorable public environment would also have to be cultivated, both in the CGU academic community and in the LDS community. Efforts in this latter respect took the form of a series of visiting lecturers and conferences involving participants of recognized eminence in both communities for what might be called a "warming up" campaign (or maybe "softening up"!). It began with a special public lecture on Joseph Smith by Richard Bushman in 2002, followed in 2003 by respected non-Mormon Jan Shipps's lecture with the engaging title "How Mormons Are Christians." These special lectures were followed by a three-day conference in 2004 titled "Positioning Mormonism" and then in 2005 by a two-day conference called "Joseph Smith and the Prophetic Tradition," featuring again Bushman, Shipps, and this time Robert Rees, Robert Millet of BYU, and several non-Mormon academics. This last event, held in October, benefited in being preceded the previous spring by the well-publicized scholarly conference on Joseph Smith under the auspices of the Library of Congress.[29] All these Claremont events were funded by members of the LDS Council on Mormon Studies, with some subsidies from the School of Religion. Many other lectures and conferences have been held since 2005, of course, on the initiative of the Mormon studies program at CGU, but those first few were intended to demonstrate, both to Mormon and to non-Mormon interest groups, the value of an academic program in Mormon studies at CGU.

In any case, with ostensibly enough of an endowment on hand in order to fund the Hunter Chair, along with a formal agreement between the foundation and CGU, Dean Torjesen and the School of Religion were given permission to start the search for a scholar to occupy the chair. The dean herself selected and chaired the first search committee, which began meeting late in the fall of 2006. Besides the dean and assistant dean, the committee included four or five faculty members from the CGU School of Religion, some of whom had joint appointments at the Claremont School of Theology (CST).[30] I was also included on the search committee as a representative of the LDS Council (required by the formal agreement between the foundation and CGU) and because of my quasi-faculty role as adjunct. Well aware that they were inaugurating a new and unprecedented relationship with a religious heritage of dubious academic standing, the committee spent the first meeting or two dealing with certain competing interests, both academic and organizational, but soon agreed on procedures for launching the search and for evaluating the candidates who would be applying for the chair. Except for me, no one on the committee had any idea of what literature or other academic resources might provide the intellectual basis for courses, theses, or dissertations in Mormon studies. I tried to help by distributing to the committee a bibliography of major academic books and journals on the Mormon experience, which apparently proved somewhat reassuring.

One of the very first issues, of course, was preparing a formal, public announcement of the search, in which criteria for acceptable applicants would be spelled out. The announcement, distributed widely in academia and through other public media in the late fall of 2006, emphasized four main criteria: senior academic rank (associate or full professor), competence and conversance in American religious history and in other fields of special focus in the curriculum of the School of Religion, a record of publication commensurate with rank, and a commitment to excellence in teaching and in collegial governance. Somewhat surprisingly, beyond a passing designation of the position as a professorship in Mormon studies, special competence in that field per se was not specified among the criteria, probably for fear of restricting an already small pool of potential candidates. Besides the dissemination of this general announcement, the LDS Council, the Hunter Foundation, and the religion faculty itself were all invited to submit names of potential candidates, who were then solicited by special letters from the dean to apply for the position. By the time the search committee began assessing the accumulated applications in the early spring of 2007, perhaps a score had been submitted, of which about a dozen came from scholars with credible credentials in religious studies or related fields, but very few with substantial interests or publications dealing *specifically with Mormons*—an outcome probably attributable to a failure of the original announcement to specify such a competence. These dozen were carefully studied by the search committee, and three of the cases were selected for the "short list" to be scheduled for campus visits and interviews during April 2007.

So few of the applications had evidence of substantial career interests in Mormon studies that the selection of these three finalists did not prove especially problematic. Beyond these finalists, only three or four additional applicants had any publications to speak of on Mormons, though their scholarship generally was not in question. A few of the applicants had devoted their careers to teaching and research at BYU, other service in the LDS Church, or both, with most of their work appearing in church-published books, journals, or magazines. In the minds of most committee members, this suggested a career history oriented largely to apologetics rather than to academic independence. Once the three finalists were selected, then, they were invited to campus for interviews and scholarly presentations from their work. All three made very impressive presentations and came across as good teachers. After a final search committee meeting in May, the finalists were reduced to two, one of whom was slightly preferred over the other and received the first offer. That offer proved unacceptable to that first finalist, given the favorable academic position that the person already held at another institution and given the inadequacy of the resources available to the new Hunter Chair from the endowment that had been raised so far. On objective grounds, one would have to concede that the offer would not have been terribly appealing to a senior scholar, who would have been expected to take the new chair partly out of altruistic motives—that is, to sacrifice a relatively secure professional position in order to help build a new program at Claremont on limited resources. That left the only other finalist, who had also been highly acceptable to the faculty, namely, Richard L. Bushman. He arrived amid high hopes to take the Hunter professorship in the fall of 2008, and he did not disappoint.[31]

As a professor recently retired from a distinguished academic chair at Columbia University, Bushman was in a position to "afford" the relatively modest salary available from the endowment, and he brought with him his wife, Claudia, also retired from a distinguished academic career, who agreed to do some additional teaching on an adjunct basis. The major motivation for them to accept the appointment was primarily, if not wholly, altruistic—namely, to provide a strong inauguration for Mormon studies at Claremont, lending their considerable prestige to the new program, and especially to the continuing efforts in building the endowment that would eventually fund it fully. They did not need the extra salary; they simply believed earnestly in the importance of the new chair and program, especially at an elite university system such as Claremont's. Yet given that they were already formally in retirement, no one expected them to make a long-term commitment to this project, so we were all appreciative of their agreement to a three-year term for Richard's appointment. In addition, Richard agreed to do some traveling and lecturing to help with the ongoing effort to finish funding the Hunter endowment. The LDS Council, for its part, agreed to continue its campaign not only to fund the basic threshold of the endowment itself, but also to raise additional amounts to cover operating expenses beyond the basic salary in the each of these three inaugural years. These expenses would go primarily to cover partial stipends for students coming to the School of Religion for graduate degrees in religion (with specializations in Mormon studies), but also to cover periodic conferences and lectures under the auspices of the Hunter Chair and one or two adjunct positions each year. Such annual "operating expenses" amounted to more than a hundred thousand dollars each year, above and beyond the capital increments being raised to complete the projected Hunter endowment itself of five million dollars.

Although the Bushmans had been selected early enough that they might have joined the faculty in the fall of 2007, their appointment was postponed until the fall of 2008 in order for them to accept a year's appointment as research fellows at the Huntington Library in nearby Pasadena. That delay turned out to be helpful, since it gave us another year to enhance the Hunter Foundation funds, and it gave the Bushmans time to do some preparation of courses and academic events that would take place under the auspices of the Hunter Chair during their pending three-year term. Even before that term began in the fall of 2008, Richard, with the assistance of the LDS Council and the emerging student association, organized a conference and a couple of lectures with visiting scholars during the spring semester of 2008. These special events, both before and after the formal beginning of Bushman's term, proved to be very rich fare indeed. In particular, the several special conferences and lectures held under Hunter Chair auspices during the 2008–10 academic years provided wide and recurrent visibility for the Mormon studies program throughout the Claremont community and much of Southern California. Especially noteworthy were the participation and leadership provided in all of this by the new Claremont Mormon Studies Student Association.[32] The students (almost all LDS) who organized themselves in this new association were the envy of many other students and faculty in the School of Religion for their initiative and leadership, not only in events sponsored by the Hunter Chair, but also in events sponsored by the school itself. In fact, the students who chaired the committee in charge of the school's own annual "Religions in Conversation" conferences for three consecutive years were CMSSA members.[33]

After Richard's term as the Hunter professor formally began in the fall of 2008, he became responsible for all the teaching under his auspices, although his own teaching was supplemented somewhat by contributions from adjunct faculty, especially Claudia Bushman. By the terms of his appointment in the School of Religion, he was obligated to teach at least one course each semester for the school's general religion curriculum, plus a second course each semester on Mormon topics. This sequence of unique and special courses provided rich intellectual fare indeed for the students who took them. Richard's courses for the general curriculum were Religion in America from First Contact to the Civil War, American Religion in the Age of Restoration, American Scripture from Thomas Jefferson to Ron Hubbard, and Religion and Politics in America. His courses under the Mormon studies rubric consisted of The Mormon Theological Tradition, The Life and Thought of Joseph Smith, Mormon Scriptures, and The Mormon Experience.[34] Some of these courses, both general and Mormon-related, were taught more than once during his three-year term. The curriculum was further enriched by several courses that Claudia Bushman also taught as adjunct faculty during these years, focused especially on Mormon women's experiences—much to the delight especially of her female students: Mormon History from the Perspective of Women, Religion in American Women's Diaries, Mormon Women's History, Contemporary Mormonism, Mormon Women in the 19th Century, and Mormon Women in the 20th Century. In addition, Claudia launched a project through which her students collected more than a hundred oral histories from living subjects recounting their experiences as Mormon women in California history.[35]

TURBULENT TIMES ARRIVE AT CLAREMONT

After the preparatory year, with the Bushmans nearby at the Huntington Library (2007–8), and then the three years of Richard's formal appointment (2008–11), I think the inauguration of the Hunter Chair and Mormon studies at CGU would have to be regarded as a great success by almost any measure. We still worried about some lag in major contributions to the Hunter endowment, but a variety of local donors had stepped up to provide at least the annual operating expenses (that is, beyond what was needed for the Hunter Chair salary itself). Even as Richard's three-year term formally began in 2008, however, the downward spiral of a national recession had already begun. Since all university endowments are heavily dependent on investments in various financial sectors, CGU's portfolios suffered along with those of other academic institutions. The Hunter endowment funds invested with CGU lost about a third of their market value, so that the book value of almost three million dollars was reduced to a market value of less than two million. Furthermore, the crisis created for CGU in general was so serious that it could not continue to guarantee the traditional 5 percent yield from endowment funds that had been invested by its various affiliates, including the Hunter Foundation. The combination of lost market value and a reduction in yield to 4 percent meant that the endowment itself could no longer cover even the basic salary of the Hunter professor (which, by contract, then had to be supplemented by CGU general funds). For this reason and several others, the budget of the School of Religion itself was seriously undermined, requiring a curtailment in resources available for all faculty and staff.

These financial exigencies combined with some crucial turnovers in leadership to create an environment of uncertainty for the university in general and the Mormon studies program in particular. To begin with, the president of CGU, Robert Klitgaard, who had been so helpful in concluding and embracing the new contract and relationship with the Hunter Foundation, came to a sudden parting of the ways with the university's board of trustees over differences in strategic plans for the future (precipitated, in large part, by the national financial downturn). He left in February 2009, just as a new treasurer (chief financial officer) of the university was arriving. Klitgaard was replaced by Joseph Hough, recently retired as president of the Union Theological Seminary in New York, who was pulled back into service as interim president at CGU (having once been on the faculty there).[36] Hough and a new treasurer then had to struggle with the deteriorating financial condition at CGU and try to correct it before the trustees found a permanent successor to Klitgaard. She turned out to be Deborah Freund, who arrived in late 2010 from the administration of the Maxwell Graduate School of Social Sciences at Syracuse University with a solid background in fund-raising and capital development—and thus with the high hopes of the entire CGU community.[37]

Meanwhile, at the School of Religion itself, Karen Torjesen, the dean who had founded the advisory councils for the various religious traditions (including the LDS Council on Mormon Studies), stepped down after ten years, reverted to regular faculty status, and departed on a well-deserved sabbatical leave. Her successor, Dean Anselm Min, was immediately saddled with the responsibility of dealing with the financial crisis and salvaging the operating budget of the School. Among other measures, Min had the unpleasant task of terminating some of his already small staff (including some untenured faculty), thereby increasing his own workload. Sincere and capable as he was, he could not be expected to have the same personal enthusiasm that Torjesen had had for the council system, which was primarily her own creation. Min's deanship, in turn, lasted only two years. Then, on the LDS side, Joseph Bentley, who had so successfully led the LDS Council and the Mormon studies program for five years, accepted a long-anticipated mission call from the church to the BYU Jerusalem Center. However, he was fortunate to recruit as his successor Randall Huff, a distinguished California church leader, who had been one of the founding members of the council before he had left on a mission of his own. It was thus against this cascade of unexpected changes that the final year of Bushman's term arrived (2010–11). Soon the search process had to be launched once again for his successor, who would have to be in place with the arrival of the next academic year (2011–12).

Given the extensive recent and projected turnovers in key players at the various organizational levels, and the uncertainties in both operational funds and capital development, the final year of the Bushman term (2010–11) began in an environment of considerable austerity, both financially and operationally. For a while the School of Religion even seemed in some jeopardy of being reduced again to departmental status and merged back into the School of Humanities from which it had come only a decade earlier. At the very least, the School of Religion, with a considerably reduced budget, could no longer provide some of the perquisites that had been supporting the activities of the Hunter Chair, nor, with reduced staff, could it any longer provide the logistical support that had made possible the large number of special conferences and lecturers brought to campus by the Hunter Foundation and LDS Council.[38] As a result, there were no special events sponsored by the chair or the council during the fall semester of 2010 and only two conferences in the spring of 2011.[39] Such a curtailment of these highly visible "Mormon-sponsored" events, presented through the School of Religion, probably also served a growing *political* necessity, since a certain amount of murmuring had been detected about a subtle (if unintended) Mormon "hijacking" of the school's image, given the frequency of these events as a proportion of the school's general calendar.

Of course, all of this created a certain amount of stress for the parties involved. I had become the LDS Council's chief budget manager, especially during the summers, since the academics, and even some of the LDS Council members, took their vacations at such times. In that capacity, I was the one left to represent the council in negotiating the annual budget reconciliations with the School of Religion. Summers could be somewhat busy with a certain amount of year-end fiscal reviewing and haggling. As each academic year ended, funds received from the council had to be brought into balance with expenditures made by the school on behalf of the council's programs. Then, with the new school year about to begin, the school and the council would have to come to an agreement about expenditures projected for the coming year and which party would be responsible for which expenditures. During the summers of 2009 and 2010, there were flurries of e-mail messages between me and the School of Religion over such issues and some face-to-face meetings as well, sometimes including a representative from the CGU treasurer.

Particularly important was one intense meeting during the summer of 2010, which produced a new, comprehensive (and, by then, very necessary) formal memorandum of agreement reconciling the various financial and operational interests of the LDS Council, the School of Religion, and the CGU treasurer in the newly austere institutional circumstances. This meeting took place in early August, just before the start of the new school year (2010–11). Besides myself, the other parties at this meeting were Dean Anselm Min; two representatives of the treasurer; the outgoing LDS Council chairman, Joseph Bentley; and his incoming successor, Randall Huff.[40] Among the agreements reached at this meeting were, first, for the remainder of the Bushmans' term, the university (CGU) was contractually obligated to cover the difference between the actual salary and benefits of the Hunter professor and the lesser amount generated by the endowment; second, except for the Hunter professor's salary, the funds for all other stipends, adjunct salaries, or other personnel disbursements requiring reports to the IRS would be deposited with the School of Religion by the end of May for the subsequent school year (and funds for student stipends as early as February); third, the council (through the school) would sponsor only two special conferences or other major events during a given academic year and would cover any and all expenses entailed by those events; fourth, the school would not be involved in the accounting or disbursement of any funds for such events (except for personnel costs requiring IRS reporting), and the council would not be responsible to the school for any of this other accounting; and finally, CGU would cover all expenses involved in the process of recruiting a scholar who would succeed Richard Bushman in the Hunter professorship starting in the 2011–12 academic year.[41]

SECURING THE FUTURE OF THE MORMON STUDIES PROGRAM

With the new mutual agreement on financial and operational "ground rules" in the relationships of the School of Religion, the CGU treasurer, and the LDS Council (for the Hunter Foundation), the academic year (2010–11) was launched with a new sense of optimism and confidence about the future of Mormon studies. In order truly to secure that future, however, two other important developments were necessary: the rest of the desired five-million-dollar endowment would have to be raised within a very few more years, and a permanent successor to Richard Bushman would have to be recruited by the spring of 2011 in order to be available for the start of the new academic year that fall. These two necessities were interconnected in certain complex ways. The existing endowment would not be sufficient to generate even the salary of a new Hunter professor, to say nothing of covering the additional operating expenses. Therefore, with the departure of Bushman, some sort of ad hoc arrangements would be necessary in order to keep the Mormon studies program going financially. In an extremity, these might have taken the form of temporary adjunct appointments (at the much lower prevailing salary rates for adjuncts). However, fortunately, the council obtained a one-time temporary infusion of funds from a special donor to cover salaries and operations for a few years and thus give the council a chance to raise a larger endowment.

In anticipation of the funding predicament, Joe Bentley had succeeded in negotiating an agreement during 2009 and early 2010 with a special out-of-state donor to provide, outside of the endowment, a hundred thousand dollars a year for five years. This pledge would cover any shortfalls in salaries or operations from the existing endowment's annual yields while that endowment was being augmented. The donor specified, however, that the actual disbursement of these funds would be contingent upon the recruitment and appointment of a new and permanent successor to Bushman. This contingency, in turn, highlighted the urgency of starting a search for the successor, so Dean Min of the School of Religion organized a faculty search committee consisting of about half of the faculty. Richard Bushman represented both the faculty and the LDS Council in this process.[42] The search committee then issued a nationwide announcement in May 2010 and began a search that was to last the rest of the year, starting with a review of all applications received by September 15. The general call for applications appeared in the usual publications of academia and was supplemented by personal invitations to apply, sent from the chairperson of the search committee to some two dozen scholars whose names were provided by Richard Bushman.

The nationwide public announcement was somewhat more specific this time about job qualifications than the 2006 announcement had been. Two new specifications in particular were added: applicants were expected to have some evidence of special competence in Mormon studies, as well as in religious studies more generally, and applicants would be expected to have access to the LDS Church archives in Salt Lake City in order to do their research.[43] For the 2006 announcement, these two criteria had been understood by the administrations of both the School of Religion and the university as a whole, but they had been left out of the public announcement itself, probably because they had not been adequately discussed with the faculty of the school during that rather truncated search period. This time, however, given the financial and operational strains that had occurred in relationships at both the university and the school levels since 2007, the entire search and recruitment process for Bushman's successor received much more scrutiny from Dean Min, his faculty, and acting president Hough as that process began in 2010. In fact, before the new search could begin, the 2006 agreement signed between CGU and the Hunter Foundation, which had established the Hunter Chair and Mormon studies program, had to be amended in a few respects. It was finally signed again in April 2010 by acting CGU president Joe Hough and by Randall Huff, the new chairman of the Hunter Foundation.

Probably the most contentious provisions (in either the original or the amended agreement) were those designed to protect the core interests of the foundation and of the university, respectively. The university, through its search committee, administration, and trustees, would naturally retain control over the recruiting and hiring process in general, as at other academic institutions. However, the Hunter Foundation and LDS Council needed protection against the prospect that the professor eventually hired with foundation funds might turn out to be a seriously biased critic of the church, even if he or she met all the other criteria.[44] To avoid such a predicament, the agreement (and the amendment) provided that any occupant of the Hunter Chair must have continuing access to the LDS Church archives, including those materials "not available to the [general] public."[45] This provision would be invoked, if necessary, only at the "short list" stage of the recruitment process, before any candidates were invited to campus for further scrutiny. In effect, this arrangement gave the Hunter Foundation a kind of "veto power" over finalist candidates without requiring an explicitly religious test, which would be illegal. The same provision could be invoked by the foundation in the unlikely event that a professor already holding the chair might later reveal an anti-Mormon agenda. In such a case, the foundation could withdraw the Hunter Chair auspices from the professor's position. The professor would still retain the tenure bestowed by the university, but in a different position, so the foundation agreed to cover the salary and benefits of said professor for the equivalent of a transitional academic year while a successor would be recruited for the Hunter Chair.

With these (and certain other) understandings now clarified and shared by the university, the school, and the foundation, the recruitment process for Bushman's successor began in earnest in May 2010 and was completed in January 2011. As an especially interested and inquisitive member of the LDS Council (though not on the search committee myself this time), I found the process surprisingly simple this time around. Despite national announcements and dozens of personal letters to potential applicants, only a half-dozen applications were ever received. A couple of those were later withdrawn by the applicants for personal reasons, and a couple more were rejected by the search committee as inappropriate for the position.

That left only two applicants for the eventual short list, each of whom was cleared by the foundation after consultation with the LDS Church Library and Archives. Each of them came to campus during November 2010 for interviews with the various interested parties and to make presentations out of their scholarly work. Both were highly qualified and accomplished, and both were currently employed at distinguished universities outside of the Mormon heartland. One was somewhat more senior, but both were qualified for an appointment as an associate professor. Negotiations were opened in December with the one ranked first by the faculty, and after some give-and-take over a period of a couple of weeks, an offer was finally made and accepted by Dr. Patrick Q. Mason, then at the Kroc Institute for International Peace Studies at the University of Notre Dame. In deference to his privacy, and to the confidentiality of various aspects of these negotiations, I will add only that the agreement thus concluded seemed to me quite a generous one under the circumstances, but Mason had been a very impressive candidate for a person who had earned his PhD degree only five years earlier. Thus, the Bushmans, their commitment fully completed, left in mid-2011 amid a celebratory send-off and profound gratitude for their hard work and self-sacrifice in launching Mormon studies at Claremont. "Well done, thou good and faithful servants!"

Mason then succeeded Richard Bushman, starting in the fall of 2011, as the occupant of the Howard W. Hunter Chair in Mormon Studies. In that capacity, he taught a course in the history of North American religion each semester as part of the general curriculum of the School of Religion, plus two courses a year, of his own design, in Mormon studies.[46] He is responsible for all the other operations under Hunter Chair auspices also, including a research program, occasional conferences and special public lectures, plus the recruitment and funding of outstanding graduate students planning to study religion (and especially Mormons). Mason arrived as a tenured associate professor, with his performance subject to review by the faculty after five years. During that period, his salary is to be covered by a combination of the large special donation of one hundred thousand dollars per year and the regular yield from the growing Hunter endowment. Under these circumstances, hopes are high among all parties that Mormon studies will become a permanent feature at CGU, but it is clear to all that permanency, in any meaningful sense, will still depend on expanding the endowment considerably within this five-year period.

It will depend also on greater stability in the leadership of CGU, the School of Religion, and the LDS Council, all of which were in transition again during 2011. In the summer of 2011, the new CGU president, Deborah Freund, was installed; Dean Min relinquished his position to yet another colleague in the School of Religion, Professor Tammi Schneider; and Randall Huff had to relinquish his position as chairman of the LDS Council on Mormon studies to accept an important new church position. Stephen Bradford, an able and enthusiastic Pasadena attorney, was chosen to succeed Huff in the chair of the LDS Council. Patrick Mason, himself only newly arrived, thus faced a largely new panorama of leaders who "knew not Joseph" (Joseph Bentley, that is!). Adding to a potentially unpredictable future is a new plan by the CGU administration to restructure the university such that the School of Religion will revert again to departmental status within the larger School of Arts and Humanities.

A Place and a Future for Mormon Studies at Claremont?

After only a relatively few years, much was achieved by the Bushmans and the LDS Council in establishing a Mormon studies chair and program at Claremont, and the prospects look good for the coming years under Patrick Mason. Yet the relationship between the program and the university remains something of an "experiment," and its long-term history remains to be lived out before it can be written. Considerable skepticism remains in some quarters about the whole idea of whether a Mormon studies program can endure, even at a secular institution, without interference from church leaders and Mormon donors. Can church leaders be expected to condone in perpetuity a curriculum and narrative about the Mormon experience that they do not control? Can potential Mormon donors, who are so often devout apologists for their religion, be expected to contribute large sums to an endowment with no "strings" attached to ensure that their money will be used for courses and professors they would approve? Indeed, is there really any such thing as "Mormon studies" as a legitimate discipline independent of parochial Mormon interests? Can occupants of a chair in Mormon studies ever be found who will not essentially be Mormon apologists or, conversely, secularized academics whose basic beliefs and commitments will be suspect to real believers?

Such questions have been raised more than once, but perhaps especially influentially in the *Wall Street Journal* by Daniel Golden, who used the particular cases of LDS scholar D. Michael Quinn and Catholic scholar Mark Jordan to illustrate the various interests that come into conflict when academic chairs and programs are proposed by any religious community, not only the Mormons.[47] Golden observed that chairs endowed for various religious communities at secular universities since the 1970s had routinely been "underwritten by donors of the same religion, who generally expect that the scholar filling the chair will be sympathetic to the faith." It should not be surprising, then, that Karen Torjesen, then dean of the CGU School of Religion, was also quoted by Golden as declaring that "we don't want any bomb-throwers" in any of the chairs she was trying to establish. Potential Mormon donors could not have made the point any better!

Among some Mormon scholars themselves there is also some skepticism about the real independence of a Mormon studies program, even in secular universities. Such was the theme of a thoughtful address by John-Charles Duffy (doctoral student at the University of North Carolina), who delivered a paper at the spring 2006 Sunstone West Symposium held at Claremont.[48] Duffy outlined some reasons for expecting Mormon studies at Claremont and elsewhere to be kept under the control of Mormonism's "faithful scholars," primarily because resources for such academic enterprises, either from the church itself or from wealthy Mormon donors, would be likely to go into the hands *only* of scholars (at any institutions) who had the trust of church leaders and would thus always be in a position to broker the application of those resources. At the same symposium, I responded to Duffy by pointing out that he might well be correct in his expectations, but there is nothing unusual about attempts to foster orthodoxies of various kinds at universities, including *secular* orthodoxies, as anyone can attest who has encountered the pressures of "political correctness" at state universities! The other side of the issue about the relation between religious orthodoxy and academic values was addressed in a 2004 lecture by BYU scholar Grant Underwood, titled "Is It Safe? Mormon History and the Secular Academy." This lecture, which opened a three-day conference at CGU in October 2004 (mentioned earlier in this chapter), concluded that it would indeed be both "safe" and beneficial for Mormon students to be exposed to "Mormon studies" in academia, but Underwood clearly recognized that a "sales job" of sorts was needed to win over the Mormon faithful.[49]

Mormonism, or at least its major denomination, the Church of Jesus Christ of Latter-day Saints, is founded upon a historical narrative of divine intervention in the history of America to call modern prophets as spokesmen for Deity in these end times. There are, of course, other religious traditions, some of them very ancient, based on claims of intervention by a personal God in history; one thinks at least of Judaism, Christianity, and Islam. For the Latter-day Saints, however, the certainty of modern revelation is accompanied by a self-perpetuating and highly centralized priesthood structure and authorized canon, which together constitute the ultimate authority in matters of faith, doctrine, and even historicity. This centralized control in organization, and to a large extent in hermeneutics as well, has traditionally left somewhat less intellectual space for the scholarly dissent and disputations than one finds in modern Judaism, Islam, or even Catholicism. Furthermore, the LDS hierarchy (usually called "General Authorities"), in exercising its power, has often been quite assertive—even heavy-handed at times—depending partly upon cultural or political threats perceived from the outside.

Yet this organizational reality has been accompanied by the seemingly contrasting injunctions throughout Mormon history in favor of as much advanced education as possible for its members, male and female. Such injunctions are found especially in the Doctrine and Covenants, where members are told (for example) that the "glory of God is intelligence," that they "cannot be saved in ignorance," that they should learn "by study and also by faith," and that they should study whatever is available "out of the best books"—including science, history, and all kinds of secular learning, not only religious.[50] Mormon teachings have also emphasized the important role of divine revelation to each person himself (herself) for guidance in matters both secular and religious, a somewhat more expansive view of individual access to Deity than just the traditional Christian idea of "conscience" or answers to prayers. So here lies the paradox: in considering a given commitment, either to belief or to action, wherein a Mormon believer sees a conflict between official church doctrine or policy, on the one hand, and his or her own lights from secular learning or personal revelation, on the other hand, *which should take priority?* This is an old paradox, not entirely peculiar to Mormonism, of course, but perhaps more specific to Mormons because of the emphasis historically given to both sides of it in Mormon teachings. The paradox has been noticed as a problem by scholars both inside and outside the church—for example, by Thomas F. O'Dea in his 1957 classic and more recently by LDS scholar Terryl Givens.[51]

If this paradox is problematic for believing Mormons, it is no less a problem for the Mormon public image, especially among skeptical academics. For a century and a half, Mormonism has been regularly portrayed as a kind of cult with sheeplike members, enthralled in obedience to their religious leaders. Mormon politicians have often been suspected of a tendency to give the demands of their religious leaders priority over their own political preferences, even as recently as the 2008 Proposition 8 campaign and the 2008 and 2012 Mitt Romney campaigns. It is not surprising, then, that in academia too, a recurrent question, sometimes openly expressed and sometimes not, is whether a believing Mormon student, or even a professor, can extricate himself from his commitment to religious apologetics long enough to consider academic issues and quandaries on the same independent basis as other academics do—especially in the study of theology, but also in history and in other fields of the humanities and social sciences. I know I am not alone among Mormon academics who have occasionally heard anecdotes *both* about such academic skepticism directed at Mormon students or professors *and* about supposed instances of Mormon apologetic and intellectual rigidity. Nor are such anecdotes always based only on unfair stereotypes. In my own personal professional experience and observations, I have seen instances that support both kinds of anecdotes.

Meanwhile, the skepticism in *academia* about Mormon intellectual imperviousness is matched by *grassroots Mormon* skepticism about the value of an academic study of religion. In Mormon worship services, Sunday-school classes, and other auxiliary activities under church auspices, the leaders, speakers, and teachers are all enjoined to stay close to the instructional curricula and materials provided from church headquarters and to avoid bringing in "outside" (that is, unapproved or secular) literature or teachings. It is the responsibility of the church to teach the truth as it is revealed in the scriptural canon and in the teachings of contemporary leaders, not to promote the ideas of the world, however valuable these might be in other settings. Reaching very far outside of the approved Mormon magisterium carries with it the risk of diluting authentic gospel teachings and undermining the faith of the Saints, especially the younger ones. Even the weekday religious instruction of students in high school "seminary" or in college "institute" classes emphasizes indoctrination and the building of "testimonies," rather than trying to reconcile their faith with some of the troublesome issues raised by their schoolteachers and professors. Ideally, all LDS college students would also attend a campus of BYU, where the faculty can be trusted not to undermine their faith by demeaning their religion, or (since BYU enrollment is limited), at least be enrolled in institute classes provided by the church near other campuses.

This protective pedagogical philosophy is a mixed blessing for the students. It works best for those who, after graduation, choose occupations where they do not confront many challenges to their faith. It works less well for those who go on for graduate work, especially in the physical, biological, and social sciences or the humanities. In particular, those who surprise their families and church leaders by choosing graduate or divinity schools for the study of religion will find quite an epistemological chasm to cross from their LDS Institute classes (or BYU religion classes) to their graduate work in academic religious studies. Also, the "folks back home" are likely to wonder why students would study religion under other auspices than their own church, where presumably they have already learned such religious truth as they need. Won't the academic study of "outside" religion simply undermine their own "testimonies" and cause them to leave the church of their youth? Why not study something practical that will bring them a good income in a secure profession, rather than "messing around with all that intellectual stuff" that will likely only get them in trouble? A concern of this kind from the Mormon grassroots tends to occur in the cases of *any* of their youth who study philosophy of any kind—and perhaps in the humanistic fields more generally—but it is particularly strong where the chosen field of graduate study is religion (or "religious studies," as it is usually called in public universities).

If this mutual skepticism, or at least wariness, between grassroots Mormonism and academic religious studies is ever significantly relaxed, such will probably occur in settings like Claremont's School of Religion, not only through constructive relationships between believing LDS students and their faculty mentors, but also in relationships between the LDS professors and their own colleagues on various faculties. The prospects seem promising but by no means assured. Non-Mormon academics will not soon be convinced about the true legitimacy of a discipline called "Mormon studies," nor can they quite understand how a true academic can sincerely believe in the founding narrative of the LDS religion. As I noted earlier, I periodically taught (as adjunct faculty) a course in Mormon history while the funding was under way for the Hunter Chair at CGU. In my early experiences with certain colleagues there, I occasionally inferred (perhaps unfairly) a certain skepticism in the questions that they would raise with me during private conversations. They seemed prepared to accept at face value my *general* credentials (and later Richard Bushman's) as part of the academic fraternity, yet seemed to wonder about our actual values and intentions—as though we could not *really* believe in something like Mormonism and still function as professional academics. In other words, my "passport" as a scholar from the *Mormon* community was sometimes suspect.

As long as my course in Mormon studies was the only one in the catalog, and it was taught only once a year, this issue did not seem especially salient to the faculty. However, once Bushman arrived as a regular member of the faculty, to begin his stint as the Hunter visiting professor, there might have been somewhat more attention paid to this issue by some of the faculty. On one occasion, not long after Bushman's arrival, a prominent member of the religion faculty, during a lunchtime conversation, asked him, "Why is it that you believe in Mormonism?"[52] I had received passing questions or comments of a similar purport once or twice on informal occasions from members of the same faculty. On the whole, however, given the financial and other resources that came to their school with an endowed chair in Mormon studies, the religion faculty seemed reconciled, if not always enthusiastic, about what clearly seemed an anomaly in their midst—a bit like having an endowed chair for Jehovah's Witnesses or "Moonies." Furthermore, Bushman himself provided a superb example of both a true academic and a sincere believer during his three years in the School of Religion and did much in the process to win over the faculty. I think the same can be expected of Patrick Mason.

In recent years, various local branches of the large LDS public affairs apparatus have periodically identified ad hoc groups of various non-LDS dignitaries and invited them on "get-acquainted" tours of important LDS institutions in Utah and elsewhere. Dedications of new temples have sometimes been occasions for such tours, which, however, have also included major Salt Lake City sites, such as the temple grounds, the Tabernacle, the museum, the Family History Center, the Church History Library and Archives, Welfare Square, and, in Provo, BYU and the Missionary Training Center. As indicated early in this chapter, a tour of this kind during 2002 included Dr. Karen Torjesen, founding dean of the School of Religion at Claremont, and helped to reinforce her plans for including the LDS religion among those that would be invited to establish endowed chairs in the new school.

Almost a decade latter, during the first week of November 2011, the LDS Public Affairs office in Los Angeles organized another such tour for five administrators of local university religion programs. These five included two from the office of the dean of religious life at the University of Southern California and the new president of the Claremont School of Theology, plus (especially important for my purposes) the new president of Claremont Graduate University, Deborah Freund, and her dean of the School of Religion, Tammi Schneider. When these two CGU women returned, they both reported on their experiences at the next meeting of the LDS Council on Mormon Studies.[53] They were effusive in their appreciation for the red-carpet treatment they had received in Utah and deeply impressed with all they had learned about the breadth and depth of LDS culture, not only in its religious aspects, but also in its educational, artistic, welfare, and humanitarian programs. The goodwill and appreciation that they brought back from their tour will greatly enhance the prospects for Mormon studies at CGU and especially the future of the Howard W. Hunter Chair there. Such goodwill is no substitute for the capital that still must be raised to guarantee that future, but it is enormously valuable in less tangible ways.

Chapter 9 | PERIODIC PASSPORT CHECKS WITH GATEKEEPERS IN THE HOMELAND

SINCE I HAVE NEVER HELD HIGH CHURCH OFFICE, MY PERSONAL ENCOUNters with church leaders have occurred mostly at the local level (ward and stake), as is true for the great majority of Latter-day Saints. I myself have, indeed, been among the leaders at those levels during my more than sixty years as an adult member in the lay priesthood. My experiences with local Mormons have almost always been reassuring about the sincerity and good intentions of ward and stake leaders. The part played by divine influence in the performance of their duties, however, has always seemed to me quite variable, ranging from imperceptible in some cases to highly probable in others. As the Saints are often reminded, the quest for divine guidance is ultimately a *personal* responsibility and achievement, so it will naturally vary with individuals, whether or not they are leaders. While still a young adult, I learned to recognize and appreciate the human fallibility in all our leaders, and thus to keep my expectations for their performance quite modest.

That attitude has blessed me with a certain immunity against disillusionment, which for many Saints has followed their confrontations with the human failings of leaders from the greatest to the least. My loyalty to the church as an institution, therefore, has never depended on my assessments of the teachings or behavior of any particular leaders at either the local or the general level. Yet their duties unavoidably include "gatekeeping" or "border checks" (formally or informally) in their relationships with members who (like me) frequently visit "outside" intellectual territories. On these occasions, I have sometimes felt a warm "welcome home"; at other times, however, I have felt a special scrutiny and rather grudging admittance.

WELCOMING ENCOUNTERS WITH LDS AUTHORITIES

My first extensive experience with a general authority of the church actually occurred on my mission, when S. Dilworth Young, then a member of the small seven-man First Council of Seventy (a remnant of the Nauvoo-Era Quorums of Seventy) was sent as president of the (then) New England Mission, where I happened to be serving as a missionary. I had been in the mission only a couple of months and was chafing under the rather heavy-handed leadership of his predecessor, but Young transformed my mission experience into a powerfully formative period in my young life. Formerly a professional Boy Scout executive, he knew exactly how to deal with boys. I have written more fully about my mission experience in chapter 1, so for now I will say only that President Young had the gift to inspire confidence, loyalty, and commitment in young men to such an extent that we followed him even as he imposed on us the regime known as "country tracting." This experience instilled—or at least called forth—character traits that served us well for the rest of our lives. For many, it also solidified our religious commitments for life, since such an intense investment of missionary effort was often accompanied by feelings of special closeness to Deity. My relationship with President Young continued to the end of his life, for he always recognized me as one of "his" missionaries. Besides occasional encounters at mission reunions, and a few visits to his home during my trips to Utah, I appreciated especially his invitation for me to bring each of my sons to be set apart by him personally as they departed on their missions. He was able to do that for my first two missionary sons, and I was deeply touched as he asked me to join him in that ordinance and blessing each time.[1]

I have had but few subsequent experiences with general authorities of such a direct and personal kind. Shortly after I returned home from my own mission, my father was called to preside over the Japan Mission of the church, which then (1949) included the entire Pacific Far East. Since Father's entire family, including me, was to accompany him to Japan, we were all invited to be present when he was set apart for his new calling under the hands of the First Presidency of the Church (then George Albert Smith, J. Reuben Clark, and David O. McKay). They all impressed me as kindly and deeply spiritual old men with the demeanor and aura that a returned missionary would expect of prophets. From my later reading of Mormon history, I came to see them all as quite human—distressingly so in some instances—but not on that auspicious occasion. I have not had many other such personal contacts.[2]

In 1990, however, I was surprised to receive a short personal letter from Elder Dallin H. Oaks of the Twelve. As background, Elder Oaks had given a talk in the April 1989 General Conference, which consisted of one long caveat about the need for discretion and good judgment as the Saints encountered "alternate voices . . . in magazines, journals, and newspapers, and at lectures, symposia, and conferences" devoted to discussions of the gospel and the church.[3] Since this talk was given during a period when certain LDS scholars were being summoned and questioned by church leaders about their speaking and writing on such topics, many of them saw this conference talk as an ominous indication of further efforts to suppress all such "alternate" expressions. During the rest of 1989, some of the discussion and commentary about the Oaks talk among LDS scholars revealed a degree of distress that I thought was rather exaggerated, given the distinctions that Elder Oaks had clearly made between constructive and destructive forms of commentary and the *variety* of motives (good and bad) that might lie behind such commentary. Accordingly, I published an article in *Sunstone* offering my own interpretation of what I thought Elder Oaks had actually meant, along with my own advice to anyone aspiring to join the ranks of the "alternate voices." I included a ten-point advisory "Decalogue for Dissenters," which I intended as realistic counsel about how we "alternate" commentators should express ourselves and what we should avoid in doing so.[4] The completely unexpected response from Elder Oaks came in a letter dated July 3, 1990, and mailed to my university office. It read in total: "Dear Brother Mauss: You gave some good advice in your April *Sunstone* piece on 'Alternate Voices.' Your article is insightful and should be helpful. Best personal regards. Sincerely, Dallin H. Oaks." I responded with a similarly brief appreciative note.

The most important personal contacts with a general authority that I have had since then have been several with Elder Marlin K. Jensen of the Seventy, until recently (mid-2012) church historian, starting with the 1997 episode, related in chapter 6, where we collaborated to seek a repudiation of traditional racist folklore in the church. Since then, I have benefited by many visits during the intervening years, either in his office or at meetings of the Mormon History Association, and we have exchanged periodic correspondence by e-mail. He is a man without guile or pretense, and he has proved to be a loyal and supportive friend to me (as to many others also, of course). Much later, in 2007, he was most helpful in connecting me also with a close colleague in the Seventy, Elder Bruce C. Hafen, then area president for the church in central Europe. The occasion was a paper that I was preparing as the "keynote address" for the upcoming inaugural conference of the European Mormon Studies Association (EMSA), which met that summer in Worcester, England.[5] In gathering material for that paper, I approached Elder Jensen seeking information about the various problems in church growth and member retention in Europe, where he had once served as area president. He agreed to meet me at his office in the Church Historical Department on May 23, 2007, where he proved very helpful in responding to a series of questions that I had sent him ahead of time and in confirming a number of my initial impressions about the difficulties in Europe. Then he referred me to Elder Hafen (his successor as area president) with an e-mail letter of introduction.

As it happened, Elder Hafen had recalled hearing of my earlier consultations with the Research Information Division (see chapter 2), and he entered into a very informative correspondence with me between June 24 and July 15, 2007. He responded fully to a long series of questions that I asked him, some of which were a little sensitive. His input was a crucial contribution to my EMSA paper and subsequent publication. He was candid both in confirming some of the impressions that I had gained elsewhere (about problems of the LDS Church in Europe) and in disagreeing with others. He even snagged an article in the *Wall Street Journal* that he knew would be helpful to my paper and commended it to my attention via e-mail.[6] Finally, he carefully read and critiqued the first complete draft of my paper, including this gratifying observation: "For someone whose own experience in Europe is relatively limited, you also reflected a grasp of some broad and important overall perspectives. And you did a nice job of including materials from our exchange, which allowed some current and specific examples. I also think it is healthy for those who hear (or read) your work to know that you and we do have the feeling of being 'in this together,' which helps all of us try to be more constructive on matters of common concern."[7]

He went on, however, to criticize part of my paper as exaggerating somewhat the actual "costs of membership" for European Saints and for some dated observations I had made about growth and retention. In this, as in our other correspondence, I felt perfectly free to argue a bit with him, based upon input I had received from European Saints, though I did make some modifications in my final draft in light of his criticisms. The main thing that impressed me about this exchange with Elder Hafen was his entire attitude so well expressed in what I quoted above about his feeling that we (that is, church leaders and independent scholars) were all "in this together." I find it difficult to imagine that a general authority of the church would have said any such thing during the 1980s or 1990s to me or to any scholar not on the church payroll (given the concern in those days about "alternative voices")—or would otherwise have been so fully forthcoming as Elder Hafen was with me during my research and writing for that paper. Times seem truly to have changed!

POTENTIALLY TENSE ENCOUNTERS WITH LDS AUTHORITIES

Except for Elders Jensen, Hafen, and earlier S. Dilworth Young, most of my contacts with general authorities have been very much of a passing and somewhat perfunctory kind. Such contacts, however, always left me feeling that my "passport" as a citizen of the LDS "kingdom" was still valid and honored. Yet certain other contacts over the years have seemed to raise questions about the validity of my passport. My most tense and potentially demoralizing contacts with general authorities have been mainly indirect and impersonal, through stake presidents, who have been required to summon me for discussions—and sometimes criticisms—about my scholarly work on church-related topics. These encounters began for me in 1983 and must be seen in the more general context of the pervasive retrenchment policy in full sway during that period. I have written elsewhere about this era in recent LDS history and referred to it earlier in this memoir (in chapters 4 and 5), so it need not be recapitulated here. It has also been discussed more recently by Terryl Givens.[8]

It will suffice here simply to say that one aspect of this retrenchment policy was an effort by the LDS leadership to assert some control over the discussion of the church's doctrine, history, and policies that had started to occur among a growing corps of young intellectuals who had become especially numerous and outspoken since midcentury.[9] Particularly worrisome to the leaders, or at least to the more conservative among them, was the candor and criticism directed by some of the intellectuals at such sensitive issues as race relations, women's rights and roles, the legacy of polygamy, doctrines of the divine feminine, and the origin and historicity of the Book of Mormon. Starting in the late 1960s, with the emergence of the privately published scholarly journal *Dialogue,* a campaign of growing intensity against unauthorized commentary on such issues began on the initiative of some of the most senior and powerful apostles. The campaign picked up momentum in the 1970s and took many forms, official and unofficial, culminating finally in several highly publicized terminations of employment for BYU professors, and excommunications or various disciplinary actions against others, during the early and mid-1990s.

The Mormon intellectuals who were the objects of this campaign were at first astonished and then increasingly alarmed and demoralized, for almost all of us had regarded ourselves as faithful members of the church with the best of intentions. In retrospect, and to the generations of younger scholars coming after us, our naïveté might now seem surprising. However, those of us who were starting our academic careers or our advanced education in the 1950s and 1960s will remember that the LDS Church leadership up to that time had not been inclined to restrict, control, or penalize what scholars did in their private capacities (except for a couple of rare cases where authors were perceived by some leaders as publicly debunking or defaming the faith).[10] Church presidents (up through midcentury) had discouraged heresy trials, and private study groups (so-called) of various stripes could be found all over Utah, including at least one at the University of Utah, which frequently took on a critical tone.[11]

Prominent individual church members occasionally criticized a church practice or policy, especially during the growing storm over the church's racial restrictions during this period. Yet it never occurred to these commentators or study groups, "intellectual" or otherwise, that they needed permission from the leaders for speaking out or writing about church matters. When *Dialogue: A Journal of Mormon Thought,* the first independent scholarly periodical to appear in decades, was founded at Stanford University in 1965, editor Eugene England and his colleagues did not feel the need to ask anyone's permission (though they did notify certain church leaders of their intentions and motives out of general deference and respect). Even many scholars then at BYU or in CES felt free from the beginning to participate in *Dialogue* (and later *Sunstone*), as authors, editorial board members, or staff, without fear of official disapproval, to say nothing of jeopardy to their church employment or church membership.

In any case, it soon became clear during the 1970s that the church leadership was transitioning *out of* that relatively permissive posture vis-à-vis private intellectual initiatives by its members and *into* a posture of greater standardization and centralization of control over the narratives and discourse about the church's history and teachings. Controversial work published in this genre by scholars in church employment continued only at the risk of losing their jobs, so it did not continue long. For scholars like myself, independent of church employment, the sanctions for "unauthorized" lecturing or publishing on topics that irritated conservative church leaders were applied through the ecclesiastical disciplinary apparatus. Such sanctions ranged from informal interviews with stake presidents or bishops all the way to eventual excommunication from the church in cases where the scholar in question was deemed by his or her local priesthood leaders to be unrepentant or incorrigible.

Outcomes of this process varied considerably depending on the attitudes of the parties involved in a given disciplinary procedure, even if it were only an informal interview. If the scholar in question was offended at even being questioned about his or her lectures or publications and reacted with indignation, the outcome might have been a breach in his or her relationship with the church. If the proceedings progressed to the point of eventual excommunication, the breach would usually be permanent. On the other hand, the initial attitude of the bishop or stake president in such cases also had much to do with the outcome. A leader who had already come to regard the member in question as a heretic or troublemaker might turn the interview (or other proceeding) into a scolding of the presumptuous scholar for having publicly said or written something regarded as unfavorable to the church. Such a posture by the priesthood leader would often cause an already tense encounter to escalate to an angry stalemate, leading, in turn, to further church discipline, further alienation, and eventual excommunication. Fortunately, my own encounters with church leaders on these occasions always remained calm, if somewhat tense, on both sides of the interview.

My first such encounter occurred in 1983, shortly after I had returned from the annual conference of the Mormon History Association (held that year in Omaha, Nebraska). There had already been nearly a decade of growing tension in relationships between the LDS general authorities and Mormon scholars or other "intellectuals," ever since the newly reorganized Office of Church Historian under Leonard Arrington had come under attack from conservative apostles and had eventually been moved to BYU as an isolated (or at least insulated) research institute.[12] During the 1983 MHA conference itself, rumors were afloat about scholars being "called in" by their bishops or stake presidents, or both, to be told that their published work was a matter of concern to "the brethren." A few at the conference reported already having had such encounters, so others, including myself, naturally wondered if our turns were coming up. I recall that one evening during the MHA conference, an informal group of us gathered around Arrington to seek his advice about what, if anything, we should do in this situation. Having himself just spent an extremely stressful and discouraging decade before being retired (first from the role of church historian and then from his BYU professorship), Arrington nevertheless remained calm and professional during this discussion, saying nothing derogatory about church leaders or about the way they had treated him and urging all of us just to "keep on doing what you are doing" and leave the rest in the Lord's hands.

Shortly after I returned from this 1983 MHA conference, I had occasion to be visiting with a close friend who happened to be a counselor to the president of my Pullman Stake. I asked him if he had any reason to believe that our stake president had been directed to contact me for this same kind of official interview. He replied in the affirmative. It happened that I needed to renew my temple recommend about that time anyway, so I made an appointment for that with the expectation that the president would take the occasion to discuss with me the recent directive about me that he had received from church headquarters. The whole encounter was wonderfully cordial and reassuring. The president, Weldon Tovey, first gave me the standard, formal interview for the temple and signed the recommend form, without even mentioning the other matter—an obvious vote of confidence in me that set the stage for a nonthreatening discussion to follow. After handing me the signed recommend, he said simply that there was one more matter that he needed to discuss with me. He proceeded to tell me that he had received a personal phone call from Elder Mark E. Petersen, of the Quorum of the Twelve, who wanted him to tell me that "the brethren are concerned about your association with apostate publications"—referring obviously to *Dialogue* and *Sunstone*. (I do not think I had actually published anything in *Sunstone* to that point, but I had been active in the Sunstone Symposia.)

The president also mentioned to me that while Elder Petersen was talking on the phone about my case, he was obviously leafing through some sort of file that had been compiled, which included the information that I was then serving as a teacher of the Sunday Gospel Doctrine class in my ward, and he wanted to know if my teaching was sound. The president told me that he responded to Elder Petersen by noting (accurately) that he had attended my Sunday-school class several times and that it was one of the best Gospel Doctrine classes he had ever witnessed. Naturally, I found all of that very reassuring from my president, who went on to tell me, however, that he was required to send a letter to Elder Petersen informing him of my response to his criticism. In that response for Elder Petersen, I simply expressed my surprise that the publications in question were considered by anyone as "apostate" in nature, for I did not so regard them, else I would not have written for them. Furthermore, I expressed the presumption that since Elder Petersen had not identified the concerned "brethren" in question, he must have been speaking for himself, and that if his views were ever shared by the First Presidency, I would expect the latter eventually to issue their own concurring counsel, which they had not yet done. Finally, as yet further reassurance of his confidence in me, my stake president told me that he would give me a copy of his required letter to Elder Petersen about my response, which he did.[13] A year or so later, this same stake president called me as group leader over the high priests of my ward, the first priesthood leadership position that I had been given since 1969. I served a decade or more in that position, during which time the president more than once publicly praised my services.

While I was yet serving as group leader of the high priests, President Tovey, who was himself an academic, was succeeded by Roy Mosman, a more conservative leader who had had a career as a small-town lawyer and judge. This new president had somewhat less sympathy for unauthorized academic commentary on LDS Church matters. Meanwhile, the personal campaigns of Elder Petersen had been regularized in the church bureaucracy through the establishment of a new institution with the deliciously Orwellian name "Committee to Strengthen

Church Members." The staff of this committee, operating under a couple of general authorities, was charged with reviewing the publications and lectures occurring in such venues as *Dialogue, Sunstone,* and other privately produced outlets and identifying excerpts of scholarly commentary that the staff considered critical of the church or its leaders.[14] The excerpted material would then be called to the attention of the appropriate area president, who would write a letter to the author's stake president about the offending excerpts, with the instruction that the stake president should summon the author for an interview. It was in about 1991, during that newly escalated environment of official surveillance, that President Mosman was required to call me in. According to a close friend of mine then serving on the stake high council, this new president was furious that one of "his" group leaders (that is, myself) should have come to the attention of church headquarters in this way. As my friend put it so colorfully to me, there was "smoke coming from every orifice" of the president. After further consultation with this high councilor, and with my ward bishop, the stake president had calmed down quite a bit before actually calling me in. This encounter was somewhat tense but turned out well enough, and I continued to get temple recommends. By the time President Mosman was released several years later, he had mellowed somewhat and treated me with considerable warmth.

My third summons of this kind was somewhat more dramatic but ultimately very reassuring. It occurred in October 1998, not long before we left Pullman and moved to Southern California in retirement. The occasion was another turnover in stake presidencies, when Elder Marlin K. Jensen, then in the Presidency of the Seventy, was the general authority sent to our stake conference to handle the transition—a matter, I believe, of sheer happenstance. Elder Jensen, as noted in chapter 6, had become acquainted with me personally during our campaign in 1997 to elicit a formal repudiation of traditional racist folklore from the First Presidency. When Elder Jensen was assigned to our stake conference in Pullman, he notified Roy Mosman, the retiring stake president, in advance, that he wanted a brief interview with me on the Saturday morning of the conference weekend. The president, in turn, told my ward bishop to ask me to appear at the appointed time and place. Both the bishop and the president (he of the smoking orifices) were convinced that I had finally gotten into serious-enough trouble with the general authorities that one of their number would have to deal with me personally! I found their demeanor on this occasion somewhat distressing, for it suggested a complete reversal in Elder Jensen's attitude toward me. I doubted that such was the case, and I found it both ironic and humorous that my interview with Elder Jensen went on for a gratifying and enjoyable forty-five minutes, during most of which time the retiring stake presidency (with their wives) were all in the ante-room patiently awaiting "farewell" interviews on the occasion of their releases.[15]

I still do not know exactly what motivated Elder Jensen to ask for this special interview with me; it could have been a suggestion from my brother, who was a good friend of his, or perhaps just a desire on Jensen's part to find out why I seemed so controversial in some quarters. In any case, as the interview began, he asked that we kneel together in prayer so that our discussion would be guided by the Holy Spirit. He then proceeded to ask me about my published work in *Dialogue* and elsewhere, including my book *The Angel and the Beehive.* He had obviously read some of my work, but I do not know how much, since he acknowledged that one of his great regrets in his current church calling was that he had no time to read much that he would like to read. Rather than question me about specific points in what I had written, he seemed more interested in knowing what was motivating me: what did I think I was doing—and other privately employed scholars were doing—through our work, that would be helpful to the church?

I did not take notes on our interview, so I cannot replicate each side of the conversation, but I do recall making the following points: first, most of the authors to whom he was referring were faithful and active members, who wished the church well even if their work sometimes seemed critical; second, I regarded my work—and that of the great majority of other privately published LDS scholars—to be fair and balanced, even if candid, and therefore more likely to be regarded as valid scholarship by non-Mormons, who were wary of anything published under official church auspices; third, all such unsponsored or "unauthorized" research and writing on the church should be treated by the leaders in exactly the way they treat the work products of the consulting firms that they occasionally hire for advice—with one major difference, namely, that they have to pay for what they get from consultants, while the work of LDS members in scholarly journals is available without charge, to be either considered or ignored as the leaders see fit; and finally, precisely because such work does not appear in church publications, the leaders are not responsible for it—unlike the case with church employees in CES or at BYU, whose public statements and writings have sometimes been embarrassing to the church. Elder Jensen seemed impressed with my observations, and we parted warmly. Since then I have had several other generous acknowledgments from him about my work or about my comments quoted in the press.

Following such a gratifying encounter with Elder Jensen, and our move to Irvine in Southern California in 1999, I assumed that I had had my last interrogation from a church leader. After all, California Mormons had a reputation for being somewhat more relaxed about unorthodox ways, an impression that was confirmed during our first year or two in Irvine. Furthermore, with the ascension in 1994 of Howard W. Hunter (briefly) as president of the church, and then of Gordon B. Hinckley in 1995, the tension between the scholars and church headquarters of the previous two decades seemed to be diminishing. I was quite surprised, therefore, to be summoned again for such an interview with the president of the Irvine Stake as late as 2002. As before, the interview began in a cordial spirit, for this president knew me as an active member and had recently issued me a temple recommend. As a fairly new stake president, he had never been put in such a position with an active member. He was frankly somewhat bewildered at having been directed by his (then) area president to question me about a comment that I had made at a Sunstone Symposium on the damage still being done from the residue of racist folklore in the church. He read my quotation from the area president's letter and then asked me if I had indeed said that. When I replied in the affirmative, he paused thoughtfully and then said, "Well, I can't see anything wrong with that." I could only concur, of course.

Perhaps because this stake president was the age of one of my sons, I somewhat presumptuously decided to take this occasion to educate him about the "unsponsored sector" of scholarship and publication in the LDS world. I first explained to him why he had received his letter from the area president, and he seemed surprised to learn that there was such an entity in the church as the Committee to Strengthen Church Members. As our discussion proceeded, he seemed unacquainted with any such developments as the 1972 appointment of Leonard J. Arrington, the distinguished church historian, or with *Dialogue, Sunstone,* or the Mormon History Association and its journal.[16] In this respect, I feel sure that he was representative of bishops and stake presidents throughout the church, even to the present day. After my explanation, I asked the president if he had any counsel for me about what I should or should not do in the future, and he offered none. He said he was satisfied with my faithfulness and would so inform his area president. I offered to furnish him with a copy of one of my books and with some back issues of *Sunstone* and *Dialogue* ("in a plain brown wrapper"), which I brought to him the next Sunday. Thereafter, our relationship became increasingly warm, and it has remained so with the new Irvine Stake president who succeeded him several years later.

Now, a decade since my last such interview, I have often wondered if the Committee to Strengthen Church Members remains in existence, for I rarely hear anymore about instances of scholars being called in by local leaders in this way, to say nothing of excommunications or other church discipline.[17] Furthermore, as a practical matter, with the recent explosion on the Internet of social media, and of blog sites devoted to Mormon, anti-Mormon, ex-Mormon, and post-Mormon discussions, no such surveillance from church headquarters seems feasible or useful, especially given the new outreach efforts of the LDS public affairs apparatus. Yet during the final decades of the twentieth century, many of my colleagues in the LDS scholarly community were subjected to official interviews like mine with their local leaders, but not always with such reassuring outcomes as I had. Indeed, from their accounts, both oral and written, it is obvious that many of these encounters were quite hostile, on one or both sides of the encounter, in several cases leading to well-publicized excommunications. I have no judgments to pass on the proceedings in any of these cases but my own, since I lack adequate information on which to base balanced judgments. To all appearances from the outside, though, I have the impression that some of them involved intemperate or hostile posturing, either by the scholars or by their priesthood leaders (or both), at or near the very beginning of the process—perhaps because of some preexisting history in their relationships.[18] My encounters, by contrast, generally occurred in a context of cordiality with my local leaders, all of whom already knew me as an active member and had regularly issued me temple recommends. For yet other disciplined scholars, even a similarly close relationship to the church, prior to being summoned, apparently provided no protection from official reprisals by indignant local or general leaders (or both).

REFLECTIONS ON A DIFFICULT ERA

As I have reflected on the period, starting in the mid-1970s, when so much tension was generated between church leaders and scholars, my general feeling is one of profound regret at the unnecessary damage done—some of it by the injudicious behavior of well-meaning LDS scholars and intellectuals, but much of it by the heavy-handed reaction of the church leadership, general and local. When scholars were harshly treated for their writings, with various forms of ecclesiastical discipline, they all too often simply left the church, and almost always their family members left with them. The numbers of such scholars and their families were not enormous, in total, and might even have been considered unavoidable "collateral damage" in some quarters. However, those who were disciplined or harassed during that period were only the most conspicuous casualties in a larger and more general malaise affecting an *entire generation* of talented, independent, and faithful intellectuals after midcentury. (See note 9 herein). In some ways reminiscent of the earlier "lost generation" identified by Edward Geary, yet this later and larger lost generation did not typically leave either the church or the

Mountain West.[19] Instead, they simply abandoned Mormon studies, or at least any scholarly work on Mormons of a controversial or critical-analytical kind.

To be sure, this abandonment was neither total nor universal. Although some did indeed leave the church or the Mormon heartland, or both, many others of that same generation of intellectuals, in response to pressures from the church leadership, simply felt that they had to choose between either continuing their dedication to wide-ranging academic studies of Mormons and Mormonism or maintaining their good standing in the church. Very few tried to stay on and do both. For those already comfortable with their work in apologetics or in church-sponsored teaching and writing, the choice was not difficult, and they went on, indeed, to make some very important contributions. Others (especially if not employed by the church) just kept doing their controversial writing or speaking and accepted such consequences as might have been forthcoming. Still others, perhaps the largest segment, however, made the choice simply to put their academic interests in Mormon studies "on hold," while burnishing their credentials as faithful members and leaders until it seemed safe to return to such studies without jeopardizing their standing with the leadership. Those who chose that path might have been the most astute of all, for they "lived to fight another day," as the saying goes. Yet such a choice was not without tensions of its own, as many of these talented intellectuals simply had to hunker down, or at least to relinquish aspirations for continued publication of innovative work in Mormon studies, in order to retain church employment, or eligibility for higher church office, or even just family tranquillity. Whatever responses the scholars in this category chose in their predicament, I think of them as another kind of "lost generation" because we will never have the full benefit of the work they might have produced in the history, social sciences, literature, and theology of the Mormon heritage. My sadness at this realization is only somewhat mitigated by the numbers of young intellectuals about the age of my grandchildren whom I now see coming back to pick up the challenge of studying the Mormon heritage in all its richness. Fortunately, this youthful generation is coming to maturity under a church leadership that now seems much more appreciative of independent scholarship in Mormon studies than were their predecessors during the era of retrenchment. Nevertheless, there will still be casualties among many of these younger intellectuals, for not all of them will be able to make their peace with the quandaries and issues in Mormon history, culture, and governance that were simply ignored or covered up by church policy for so many years.

Meanwhile, the damage done to the church itself by its long campaign against the earlier independent scholarship seems finally to have become apparent with the arrival of the new century, as a newer generation of church leaders has recognized the folly of trying to suppress, control, or sanitize the narrative of Mormon history in the age of the Internet. Not only are the skeletons in the Mormon historical closet, and even its sacred temple rites and clothing, now increasingly accessible electronically to the whole world, but, more important, the same has become accessible to any of the faithful with the curiosity to browse a variety of Mormon-related websites—including many sites devoted especially to exposés of the Mormon past.

Increasingly the contemporary LDS leadership is recognizing that the faithful have not been prepared by their curricula in Sunday school, seminary, institute, or elsewhere for understanding or intellectually assimilating certain disturbing events in LDS history. One result has been a recurring intellectual turmoil and a noticeable departure from church activity by younger members, including many of the temple-married and the returned missionaries. This predicament was acknowledged with surprising candor on November 11, 2011, by the outgoing church historian Marlin K. Jensen, who has been a major promoter of the new LDS policy of transparency about its history and has been deeply concerned about the growing member dropout rates.[20]

Even though, like other scholars involved in independent intellectual activity, I have often felt personally this tension between church leaders and scholars, I have usually found it helpful to maintain a certain intellectual and emotional detachment learned from my sociological training.[21] I try to keep in mind the larger historical context in which the church as an institution has been evolving (with periodic retrenchments) toward increasing assimilation with modern society (especially in the United States). This process has required regular reconsiderations and adjustments in the boundaries that define the identity and behavior of Mormons as a separate people, changes also in the nature of the "brand" that defines the identity of the church as an institution, and, changes, indeed, in the prerogatives of church leaders, both collectively and individually. Such changes occur across time at all these organizational levels, *largely independently of the intentions of individuals,* each of whom is likely acting in what he (or she) takes to be the values and interests of whatever roles he or she appropriates. Whatever the intentions of individual actors, it is the collective and cumulative effects of their actions, along with the reactions from elsewhere within their operating environments, that produce the changes—including unintended consequences—in the institutional church and its history.

Not that individual actors in organizations do not have intentions. Certainly, LDS Church leaders take seriously their roles as guardians of the flock and spokesmen for Deity, encouraging faithfulness and sometimes acting in opposition to whatever they believe undermines either their own authority or the faith of their followers—or, in other words, acting in their own organizational interests. Lay members of the church presumably share those interests, for the most part, but also have separate interests and values of their own, whether based on their occupations, their hobbies, or their artistic or intellectual orientations. Members sometimes create formal organizations and publications, independent of the church, to promote these other kinds of interests—for example, the J. Reuben Clark Law Society or the Association for Mormon Letters (AML). Of course, not all Mormon lawyers belong to the former, but there is a somewhat amorphous informal constituency that will share a community of interests and values with that organization, even if they are not members of it. The same can be said of the AML and the extended constituency of Mormon writers who might share its interests and values. Similarly, there is also an amorphous "community" or constituency of Mormon "intellectuals," as they are sometimes called, who share common interests in exploring ideas and issues in the history, doctrines, and culture of the Mormon people and their religion—often outside the auspices or control of the institutional church. Some, probably a minority, of such intellectuals belong to formal organizations such as the Mormon History Association and subscribe to *Dialogue, Sunstone,* or *BYU Studies* and attend conferences sponsored by such organizations. Some are professional scholars employed by academic institutions, including BYU, but most are not so employed. All would be included, though, in what I am here calling a constituency of Mormon "intellectuals."

Whether within formal organizations or in these amorphous constituencies, individuals are also quite capable of acting in their own *political* interests—that is, in ways that will *maximize their influence* among their own colleagues. No matter how much underlying collegial affection there might be, there are also individual differences in power and influence resulting from rank or position, from tenure or seniority (often age based), from family ties, from friendship ties, from ethnicity, from gender, from special social skills or charisma, or from some combination of these. On some of these criteria, certain personalities, within a given organization or its surrounding constituency, will prove more influential than others, and cliques will likely arise, sometimes seemingly on the basis of such vague orientations as "liberal" or "conservative." These are all standard political processes that will be found in the bureaucracies of large formal organizations, including the LDS Church, as well as in amorphous constituencies such as "Mormon intellectuals." Wherever these constituencies occur, the actors will always cite important values and myths in their shared experiences to justify and explain their actions and policies. Given this sociological perspective, I have never found it necessary or helpful to question the sincerity of any of the actors, ecclesiastical or otherwise, in order to understand their behavior.

As one who identifies with that amorphous constituency sometimes called "Mormon intellectuals," I have tried to understand the tension with church leaders in light of all the historical and sociological considerations outlined just above. In today's large, contemporary church (unlike the smaller, more familial one of the nineteenth and early twentieth centuries), I expect LDS hierarchs, and the bureaucrats who work under them, to operate pretty much like those in any other complex and centralized organization. When they feel that they have been publicly criticized, or that there has been a public challenge to their authority or teachings, they are likely to respond with public and private reproofs or, in aggravated cases, with some sort of discipline or reprisal. Such responses might sometimes seem excessive, especially to outside observers, and they often have unintended consequences. Yet they are responses structured, if not always required, by the roles that the priesthood leaders and bureaucrats occupy, sometimes moderated and sometimes exaggerated by individual characteristics, but to me essentially understandable. Of course, when a church leader thus speaks out, we are always entitled to consider time, place, circumstances, and the nature of his role in deciding whether he is speaking for the church or only for himself—or, indeed, whether he is "exercising unrighteous dominion," in Mormon parlance.

Similarly, when LDS intellectuals speak or write publicly about the significance of their research or analysis, they too are acting out certain roles. Often the role in question is very informal—perhaps nothing more than "a regular commentator" or even "gadfly." In other cases, the intellectual in question might be a frequently published author whose work has demonstrated a degree of expertise on given topics, or one who has gained academic or other special credentials. Even more formally, the intellectual might be an elected or appointed leader in an organization formed to promote intellectual or artistic work or activities. Examples here would again include the Mormon History Association, Dialogue (foundation and journal), *Sunstone,* and the AML. In all these cases, too, we are entitled to evaluate the time, place, circumstances, and nature of the intellectual's role in deciding whether she or he is speaking for a given organization, a certain informal constituency, or only for himself or herself. We are also well advised to consider whether the proffered observations and opinions reflect careful and balanced analysis, as contrasted with simply the interests and agenda of a certain intellectual or political constituency, or gratuitous intellectual arrogance—or even sheer spleen, all of which are constant hazards in the world of intellectuals.

During my decades among Mormon intellectuals, I have seen roles ill-performed both by church leaders (local or general) and by certain of my intellectual colleagues. Most, on either side, have been cases of excessive zeal in the service of good intentions. To me and some of my colleagues, who were targeted by church leaders or bureaucrats to give account of our scholarly work in Mormon studies, we often felt that we were seeing cases of "unrighteous dominion," especially when some of the local leaders aggravated the interviews with unjustified criticisms or threats of church discipline. Especially regrettable were cases of scholars with long records of faithful church service who saw their loyalty to the church seriously questioned; many of these, and their family members, could never again feel the same about the church. On the other hand, some of these scholars themselves have been responsible for publications or public statements that have been gratuitously offensive to church leaders and ordinary members, revealing on the author's part a tendency toward arrogance and a lack of appreciation for the roles and prerogatives of leaders.

To be sure, what gives offense from either side is often mainly in the eye of the beholder (or recipient), but the risk of a permanent and unnecessary rupture in long-standing relationships between leaders and intellectuals should always be taken carefully into account in any transaction. For me personally, the net result of all my encounters with church leaders has been to help me see them primarily as well-meaning and conscientious human vessels, with a strong fiduciary sense on behalf of the church, rather than as near-infallible spokesmen for Deity. My main feelings toward all of them collectively are respect and appreciation, not adulation or anything of the kind. Of course, among those who have been the most prominent and influential in the church during my lifetime, I have gained more appreciation for some than for others.

Concluding Apologia

How might I summarize this memoir in the metaphorical language of borders and passports, with which I began? I grew to maturity understanding myself as a loyal citizen of the kingdom of God in an intellectual territory that was expanding along with its population. As I negotiated my passport in other intellectual territories—during my mission, during my undergraduate studies in Japan, during my graduate studies at UC-Berkeley, and in my sojourns through the skeptical territories of academia—the passport received much handling, sometimes rather rough. Yet I never considered replacing it with citizenship or a passport from any other territory; I always regarded my original kingdom as my true home. With the passage of time, however, I noticed that each of my reentries into the kingdom seemed to become a little more difficult and complicated, partly because my home intellectual territory, once so expansive, had narrowed, and partly because the border guards seemed to have become less friendly to citizens who were bringing home alternative ideas from abroad. Indeed, ironic as it may seem, my passport sometimes received more wear and tear at the hands of the gatekeepers, questioning its authenticity in my own kingdom, than it did in my foreign sojourns. I see signs now, however, that our intellectual territory seems to be expanding once again and that my sojourns in the outside intellectual world no longer make my passport seem so suspect at home. I feel somewhat more welcome there now, in the new century, than I did a couple of decades ago.

I do not regard my intellectual life, or my academic career, as having been especially noteworthy except in one respect: they have developed in a dialectical relationship with a religious outlook that itself continues to evolve even now. I cannot say exactly what the relationship is between my religious and my other intellectual commitments. I can say only that the relationship is complicated and that I do not ever expect to be quite at peace with it. In 2010 I responded to a request from BYU colleagues to post a statement of my religious commitments on a website called *Mormon Scholars Testify*, to which I would refer readers who might be interested.[1] I offered that statement mainly in the traditional language of a believing Latter-day Saint, but with an acknowledgment of how little I could claim to believe with any certainty. In the LDS tradition, such certainty is ultimately dependent on the confirmation of the Holy Spirit. My level of certainty has waxed and waned many times during my lifetime, and frankly I am not sure whether such emotional confirmations as I have felt can be attributed to a supernatural source. The social scientist in me finds it difficult to distinguish spiritual emotions from any other kind. And yet . . . and yet . . . there have been times when my certainty has seemed sublime and deeply satisfying, a condition I find myself striving to recover from time to time.

My Epistemology: A Work in Progress

In writing for academic readers, however, I use the language and epistemology of social science, explicitly acknowledging that my religion is a *social construction* that I have embraced and adapted from my cultural and religious heritage to fulfill my own need for meaning. It is, in other words, a construction of reality that I have *chosen,* and such *certainty* as I feel about it is largely emotional in nature, or *intuitive,* rather than rational and intellectual. Each person must similarly construct the reality by which to live his or her life, and that construction will inevitably be based partly on rational and partly on emotional elements, none of which can really ever be certain, much as we may think and hope otherwise. Nor do I feel any embarrassment about taking this act of faith, for the embrace of unfalsifiable hope is among the most common human resorts. In science, an unfalsifiable premise might not be acceptable, since it cannot be tested empirically.[2] In real life, however, the unfalsifiable hope is often the source of motivation for many of the decisions and commitments that we make. We act regularly upon such hope when we decide to marry, or to have children, or to select a career, or to buy stock, or to make any other kind of investment for which the long-term outcome cannot be known in advance. We might take hope from the examples or the testimonies of others, but given the recurrent human failures with all such investments, we know that there is no advance certainty with any of them. Unfalsifiable hopes about the supernatural, or about the "next world," are not so different. Those of us who make such "religious investments," whatever may be our ultimate reasons for doing so, are acting on the most ordinary human impulses. Nor are the intellectually fashionable secular ideologies and theories any less unfalsifiable—one thinks here of Marxism or of Freudian psychology—but that does not prevent them from gaining new adherents year after year.[3]

Having arrived at that realization, I have become increasingly impatient over the years with theological claims and arguments, whether in the LDS religion or elsewhere. Obviously, my general intellectual outlook and my religious thinking have influenced each other throughout my lifetime, and that mutual influence is probably reflected in my published work, but it is perhaps easier for others than for me to articulate exactly how. One's own subjective thoughts and feelings are sometimes difficult to analyze objectively for oneself, lacking the benefit of external and impersonal detachment.

Conversely, of course, outside individuals are in no position to appreciate the depth or exact quality of another's subjective feelings. For that reason, I sometimes encounter LDS friends who seem to question my religious commitments, having found me lacking in the fervency of orthodox expression that they have come to expect of deeply converted Mormons. All I can do is protest that they are in no position to judge the depth of my religious faith. Yet I must confess that I am sometimes reciprocally guilty of the opposite—that is, a certain skepticism about the strength and durability of the emotionally based expressions of faith and testimony by others. I have known too many people across the years who, after tests of their faith, have experienced disillusionment at a depth roughly proportional to that of the emotional fervor of their earlier testimonies. Subjective feelings are by definition not really replicable from one person to another, so it is always hard to assess the authenticity of another person's claims based on his or her expressed feelings.

INTELLECT, EMOTION, AND DISENCHANTMENT

Indeed, I have found it difficult in general to cope with the gradual displacement of the rational by the emotional element in the LDS ecclesiastical culture during my lifetime. Compared to the church of my boyhood, and even of my missionary days, the current ecclesiastical culture seems to prefer tearful pulpit renditions of faith-promoting stories to the reasoned scriptural discourses of my youth. Today's pulpits rarely feature a stack of scriptures for easy resort by the speaker, but the box of tissues is nearly universal. That says it all. Missionaries no longer have a library of pamphlets to hand out on key doctrines with scriptural reasoning, but instead seek to cultivate in their investigators a certain *feeling* identified as the Holy Spirit. Even the majestic religious music of the classical masters, routinely sung by ward choirs in my youth, has been replaced, as a matter of policy, by simple but emotionally touching hymns and hymn arrangements—some of which, indeed, show the influence of soft "Christian rock." Thus, I no longer find it challenging or inspiring to sing in ward choirs.[4] I feel all this as a deep personal loss, but younger church members do not understand my feelings, since, of course, they have no memory of the Mormon world at midcentury or earlier, and thus no basis for comparison.

My relationship to the LDS Church as an institution (in contrast to the religious culture) has evolved in ways that are rational as well as emotional. I would summarize by saying that it has been one long process of disenchantment to which the changing ecclesiastical culture has contributed but not caused. Note that I use the term *disenchantment,* not *disillusionment.*[5] Perhaps I could just as well say *disenthrallment.* I mean only that for me, the institutional church and its leaders no longer embody an otherworldly *mystique,* as they did when I was a young man. I confess that sometimes I miss the sense of security and certainty about church leaders that I had as a youth, when I saw LDS prophets and other leaders as virtually infallible spokesmen for Deity. However, my personal experiences with them over the years, both direct and indirect, along with my academic study of the church, both as a historic movement and as a modern organization, have all combined to help me see the leaders at all levels as all too human and fallible. Whatever part Deity played in its origins, the church soon came to operate and develop a lot like other human institutions and organizations. Therefore, the behavior of the leadership, and the development of the organization, can be understood, in large part, through sociological analysis. Such analysis might not be all that is necessary for our understanding, given the potential role of many unmeasurable factors (including divine guidance), but the sociological view is *necessary,* if not always *sufficient.* It was my understanding of this reality that gradually brought my disenchantment.

I have seen cases among my more intellectual LDS friends and colleagues in which such *disenchantment* has been followed soon by *disillusionment,* and then by an urge to attack the church—or at least to attack certain leaders, doctrines, or policies in the church. My sociological understanding, however, has inclined me to respond differently. I am as offended as other intellectuals—or as other members generally—when I see policies and practices in the church that I consider harmful, or just plain wrong, either for the institution or for the membership, or, for that matter, for society more generally. Yet I have always understood the nature of the LDS ecclesiastical polity: I know that the church is not a democracy and does not claim to be one. It is a corporate, centralized bureaucracy, in which change usually occurs slowly, as certain vested interests among the apostles (including the presidency) have to be reconciled in the pursuit of *consensus*— a process not so different from that which occurs on other corporate boards of trustees, except for the expectation that the consensus finally reached represents the will of the Holy Spirit. My loyalty to this corporate institution is long and deep, but it is not unconditional. I recognize the legitimacy of the apostolic authority and the appropriate channels, formal and informal, for bringing about change. I remain free to leave the church, as I remain free to leave the nation itself, if ever I come to believe that either the leadership or the process of governance has become fundamentally corrupt. Meanwhile, I might criticize certain policies and conditions, but my loyalty does not, and should not, ever depend on having my own preferences prevail in any particular instance.

Neutralizing Disillusionment

With this perspective, my public comments and critiques on LDS matters over the years have perhaps made me seem more conservative than certain other LDS intellectuals in the "unsponsored sector," who take more strident postures, theologically, politically, or both. My perspective on the LDS Church does, in fact, have a certain congruence with my political perspective, which also has a generally conservative bent—as no doubt my readers will have realized by now. Yet American conservatism has always had a strong libertarian strand, with which I have increasingly identified as the years have passed.[6] All of this leads to a certain complexity in my attitude toward the LDS Church. On the one hand, I favor a certain amount of tradition, institutional integrity, and predictability in the church. Given the LDS tradition of continuous revelation, I also expect our prophets to "stand for something"[7] in this world of moral and political chaos, and thus occasionally to take public positions on issues that they consider critical to the well-being of the church or of civilization more generally, even if those positions are unpopular—and even if I think they are ill-advised.

On the other hand, I deeply resent any intimation of "unrighteous dominion" or abuse of power on the parts of church leaders, whether collective or individual, formal or informal, local or general. In my own personal experience, I have not seen such abuse very often, but from the firsthand accounts of other church members whom I respect, including especially scholars and intellectuals, I suspect that many instances of unrighteous dominion, in its various forms, did occur during the recent period of retrenchment in the church, especially throughout the two decades between the early 1970s and the early 1990s. I have alluded to some of those instances in a previous chapter.[8] At the same time, I have been critical of some of my colleagues for unnecessarily antagonizing church leaders. I have also learned to be skeptical about cases where only one side of a controversy is available, as in most cases of church discipline, and my usual policy is to withhold judgment, especially during public discussions of such cases. Yet I share the outrage of some whose cases I have come to know well enough to suspect real mistreatment by church leaders.

In my own case, I have resisted the occasional effort of a church leader (general or local) to intimidate me for my independent thinking or expression. My resistance is born of at least three factors: my libertarian streak—or, in LDS terms, a jealous regard for my own agency; the faith that unjust church discipline or other treatment would not be recognized by Deity; and, on a more pragmatic level, an absence of the slightest inclination to seek professional employment with the church, or, in other words, to allow my intellectual independence to be compromised by concerns over my livelihood. So it is that my attitude toward the church has that "complexity" that I mentioned above. This complexity has imposed a degree of personal anguish for me whenever the church has sought to achieve member conformity on public positions that have seemed wrong to me. I have always defended the *right* of the church to do so and have decried the sneers of critics who would punish the church for asserting that right—backed by its resources, if necessary. On the other hand, I have no control over what the leaders decide in such cases, and I expect them to take the responsibility for the outcomes of their decisions on a cost-benefit basis.

Thus, for example, on the race issue (as discussed in chapter 6), I always thought the church was lacking a doctrinal basis for withholding the priesthood from black people, and increasingly during the intervening years, I came to believe that such a policy was both unnecessary and badly mistaken. Yet I always insisted that the church had the right to maintain that policy within its own institutions, whatever consequences might result. On the campaign against the Equal Rights Amendment, during the 1970s and 1980s, I thought the church had every right to assert itself politically, but I deplored some of the tactics used, especially the surreptitious ones that I experienced in my stake at the time, and I thought the church's intervention was both unnecessary and counterproductive.[9] Yet I deeply sympathized (and still do) with the motivation of church leaders fearful of the unintended consequences of new national laws and policies for the family as an institution. I am pleased to see the greater autonomy and opportunity today for women as individuals, both in the nation and in the church—even without a national Equal Rights Amendment—but I doubt that anyone, inside or outside the church, would claim that the family as an institution is stronger today, either because of the feminist movement itself or because of the church's opposition to it.

Then, in the more recent campaigns against same-sex marriage, the church president and his colleagues once again raised a prophetic voice against state and national policy proposals that they believed would further undermine the integrity of the family as an institution, and they mobilized the political and economic resources that perhaps made a difference in the outcome of elections, at least in California. Once again, I supported their right to do this as spokesmen for the church, only one of several legitimate pressure groups over this issue in the nation. I should note that as a libertarian, if I had my way constitutionally, the state would have no role at all in defining or legitimating marriage per se; rather, each religion (or other institution) would have its own rules about marriage. The state could opt to back any number of different kinds of civil contracts, and it could impose obligations on the parties to those contracts, but these would not carry the implications of sanctity traditionally attached to the institution of marriage. Sanctity would be bestowed only according to the beliefs of the institution performing the marriage. On the other hand, the conservative in me would prefer to see us preserve the integrity of the marriage institution as understood, at least in Euro-American culture, for thousands of years. (And, since you ask, yes, I do, in fact, believe that Mormon polygamy also was and is subversive of the traditional marriage institution, so at least I am consistent here!)[10]

Yet, in most respects, such questions are moot at present, for in our nation, every state—and to some extent the federal government—has been empowered to regulate marriage by law, and as long as that is so, the LDS Church should have the same right as any other interest group to try to influence the law. The leaders might well have underestimated the adverse consequences for the church, including the "blowback" in public relations from its intervention in the campaigns against same-sex marriage. The issue also proved rather divisive among church members themselves, and I know from firsthand accounts that a great deal of pressure—including what I would consider "unrighteous dominion"—was applied in some stakes to get members to donate time and money to the Proposition 8 campaign in California and to silence the expression of opposition, or even of misgivings. I hasten to add that I am unaware of any such pressure in my own stake, but I know it did occur in some wards and stakes. It seems unlikely to me that the church leaders are unaware of the costs that have been exacted by any of the political campaigns that they have decided to enter in a significant way.[11] I believe that they have been acting on what might be called the "prophetic imperative" in the LDS tradition—that is, the obligation they feel for forceful words and actions at times of special peril. Otherwise, what are prophets for? Yet the cost-benefit assessment is something else again, and they will not be able to ignore that in either their spiritual or their corporate roles.

Faith, Hope, and Charity

So it is that I have continued to value my membership in the LDS Church and kingdom and to give it my voluntary loyalty, even when I have believed church policies to be in error in certain respects and even on several occasions when I have felt personally offended. Well into my ninth decade of life, I have felt no more inclination to leave the church than I have felt to leave the nation, though, as I said, I have become disenchanted or disenthralled.[12] Yet—and this is important—it has been precisely my *disenchantment* that has inoculated me against *disillusionment,* because of the concomitant reductions in my expectations. That is, an understanding of the church and its leaders as human and mortal has kept me from holding out unrealistic expectations for their performance. This has left me free to offer them my own support, loyalty, respect, and appreciation as fellow laborers in the vineyard, but not as contingent on an inerrant execution of their duties.

When I have been critical of church policies, practices, or leaders, this kind of emotional detachment has also left me free to express myself, in fair and respectful terms, without an accompanying anger that might have led to my departure from the church. During those occasions, described in chapter 9, when I was called in by leaders for interviews about my publications, I was able to arrive without indignation, because I had long since learned to see the church as an impersonal bureaucracy, with the local leaders simply doing their best to cope with unpleasant responsibilities sometimes imposed on them by their roles. I entered these interviews expecting to be treated fairly. I was prepared to hear and consider criticism, but I was never obsequious. I saw my relationship to the church as separate from my relationship with Deity, so that if I were to be unfairly treated or disciplined by church leaders, I could count on Deity eventually to make things right. In these respects, I guess one could say that I have always tried to look on the church and its leaders with faith, hope, and charity, even while keeping my expectations modest. I suspect they might say the same about me.

EDUCATION

BA, 1954: History and Asian studies, Sophia University, Tokyo, Japan
MA, 1957: History, Asian studies, and sociology, University of California, Berkeley
PhD, 1970: Sociology and history, University of California, Berkeley

ACADEMIC CAREER

1957–62: Teacher in social studies and English, secondary schools of Lafayette, California
1962–67: Instructor in the social sciences, Diablo Valley College, Pleasant Hill, California
1967–69: Associate professor of sociology, Utah State University, Logan
1969–99: Professor of sociology and religious studies (and earlier ranks), Washington State University, Pullman (emeritus since 1999)
1979, 1980, 1985 (summer terms): Visiting professor of sociology, University of Lethbridge, Alberta
1983 (summer term): Visiting professor of sociology, University of Calgary, Alberta
1985 (spring and fall terms): Visiting professor of sociology and religious studies, University of California, Santa Barbara
1989–92: Editor in chief, *Journal for the Scientific Study of Religion,* published by the Society for the Scientific Study of Religion
1999 (spring term): Visiting fellow in theology, College of St. Hild and St. Bede, Durham University, Durham, UK
2005–9: Visiting scholar and adjunct faculty, School of Religion, Claremont Graduate University, Claremont, California

PUBLICATIONS OF SCHOLARLY BOOKS AND ARTICLES

Monographs

Social Problems as Social Movements. Philadelphia: J. B. Lippincott, 1975.
The Angel and the Beehive: The Mormon Struggle with Assimilation. Urbana: University of Illinois Press, 1994.

All Abraham's Children: Changing Mormon Conceptions of Race and Lineage. Urbana: University of Illinois Press, 2003.

Shifting Borders and a Tattered Passport: Intellectual Journeys of a Mormon Academic. Salt Lake City: University of Utah Press, 2012.

Edited Collections

The New Left and the Old. Ann Arbor, MI: Society for the Psychological Study of Social Issues, 1971. Published in *Journal of Social Issues* 27, no. 1.

This Land of Promises: The Rise and Fall of Social Problems in America (with Julie C. Wolfe). Philadelphia: J. B. Lippincott, 1977.

Neither White nor Black: Mormon Scholars Confront the Race Issue in a Universal Church (coeditor with Lester E. Bush Jr. of our own collected essays). Salt Lake City: Signature Books, 1984.

The Sociological Study of Mormon Life. Storrs, CT: Religious Research Association, 1984. Published in *Review of Religious Research* 26, no. 1.

Mormons and Mormonism in the Twenty-First Century: Prospects and Issues. Salt Lake City: Dialogue Foundation, 1996. Published in *Dialogue: A Journal of Mormon Thought* 29, no. 1.

Articles
(By topic, in reverse chronological order)
Social Movements

"Research in Social Movements and in New Religious Movements: The Prospects for Convergence." In *Handbook of Cults and Sects in America,* edited by David G. Bromley and Jeffrey K. Hadden, vol. 3, pt. A, 127–51. Greenwich, CT: JAI Press, 1993.

"Beyond the Illusion of Social Problems Theory." In *Perspectives on Social Problems,* edited by Gale Miller and James A. Holstein, 1:19–39. Greenwich, CT: JAI Press, 1989.

"The Lost Promise of Reconciliation: New Left vs. Old Left." *Journal of Social Issues* 27, no. 1 (1971): 1–20.

"On Being Strangled by the Stars and Stripes: The New Left, the Old Left, and the Natural History of American Radical Movements." *Journal of Social Issues* 27, no. 1 (1971): 183–202.

"The Reluctant Right: Right-Wing Anti-communism among Libertarian University Students." *Sociology of Education* 40, no. 1 (1967): 39–54.

Sociology of Religion and Religious Movements

"Attaining a 'Sophisticated Maturity': A Brief History of the *Journal for the Scientific Study of Religion*'" (with Stacy A. Hammons). *Journal for the Scientific Study of Religion* 39, no. 4 (2000): 449–73.

"Apostasy and the Management of Spoiled Identity." In *The Politics of Apostasy: The Role of Apostates in the Transformation of Religious Movements,* edited by David G. Bromley, 51–73. New York: Praeger, 1998.

"Glock, Charles Young (1919–)." In *Encyclopedia of Religion and Society,* edited by William A. Swatos, 210–11. Walnut Creek, CA: Sage, Altamira Division, 1998.

"The Impact of Feminism and Religious Involvement on Sentiment toward God" (coauthor with Sherrie Steiner-Aeschliman). *Review of Religious Research* 37, no. 3 (1996): 248–59.

"Strictly Speaking . . . : Kelley's Quandary and the Vineyard Christian Fellowship" (coauthor with Robin D. Perrin). *Journal for the Scientific Study of Religion* 32, no. 2 (1993): 125–35.

"Saints and Seekers: Sources of Recruitment to the Vineyard Christian Fellowship" (coauthor with Robin D. Perrin). *Review of Religious Research* 33, no. 2 (1991): 97–111.

"The Great Protestant Puzzle: Retreat, Renewal, or Reshuffle?" (coauthor with Robin D. Perrin). Chap. 7 in *In Gods We Trust: New Patterns of Religious Pluralism in America,* edited by Thomas Robbins and Dick Anthony, 2nd ed. New Brunswick, NJ: Rutgers University Press, 1990.

"Conversion or Commitment? A Reassessment of the Snow and Machalek Approach to the Study of Conversion" (coauthor with Clifford Staples). *Journal for the Scientific Study of Religion* 26, no. 2 (1987): 133–47.

"Religion and the Right to Life: Correlates of Opposition to Abortion" (coauthor with Larry R. Petersen). *Sociological Analysis* 37, no. 3 (1976): 243–54.

"Les 'Jesus Freaks' et le retour à la respectabilité" [Prodigals as Preachers: The 'Jesus Freaks' and the Return to Respectability] (with Donald W. Petersen). *Social Compass* 21, no. 3 (1974): 283–301.

"Skidders and Their Servants: Variable Goals and Functions of the Skidroad 'Rescue Mission'" (coauthor with Reginald W. Bibby). *Journal for the Scientific Study of Religion* 13, no. 4 (1974): 421–36.

"The Cross and the Commune: A Sociological Interpretation of the 'Jesus Freaks'" (coauthor with Donald W. Petersen). In *Religion in Sociological Perspective: Essays in the Empirical Study of Religion,* edited by Charles Y. Glock, 261–79. Belmont, CA: Wadsworth, 1973.

"Dimensions of Religious Defection." *Review of Religious Research* 10, no. 3 (1969): 128–35.

Sociological and Other Studies of the Mormon Experience

"Authority and Dissent among the Latter-day Saints." In *The Oxford Handbook of Mormonism,* edited by Terryl L. Givens and Philip Barlow. Oxford: Oxford University Press, in press.

"Mormonism and Race." In *The Mormon World,* edited by Richard Sherlock and Carl Mosser. Routledge Worlds. New York: Routledge Books, in press.

"Living Indefinitely with Ambiguity." In *Why I Stay: The Challenges of Discipleship for Contemporary Mormons,* edited by Robert A. Rees, 39–44. Salt Lake City: Signature Books, 2011.

"Rethinking Retrenchment: Course Corrections in the Ongoing Campaign for Respectability." *Dialogue: A Journal of Mormon Thought* 44, no. 4 (2011). Hereinafter this journal will be cited simply as *Dialogue.*

"Mormonism and Race." In *Mormonism: A Historical Encyclopedia,* edited by W. Paul Reeve and Ardis E. Parshall. Santa Barbara, CA: ABC-Clio, 2010.

"The Mormon Church and Its Intellectuals: Traditions and Transitions." *Archivo Teologico Torinese* (Facolta Teologica dell'Italia Settentrionale, Sezione Parallela di Torino) 15, no. 2 (2009): 358–85.

"From Near Nation to World Religion." In *Revisiting O'Dea's "The Mormons": Persistent Themes and Contemporary Perspectives,* edited by Cardell Jacobson, Tim Heaton, and John Hoffman. Salt Lake City: University of Utah Press, 2008.

"Mormons and Race." In vol. 2 of *Encyclopedia of Race, Ethnicity, and Society,* edited by Richard T. Schaefer. Thousand Oaks, CA: Sage, 2008.

"The Peril and Promise of Social Prognosis: O'Dea and the Race Issue." In *Revisiting O'Dea's "The Mormons": Persistent Themes and Contemporary Perspectives,* edited by Cardell Jacobson, Tim Heaton, and John Hoffman. Salt Lake City: University of Utah Press, 2008.

"Seeking the 'Second Harvest'? Controlling the Costs of Latter-day Saint Membership in Europe." *Dialogue* 41, no. 4 (2008): 1–54, and in *International Journal of Mormon Studies* (online journal of the European Mormon Studies Association) 1, no. 1 (2008): 1–59.

"The Emergence of Mormon Studies in the Social Sciences." In *American Sociology of Religion: Histories,* edited by Anthony J. Blasi, 121–50. Leiden and Boston: Brill Academic Publishers, 2007.

"Children of Ham and Children of Abraham: The Construction and Deconstruction of Ethnic Identities in the Mormon Heartland." In *Race, Religion, Region: Landscapes of Encounter in the American West,* edited by Fay Botham and Sara M. Patterson, 115–24. Tucson: University of Arizona Press, 2006.

"Maturing and Enduring: *Dialogue* and Its Readers after Forty Years" (coauthor with Robert W. Reynolds and John D. Remy). *Dialogue* 39, no. 4 (2006): 82–106.

"Feelings, Faith, and Folkways: A Personal Essay on Mormon Popular Culture." In *Proving Contraries: A Collection of Writings in Honor of Eugene England,* edited by Robert A. Rees, 23–38. Salt Lake City: Signature Books, 2005.

"Casting Off the 'Curse of Cain': The Extent and Limits of Progress since 1978." In *Black and Mormon,* edited by Newell G. Bringhurst and Darron T. Smith, 82–115. Urbana: University of Illinois Press, 2004.

"Dispelling the Curse of Cain; or, How to Explain the Old Priesthood Ban without Looking Ridiculous." *Sunstone,* October 2004, 54–59.

"Flowers, Weeds, and Thistles: The State of Social Science Literature on the Mormons." In *Mormon History,* edited by Ronald W. Walker, David J. Whittaker, and James B. Allen, 153–97. Urbana: University of Illinois Press, 2001.

"Mormonism's Worldwide Aspirations and Its Changing Conceptions of Race and Lineage." *Dialogue* 34, nos. 3–4 (2001): 103–33.

"On 'Defense of Marriage': A Reply to Quinn." *Dialogue* 33, no. 3 (2000): 53–65.

"Topical Guide to Published Social Science Literature on the Mormons" (with Dynette I. Reynolds). In *Studies in Mormon History, 1830–1997,* edited by James B. Allen, Ronald W. Walker, and David J. Whittaker, 1057–1152. Urbana: University of Illinois Press, 2000.

"God of Gods: Some Social Consequences of Belief in God among the Mormons." Chap. 3 in *Social Consequences of Religious Belief,* edited by William R. Garrett. New York: Paragon House, 1999. Reissue of 1989 book of similar title.

"In Search of Ephraim: Traditional Mormon Conceptions of Lineage and Race." *Journal of Mormon History* 25, no. 1 (1999): 131–73.

"Smith, Joseph Jr. (1805–1844)." In *Encyclopedia of Religion and Society,* edited by William A. Swatos, 471. Walnut Creek, CA: Sage, Altamira Division, 1998.

"Young, Brigham (1801–1877)." In *Encyclopedia of Religion and Society,* edited by William A. Swatos, 569. Walnut Creek, CA: Sage, Altamira Division, 1998.

"Agency, Authority, and Ambiguity: The Elusive Boundaries of Required Obedience to Priesthood Leaders." *Sunstone,* March 1996, 20–31.

"Identity and Boundary Maintenance: International Prospects for Mormonism at the Dawn of the Twenty-First Century." In *Mormon Identities in Transition,* edited by Douglas J. Davies, 9–19. London and New York: Cassell, 1996.

"Mormonism in the Twenty-First Century: Marketing for Miracles." *Dialogue* 29, no. 1 (1996): 236–49.

"The Mormon Struggle with Assimilation and Identity: Trends and Developments since Midcentury." *Dialogue* 27, no. 1 (1994): 129–49.

"Refuge and Retrenchment: The Mormon Quest for Identity." In *Contemporary Mormonism: Social Science Perspectives,* edited by Marie Cornwall, Tim Heaton, and Lawrence Young, 24–42. Urbana: University of Illinois Press, 1994.

"Church, Sect, and Scripture: The Protestant Bible and Mormon Sectarian Retrenchment" (with Philip L. Barlow). *Sociological Analysis* (renamed *Sociology of Religion*) 52, no. 4 (1991): 397–414.

"Alternate Voices: The Calling and Its Implications." *Sunstone,* April 1990, 7–10.

"Mormons as Ethnics: Variable Historical and International Implications of an Appealing Concept." Chap. 16 in *The Mormon Presence in Canada,* edited by B. Y. Card, H. C. Northcott, J. E. Foster, Howard Palmer, and G. K. Jarvis. Edmonton: University of Alberta Press, 1990.

"Assimilation and Ambivalence: The Mormon Reaction to Americanization." *Dialogue* 22, no. 1 (1989): 30–67.

"Mormon Assimilation and Politics: Toward a Theory of Mormon Church Involvement in National U. S. Politics" (with M. Gerald Bradford). In *The Politics of Religion and Social Change,* edited by Anson D. Shupe and Jeffrey K. Hadden. Religion and the Political Order, vol. 2. New York: Paragon House, 1988.

"Culture, Charisma, and Change: Reflections on Mormon Temple Worship." *Dialogue* 20, no. 4 (1987): 77–83.

"The Unfettered Faithful: An Analysis of the *Dialogue* Subscribers Survey" (with John Tarjan and Martha Esplin). *Dialogue* 20, no. 1 (1987): 27–53.

"Comprehensive Bibliography of Social Science Literature on the Mormons" (with Jeffrey R. Franks). *Review of Religious Research* 26, no. 1 (1984): 73–115.

"Introduction: Conflict and Commitment in an Age of Civil Turmoil." In *Neither White nor Black: Mormon Scholars Confront the Race Issue in a Universal Church,* edited by Lester E. Bush Jr. and Armand L. Mauss, 1–8. Salt Lake City: Signature Books, 1984.

"Sociological Perspectives on the Mormon Subculture." *Annual Review of Sociology* 10 (1984): 437–60.

"The Angel and the Beehive: The Mormon Quest for Peculiarity and the Struggle with Secularization." *BYU Today* 37 (August 1983): 12–15.

"The Fading of the Pharoahs' Curse: The Decline and Fall of the Priesthood Ban against Blacks in the Mormon Church." *Dialogue* 14, no. 3 (1981): 10–45.

"White on Black among the Mormons: A Critique of White and White (with Response from White and White)." *Sociological Analysis* 42, no. 3 (1981): 277–78.

"Shall the Youth of Zion Falter? Mormon Youth and Sex—a Two-City Comparison." *Dialogue* 10, no. 2 (1976): 82–84.

"Moderation in All Things: Political and Social Outlooks of Modern Urban Mormons." *Dialogue* 7, no. 1 (1972): 57–69.

"Saints, Cities, and Secularism: Religious Attitudes and Behavior of Modern Urban Mormons." *Dialogue* 7, no. 2 (1972): 8–27.

"Mormon Semitism and Anti-Semitism." *Sociological Analysis* 29, no. 1 (1968): 11–27.

"Religious and Secular Factors in the Race Attitudes of Logan (Utah) Residents" (with Ella D. Lewis Douglas). *Proceedings of the Utah Academy of Sciences, Arts, and Letters* 45, no. 2 (1968): 467–88.

"Mormonism and the Negro: Faith, Folklore, and Civil Rights." *Dialogue* 2, no. 4 (1967): 19–39.

"Mormonism and Secular Attitudes toward Negroes." *Pacific Sociological Review* 9, no. 2 (1966): 91–99.

Deviant Behavior, Social Problems, and Alcohol Studies

"Social Problems" (with Valerie Jenness). In *Encyclopedia of Sociology,* edited by Edgar F. Borgatta and Rhonda J. V. Montgomery, 2759–66. 2nd ed. New York: Macmillan, 2000.

"Changing Perceptions of Peer Norms as a Drinking Reduction Program for College Students" (third author with Lisa Barnett, Jeanne Far, and John A. Miller). *Journal of Alcohol and Drug Education* 41, no. 2 (1996): 39–62.

"The 'Here's Looking at You' Series." In the *Encyclopedia of Drugs and Alcohol,* edited by Jerome H. Jaffe. New York: Macmillan, 1994.

"Social Problems." In *The Encyclopedia of Sociology,* edited by Edgar F. and Marie L. Borgatta, 1916–21. New York: Macmillan, 1992.

"Science, Social Movements, and Cynicism: Appreciating the Political Context of Sociological Research in Alcohol Studies." In *Alcohol: The Development of Sociological Perspectives on Use and Abuse,* edited by Paul M. Roman, 187–204. New Brunswick, NJ: Rutgers University Press, 1991.

"The Problematic Prospects for Prevention: Should Alcohol Education Programs Be Expected to Reduce Drinking by Youth?" (first author with Ronald H. Hopkins, Ralph A. Weisheit, and Kathleen A. Kearney). *Journal of Studies on Alcohol* 49, no. 1 (1988): 51–61.

"The School as a Setting for Primary Prevention" (fourth author with Ralph A. Weisheit, Ronald H. Hopkins, and Kathleen A. Kearney). *Journal of Alcohol and Drug Education* 30, no. 1 (1984): 27–35.

"Draughts and Drunks: The Contributions of Bars and Taverns to Excessive Drinking in America" (second author with Michael Nusbaumer and Dave Pearson). *Deviant Behavior* 3, no. 4 (1982): 329–58.

"Salvation and Survival on Skid Row: A Critical Comment." *Social Forces* 60, no. 3 (1982): 898–904.

"Substance Abuse, Non-conformity, and the Inability to Assign Problem Responsibility" (fourth author with Ralph A. Weisheit, Ronald H. Hopkins, and Kathleen A. Kearney). *Journal of Drug Issues* 12, no. 2 (1982): 72–81.

"Perils and Potshots in Prevention Research: A Comment" (with Ronald H. Hopkins, John Tarnai, and Kathleen A. Kearney). *Journal of Studies on Alcohol* (renamed *Journal of Alcohol and Drugs*) 41, no. 9 (1980): 959–62.

"Promises and Problems in American Society." In *This Land of Promises: The Rise and Fall of Social Problems in America,* edited by Armand L. Mauss and Julie C. Wolfe, 1–23. Philadelphia: J. B. Lippincott, 1977.

"Social Problems: A Review Essay." *Contemporary Sociology: A Journal of Reviews* 6, no. 5 (1977): 602–6.

"Waves from Watergate: Evidence Concerning the Impact of the Watergate Scandal upon Political Legitimacy and Social Control" (coauthor with Roger Dunham). *Pacific Sociological Review* 19, no. 4 (1976): 469–90.

"Anticipatory Socialization toward College as a Factor in Adolescent Marijuana Use." *Social Problems* 16, no. 3 (1969): 357–64.

Evaluation Research and Methodology

"Recommendations for Aspiring Authors" (at editor's request). *Sociology of Religion* 55, no. 4 (1994): 481–86.

"Comprehensive Evaluation of a Model Alcohol Education Curriculum" (second author with Ronald H. Hopkins, Kathleen A. Kearney, and Ralph A. Weisheit). *Journal of Studies on Alcohol* 49, no. 1 (1988): 38–50.

"Social Margin and Social Re-entry: Evaluation of a Rehabilitation Program for Skid Row Alcoholics" (coauthor with Ronald Fagan). *Journal of Studies on Alcohol* 47, no. 5 (1986): 413–25.

"Self-Generated Identification Codes for Anonymous Collection of Longitudinal Questionnaire Data" (third author with Kathleen A. Kearney, Ronald H. Hopkins, and Ralph A. Weisheit). *Public Opinion Quarterly* 48 (1984): 370–78.

"Sample Bias Resulting from a Requirement for Written Parental Consent" (third author with Kathleen A. Kearney, Ronald H. Hopkins, and Ralph A. Weisheit). *Public Opinion Quarterly* 47 (1983): 96–102.

"Reluctant Referrals: The Effectiveness of Legal Coercion in Outpatient Treatment for Problem Drinkers" (coauthor with Roger Dunham). *Journal of Drug Issues* 12, no. 1 (1982): 5–20.

"On Re-tooling the Teachers: An Evaluation of Teacher Training in Alcohol Education" (fourth author with John Tarnai, Nancy J. M. Fagan, Ronald H. Hopkins, and Monica Eichberger). *Journal of Alcohol and Drug Education* 27, no. 1 (1981): 34–46.

"Evaluation of Treatment Programs: Statistical Resolution of Selection Biases Using the Case of Problem Drinkers" (coauthor with Roger Dunham). *Evaluation Quarterly* (renamed *Evaluation Review*) 3, no. 3 (1979): 411–26.

"An Evaluation of Workshops Designed to Prepare Teachers in Alcohol Education" (fourth author with William L. Rankin, John Tarnai, Nancy J. M. Fagan, and Ronald H. Hopkins). *Journal of Alcohol and Drug Education* 23, no. 3 (1978): 1–13.

"Padding the Revolving Door: An Initial Assessment of the Uniform Alcoholism and Intoxication Treatment Act in Practice" (coauthor with Ronald Fagan). *Social Problems* 26, no. 2 (1978): 232–46.

Dozens of book reviews appearing since 1970 in a variety of scholarly journals, including the *American Sociological Review*, the *American Journal of Sociology*, *Contemporary Sociology*, the *Canadian Journal of Sociology*, the *Journal of Studies on Alcohol*, the *Journal for the Scientific Study of Religion*, *Sociological Analysis* (renamed *Sociology of Religion*), the *Review of Religious Research*, *Dialogue: A Journal of Mormon Thought*, the *Journal of Mormon History*, *BYU Studies*, *Sunstone*, and others.

ACTIVITIES IN PROFESSIONAL SOCIETIES

American Sociological Association

1980–82: Founding member, Executive Council, Section on Collective Behavior and Social Movements

Pacific Sociological Association

1981–84: Chair, Awards Committee
1984: Vice presidential nominee
1988: Presidential nominee

Society for the Study of Social Problems

1979–81: Chair, Drinking and Drugs Division
1983: Vice presidential nominee

Society for the Scientific Study of Religion

1985–88: Treasurer
1989–92: Editor of the *Journal for the Scientific Study of Religion*
1993: Presidential nominee

Association for the Sociology of Religion

1981–83 and 1993–96: Executive Council
1990: Presidential nominee

Religious Research Association

1986–88: Book review editor, *Review of Religious Research*
1997: Presidential nominee

Mormon Social Science Association

1977–79: Founding vice president
1979–81: President

Mormon History Association

1996–97: General chairman, Awards Committee

1996–99: Council member
1997–98: President
2007–10: Chair, Student Awards Subcommittee
2010–13: Chair, Leonard J. Arrington Award Subcommittee

Dialogue Foundation (publisher of Dialogue: A Journal of Mormon Thought)
1979–98: Editorial and advisory boards
1998–2008: Board of directors of the foundation (chair, 1999–2003)

AWARDS FOR SCHOLARSHIP

1973: Dialogue Silver Foundation Award for Best 1972 *Dialogue* Articles in Social Literature

1982: Invited lectureship, Charles Redd Center for Western Studies, BYU, Provo, Utah
1995: Mormon History Association's Chipman Award for Best First Book in Mormon Studies
1995: Mormon History Association's Grace F. Arrington Award for Historical Excellence
1997: Dialogue Foundation Award for Best 1996 *Dialogue* Article in Issues and Essays
2004: Mormon History Association's Award for Best Book Published in 2003

PROLOGUE

1. The epigraph is quoted by Elder Bruce C. Hafen (biographer of Maxwell) in "Elder Neal A. Maxwell: An Understanding Heart," *Ensign,* February 1982, 6. A fuller version of the same statement will be found in Neal A. Maxwell, *Deposition of a Disciple* (Salt Lake City: Deseret Book, 1976), 15.
2. Quoted by Elder Bruce C. Hafen in his "Second Annual Neal A. Maxwell Lecture," *Insights* 28, no. 3 (2008). His analogy at times seems to confuse a passport with a visa, but that is only a quibble for my rhetorical purposes here.

1. NOT A BORING LIFE

1. Any readers with further interest in my family history can consult various documents that I have archived with the Utah State Historical Society on the origins of the Linds and Westlunds, and on the Mauss family of Utah. Late though my Mauss family's arrival in Utah was, it was early enough for it to acquire the taint of post-Manifesto polygamy through its connections to the Kelsch and Wright lines. Family stories about all that have been somewhat suppressed, and are in any case peripheral, but not without drama.
2. For a study of the early LDS mission in Japan, see Reid L. Neilson, *Early Mormon Missionary Activities in Japan, 1901–1924* (Salt Lake City: University of Utah Press, 2010).
3. See the long interview of Vinal G. Mauss by Matthew K. Heiss under the James Moyle Oral History Program, September 1989, available at the LDS Church History Library.
4. On the National Federation of Music Clubs, see http://www.nfmc-music.org/.
5. Mother left me a collection of a dozen or so newspaper clippings, some or all of which came from the *Salt Lake Tribune* during the period 1921 through 1926. These clippings report on a variety of public musical events in which she was the principal performer as soprano soloist. Unfortunately, she did not provide dates or other citation information for most of these clippings, but at least one of them is from the *Salt Lake Tribune* and is dated January 2, 1921.
6. Douglas Stanley died in 1969. For information on his main book, see Douglas Stanley and J. P. Maxfield, *The Voice: Its Production and Reproduction* (New York: Pitman, 1933). For a more recent representation on YouTube of his work and student commentary, see http://www.youtube.com/watch?v=mEvX3VYay8g. In recalling these details (and several others) about Mother's vocal study and teaching during these years, I have

benefited by an exchange of correspondence with Claude Heater (back and forth, on April 1, 2012), who was a friend from my teen years and, more important, my mother's star student during the mid-1940s. After three months of study with Mother, Claude went on to study for several weeks each with both Robinson in Los Angeles and Stanley in New York City. He then started singing in Broadway musicals and eventually had a long and distinguished operatic career, much of it in Europe. See his website at http://www.claudeheater.com and his entry in *Wikipedia*. He agreed with me that Mother had a world-class soprano/contralto voice and could have had a very successful operatic career. I treasure an old recording I have of her singing Schubert's *The Almighty* with the Mormon Male Chorus in Oakland, California, in 1947.

7. For some of my career history that follows in the rest of this chapter, I was interviewed by William G. Hartley, then of the LDS Historical Department, under the auspices of the James Moyle Oral History Program. A bound transcript of those interviews, some 150 pages, dated December 1981, will be found in the LDS Church History Library. I would expect my recollections here to be consistent with those in that interview, but I did not consult that transcript in writing this chapter.

8. The young woman in question was June Butts. Years later she wrote of the origins and growth of the church in the Torrington area: June Lorraine Butts Zeiner, "History of the Goshen Ward of Connecticut," 1994. Elder Turner and I are acknowledged on page 3. This document remains in my personal files for the time being.

9. I was apparently even too humiliated to mention this experience in my missionary diary, though my memory of it remains vivid after all these years. I hasten to add that this experience was not typical of our several weeks' sojourn in Torrington. It was our one and only visit to a parsonage, and most of our time was spent in the tedium of "tracting."

10. New England was not the only mission in which this approach was tried in the years immediately after World War II, but it was the first and the "model" for the other attempts, none of which was as durable. See Jessie L. Embry, "Without Purse or Scrip," *Dialogue: A Journal of Mormon Thought* 29, no. 3 (1996): 77–94, starting especially on page 82. See also the early report of S. Dilworth Young to the *Deseret News*: "Successful New England 'Purse or Scrip' Experiment Reported," *Deseret News*, November 15, 1947, 8.

11. As indicated in a letter to me on Mission stationery, October 6, 1948, in my files. It should be noted here that Dilworth Young not only appreciated the arts but was a gifted poet and painter in his own right. See, for example, his collection of poems in *The Long Road from Vermont to Nauvoo* (Salt Lake City: Bookcraft, 1967).

12. The fiftieth anniversary reunion of all the missionaries who had served under S. Dilworth and Gladys Pratt Young was held in the Salt Lake Hilton Hotel on May 17, 1997. The Sunstone Symposium for 1999 was held at the Salt Palace Convention Center, July 14–17. Ardean's manuscript for the text and music appears on page 19 of the final program for that symposium.

13. My missionary diary, for March 21, 1949, briefly describes this experience. Though initially feeling encouraged about my prospects from this experience, I was sobered as I reflected on the enormity of the investment I would have to make in such a career.

Incidentally, Dwain Bracken, of Nephi, Utah, traveled to the mission field with me at the beginning. We remained in regular and friendly contact, and then, at the end of our mission, we drove back to Utah together in a new truck that his father had arranged for him to purchase in New York City. That trip home provided some adventures of its own.

14. I confess that in more recent years, I have somewhat wistfully thought back on my brief New York flirtation with an operatic career and wondered if I might, after all, have found some way to have achieved a successful and satisfying career—and what I might have sacrificed to get it. On balance, I have no regrets.

15. See the following brief article on these developments: R. Lanier Britsch, "The Blossoming of the Church in Japan," *Ensign,* October 1992, http://lds.orgnsign/1992/10/the-blossomi-of-the-church-in-japan?lang=eng. For a more thorough treatment, see the pair of articles by Shinji Takagi in the *Journal of Mormon History:* "The Eagle and the Scattered Flock: LDS Church Beginnings in Occupied Japan, 1945–49," 28, no. 2 (2002): 104–38, and "Riding on the Eagle's Wings: The Japanese Mission under American Occupation, 1948–52," 29, no. 1 (2003): 200–232. See also the above-cited interview of Vinal G. Mauss by Matthew K. Heiss.

16. At this point the mission was called the Far East Mission, indicating the extensive territory that my father was actually responsible for. A year or so later, the mission was divided into the Northern and the Southern Far East Missions.

17. Since I had reached the age of majority, I would have to cover the cost of my own travel.

18. Sophia University of Tokyo, Japan, had been in operation since about the beginning of the twentieth century. See http://en.wikipedia.org/wiki/Sophia_University.

19. Andrus was later (1955–62) called as mission president, the first one ever to fill that role with a fluency in the language on arrival.

20. My attempt at poetry was an irrepressible (if somewhat primitive) product of those heady romantic days. See my "Sonnet to a Japanese Spring," *Dialogue* 40, no. 3 (2007): 183.

21. Our sealing as a family with our first two children (and one in the "oven") took place in the Salt Lake Temple in April 1954.

22. Yet I must confess some retrospective embarrassment as I review correspondence in my files from my first year in Japan and see how naive, judgmental, and condescending I was about the Japanese and their religious traditions. I certainly became more expansive during the succeeding years there, but I never realized the true richness of the Japanese culture while I was living there. I guess I was just too young.

23. In those days, the stake mission was a major stake auxiliary with a presidency reporting directly to the stake president. In 1955 the Spokane Stake Mission had about fifty missionaries, men and women of all ages who did their work mainly in the evenings. The mission presidency was responsible for the training and preparation of these missionaries for service. A copy of the syllabus for the course I developed, complete with exercises and quizzes, will be found in my files as "Missionary School Training Curriculum," by Elder Armand L. Mauss of the Spokane Stake Mission Presidency (1955).

Stake missions have not existed for many years now. Local missionaries are called and supervised at the ward level these days.

24. This idea was fought out in the pages of the periodic faculty bulletin *DVC Forum*, among other places. See the DVC history by Don Mahan, Ruth Sutter, and Greg Tilles, *Diablo Valley College: The First Forty Years, 1949–1989* (Pleasant Hill, CA: privately published, 1990), especially part 2, chapters 4–5. My pedagogical and intellectual positions on all such issues are made clear on pages 80–88, 105, 115, and 149.

25. Actually, I often *combined* teaching and research by teaching *about* research, even with community college students. An example was the project on marijuana use, discussed briefly in chapter 2, which was touted by the DVC administration and received a lot of coverage in the local press (for example, "Use of Pot Plumbed," *Oakland Tribune*, July 12, 1967, Teenage section, 25)—all much to the chagrin of my faculty critics there.

26. See especially two articles by Gary James Bergera, "The Richard D. Poll and J. Kenneth Davies Cases: Politics and Religion at BYU during the Wilkinson Years," *Dialogue* 45, no. 1 (2012): 43–73; and "The 1966 BYU Student Spy Ring," *Utah Historical Quarterly* 79, no. 2 (2011): 164–88. A principal victim in the spy scandal was Professor Ray C. Hillam, who had served with me in the leadership of an LDS Servicemen's Branch in Japan during the 1950s.

27. During the previous academic year, I had had three articles published, or accepted for publication, in good academic journals.

28. This predicament was understandable in view of the reality that this introductory course had been taught in the past by an older part-time woman with a pleasant, maternal disposition and a reputation as an easy grader. In my first quarter as her successor, and through my regular quizzes, I did my best to disabuse the students of such expectations about the grading, but to no avail. The situation greatly improved in subsequent quarters as the word got around about the new regime.

29. The production took place under the auspices of the then new Radio and TV Center at USU, headed by Burrell Hansen, with a federal grant of some kind. Donigan, in a communication to me of September 8, 2009, believed that it was the only such TV "pilot project" attempted with any USU course during that general period. The resulting videotapes failed to survive the various stages of technological updating at either USU or WSU and never got as far as DVD preservation, as far as I know. However, I have personally retained audiotapes of these lectures with the sound effects.

30. I was able to take copies of this video course with me when I left Utah for Washington State, where I used them for my first two years there.

31. See J. R. Allred, "Higher Education Comes to Eastern Utah Outpost," *Logan (UT) Herald Journal*, May 25, 1969, 10.

32. At this time, the Department of Sociology, Social Work, and Anthropology was in the College of Business and Social Science (or similar name), but in the early 1970s this department was placed in the newly created College of Humanities, Arts, and Social Science.

33. This conclusion was drawn on the basis of correlating students' scores on entrance exams with their actual grade averages. I cannot recall now whether the entrance scores used were SATs or ACTs, supposedly predictors of college success. The logic

was that the stronger the correlation of these scores with actual grades, the more valid were the grades in a given course—or at least in a given department.

34. See Box 21 of my papers archived at the Utah State Historical Society for more information on these three student projects: http://history.utah.gov/FindAids/B01015/B1015ff.XML.

35. See Armand L. Mauss and Ella D. Lewis Douglas, "Religious and Secular Factors in the Race Attitudes of Logan (Utah) Residents," *Proceedings of the Utah Academy of Sciences, Arts, and Letters* 45, no. 2 (1968): 467–88.

36. One of these was a study of the intellectually "incestuous" nature of the USU faculty, the great majority of whom had their degrees from USU or other Utah institutions. Another was a survey of potential student interest in a black studies curriculum at USU. Both topics were eventually vetoed by the department chairman. The chairman suddenly removed me as a thesis adviser over these projects and turned the students over to other members of the faculty with whom they had to negotiate different thesis topics. Little did I know, at the time, that "Ross Wellington" (as I shall call him here), one of the semiretired, old-guard faculty, had quietly made the entirely false allegation to the chairman (and perhaps others) that I was having an affair with one of those students, a young woman named Sonya. I had forgotten these details until 2009, when Sonya, who had recently encountered an article about me on the Internet, initiated a brief e-mail exchange with me about the "old times" we had shared at USU. Sonya (surname withheld) to author, September 10, 2009.

37. I will note here that Arrington, during the years to come, intervened more than once in my career to give me encouragement and recognition in ways that will become clear in later chapters. He had much to do with my eventual decision to spend the last half of my own career in Mormon studies.

38. Such was the claim of department chairman Mel DeFleur in a letter circulated to the sociology faculty on September 9, 1969 ("National Rankings of WSU Sociologists"), copy in my files. In this letter, DeFleur cites a published article by D. D. Knudson and T. R. Vaughn, "Quality in Graduate Education," *American Sociologist* 4, no. 1 (1969): 12–18, and an unpublished (prepublication) paper by Norval D. Glenn and Wayne Villemez, "The Productivity of Sociologists at 45 American Universities" (Austin: University of Texas, 1969).

39. It is situated in southeastern Washington near the Idaho border and, indeed, eight miles from the University of Idaho in Moscow, which made possible some mutually beneficial collaboration between the two universities.

40. The ward was divided in two while we were there, and the student branch became a ward. Also, in 1974 a new LDS stake was created containing the wards and branches in both Pullman and Moscow. After we left Pullman, the stake itself was divided, but not geographically. One of the stakes there is a regular resident stake, but the other is a student stake. Both now carry the name of Moscow, not Pullman.

41. In 1987, as part of a project in the WSU Department of History to produce an institutional history of the university for its centennial in 1990, I was interviewed extensively about my career at WSU by J. Muriel Backus. The transcript of this interview will be

found in the WSU archives under the call number F 891/C46X/1988, and the MASC location is UA 202, Box 13.

42. Indeed, a few students admitted for graduate work were serious misfits, one of whom attempted to kill me in the belief that I had washed him out of graduate school. This resulted in a long prison sentence for him. My relationship with him is a long and sad story in its own right—and continues to the present day, though in diminishing degrees.

43. The politics of national agenda setting is itself an interesting study in social and political movements.

44. My first publication from this project (with Reginald W. Bibby) was "Skidders and Their Servants: Variable Goals and Functions of the Skidroad 'Rescue Mission,'" *Journal for the Scientific Study of Religion* 13, no. 4 (1974): 426–36.

45. See "Social Margin and Social Re-entry: Evaluation of a Rehabilitation Program for Skid Row Alcoholics" (with Ronald W. Fagan), *Journal of Studies on Alcohol* 47, no. 5 (1986): 413–25.

46. "Padding the Revolving Door: An Initial Assessment of the Uniform Alcoholism and Intoxication Treatment Act in Practice" (with Ronald W. Fagan), *Social Problems* 26, no. 2 (1978): 232–46.

47. A list of the dissertations that resulted from this "skid road" research will be found in my research note "Salvation and Survival on Skid Row: A Critical Comment," *Social Forces* 60, no. 3 (1982): 898–904.

48. Among the publications out of this project were two major articles evaluating the efficacy of the prevention program, both of which were jointly authored with our graduate students and appeared in the same 1988 issue of the *Journal of Studies on Alcohol:* "Comprehensive Evaluation of a Model Alcohol Education Curriculum," 49, no. 1: 38–50, and "The Problematic Prospects for Prevention: Should Alcohol Education Programs Be Expected to Reduce Drinking by Youth?" 49, no. 1: 56–61. I was second author of the first of these articles and first author of the second one. See also my critique of this alcohol education program in "The 'Here's Looking at You' Series," in *Encyclopedia of Drugs and Alcohol,* edited by Jerome H. Jaffe (New York: Macmillan, 1994).

49. I calculate that during my career at WSU, I (and my collaborators) brought in almost a million dollars for research in alcohol or drug abuse or both.

50. See the account included in David Weddle, "The Gang That Couldn't Smoke, Drink, or Shoot Straight: How the Mormon Mafia Turned the FBI's L.A. Office into the Laughingstock of Law Enforcement," *California,* October 1988, 66–73.

51. William Overend, "Miller Trial—'Intellectual Challenge,'" *Los Angeles Times,* October 7, 1985, Metro section, 1.

52. William Overend, "Jurors Have Testimony of Three Witnesses in Trial of Miller Reread," *Los Angeles Times,* October 25, 1985, Metro section, 2.

53. See "Transcript of Proceedings," *U.S. vs. Richard W. Miller,* No. CR 84-972 (A) DVK, October 1, 1985, 46–83 ("Armand Mauss—Defendant's Witness").

54. William Overend, "Mistrial Declared in Spy Case," *Los Angeles Times,* November 7, 1985, 1.

55. At the retrial in June 1986, I was not again called to testify. This time the result was the expected verdicts of guilty for the most serious charges, and Miller was given what amounted to a life sentence. This sentence, however, was overturned on the grounds that the judge had wrongly admitted polygraph evidence against Miller, and yet another trial in October 1990 again yielded a conviction, this time with a sentence of twenty years. That sentence, in turn, was later reduced by a federal judge to thirteen years, and with credit for good behavior, Miller was finally released in May 1994. At last report, he was living in northern Utah with his second wife.

56. These periodic meetings included not only religious lessons but also the evolving family policies and disciplinary procedures from time to time, as well as notes on developments in the "personal history" of each family member. These minutes have been transcribed and compiled in a document of some five hundred pages titled *Mauss Family Home Evenings: Two Decades of Minutes, Minutiae, and Mutual Refining* (privately published, 2011). Public access is available by request. Eventually, this document will be placed among my materials archived at the Utah State Historical Society.

2. Earning the Passport as a "Defender of the Faith"

1. I am using the term *intellectual* here to refer to one who lives largely in academia or in the world of ideas. By *apologist,* of course, I mean one devoted to defending an idea, a philosophy, or an institution.

2. Paul eventually finished his PhD in Asian studies and joined the faculty at BYU, where he spent his entire academic career as a China specialist, with interests also in China border societies such as Mongolia. Eventually, he headed the David M. Kennedy Center for International Studies at BYU and took assignments (with his wife) first as temple president and then as mission president in Taiwan.

3. Thomas A. Blakely, "The Swearing Elders: The First Generation of Modern Mormon Intellectuals," *Sunstone,* December 1985, 8–13.

4. Thomas F. O'Dea, *The Mormons* (Chicago: University of Chicago Press, 1957). A couple of later editions occurred in paperback. Juanita Brooks's *Mountain Meadows Massacre* had been out since 1950, but Arrington's *Great Basin Kingdom* was yet to appear.

5. Probably my most helpful guide in all of that was Professor Aloysius J. Miller, SJ, who was also director of the International Division of the university at that time (equivalent to a dean).

6. Talmage had died in 1933, of course, but his work still had great currency and carried great authority among the Mormon rank and file, as well as among the leaders.

7. Nibley's work on Mormon scriptures was rarely reviewed by non-Mormon peers, and in more recent years, even some of his Mormon peers, though generally appreciative, have found frequent flaws in his citations to sources. See, for example, Kent P. Jackson, foreword to *The Collected Works of Hugh Nibley: Old Testament and Related Studies* (Salt Lake City: Deseret Book, 1986); William J. Hamblin, "Time Vindicates Hugh Nibley," *FARMS Review of Books* (Maxwell Institute) 2, no. 1 (1990): 19–27; Eric Jay Olson, "The Extremes of Eclecticism," *Dialogue: A Journal of Mormon Thought* 15, no.

4 (1982): 123–25; and Douglas F. Salmon, "Parallelomania and the Study of Latter-day Saint Scripture: Confirmation, Coincidence, or Collective Unconscious," *Dialogue* 33, no. 2 (2000): 129–56.

8. Installments of his *Lehi in the Desert and the World of the Jaredites* appeared in successive months from January through October 1950 and from September 1951 through July 1952 (*Improvement Era* 53, 54, and 55), and the series was eventually published as a book by the same title (Salt Lake City: Bookcraft, 1952). Nibley's book *An Approach to the Book of Mormon* (Salt Lake City: Council of the Twelve Apostles of the LDS Church, 1957) was the Melchizedek priesthood manual for that year and was published again as a 1964 book by Bookcraft.

9. James L. Barker, *Apostasy from the Divine Church* (Salt Lake City: Council of the Twelve Apostles, 1952–54). The three were later combined into a single volume and published as a book (Salt Lake City: Bookcraft, 1960). Of course, this work had an explicitly apologetic purpose, but its portrayal of the transformation of the ancient church, even if somewhat selective, was based on responsible scholarship. These works by Nibley and Barker (along with other scholarly works in the church curriculum during this period) create a painful contrast to the intellectually thin pablum served up by church manuals in recent years.

10. *Cumorah—Where?* (his first book, seventy-three pages) was privately published (Press of Zion's Printing and Publishing, 1947). It was already getting some noteworthy comment around the church when I left on my mission to New England. During a mission conference, I remember asking President S. Dilworth Young what he thought about Ferguson's conjecture that the original Hill Cumorah was in Mesoamerica. Young answered crisply and definitively, "The Hill Cumorah is in New York State because that's where the Prophet said it was!" Not many general authorities of the church in those days were prepared to entertain new notions about the Book of Mormon or anything else in the traditional Mormon narrative.

11. The NWAF was incorporated under the laws of the state of California in 1952 but moved to BYU in 1961.

12. During these years, his main publications were *Ancient America and the Book of Mormon,* on which he was coauthor with the scholarly Milton R. Hunter (Oakland: Kolob Book, 1950), and *One Fold and One Shepherd* (Oakland: Books of California, 1958), 394 pages, revised and updated by Bruce W. Warren as *The Messiah in Ancient America* (Provo, UT: Book of Mormon Research Foundation, 1987).

13. Who had the benefit of a modern Egyptian lexicon, not available in Smith's time.

14. This story is told by Stan Larson in *Quest for the Gold Plates: Thomas Stuart Ferguson's Archaeological Search for the Book of Mormon* (Salt Lake City: Freethinker Press and Smith Research Associates, 1996), with a shorter version as an article: "The Odyssey of Thomas Stuart Ferguson," *Dialogue* 23, no. 1 (1990): 55–93. Larson's accounts have been criticized and supplemented in Daniel C. Peterson and Matthew Roper, "Ein Heldenleben? Thomas Stuart Ferguson as an Elias for Cultural Mormons," *FARMS Review of Books* (Maxwell Institute) 16, no. 1 (2004): 175–219.

15. "FARMS" is an acronym for the Foundation for Ancient Research and Mormon Studies, an originally private think tank that has since been subsumed as part of the Maxwell Institute for Religious Scholarship at BYU.

16. I think this stipend would amount to ten times that figure in today's dollars.

17. On this history, see, for example, my *The Angel and the Beehive: The Mormon Struggle with Assimilation* (Urbana: University of Illinois Press, 1994), 95–99.

18. As an example of this policy, see Russel B. Swensen, "Mormons at the University of Chicago Divinity School," *Dialogue* 7, no. 2 (1972): 37–46. A more recent and fuller treatment will be found in Casey Paul Griffiths, "Joseph F. Merrill and the 1930–1931 LDS Church Education Crisis," *BYU Studies* 49, no. 1 (2010): 93–134.

19. See J. Reuben Clark Jr., "The Charted Course of the Church in Education," *Address to Seminary and Institute Religion Teachers,* August 8, 1938, BYU Summer School in Aspen Grove, Utah (reprinted in various publications and excerpted in the September 2002 issue of the *Ensign*).

20. This historic retrenchment process and its implications constitute the general theme of my book *The Angel and the Beehive,* cited above.

21. I shall have more to say in a later chapter about my intellectual and educational debt to Glock.

22. This arrangement constituted a rather primitive and fragmentary research program that was eventually replaced, a decade or so later, by a much more elaborate and professional operation in central church headquarters called the "Research Information Division," of which I will have somewhat more to say later.

23. "Aaronic adults" referred mainly to adult males who had not retained sufficient church activity to have advanced to the higher or "Melchizedek" order of the lay priesthood. "Aaronic youth" referred to boys between the ages of twelve and nineteen who were advancing through the ranks of the "lesser" or Aaronic priesthood more or less on schedule.

24. My recollections of these developments are augmented by records deposited in my personal archives at the Utah State Historical Society (Catalogue No. B-1015). See especially Box 22, Folder 12, containing the minutes of this Bay Area committee for January 23, 1966. The proposal to do the survey is found in Folder 3, and a draft of the report of this committee, dated February 24, 1966, is found in Folder 4. The proposals in Folders 3 and 4 both contain references to the need for identifying different "dimensions of separation" among religiously inactive men. A refined and empirically validated typology of these different modes of "separation" was eventually published in my article "Dimensions of Religious Defection," *Review of Religious Research* 10, no. 3 (1969): 128–35. Copies of the actual survey instrument (questionnaire), some blank and some filled out, are found in Folders 6–11, and comments from respondents on postcards (mailed separately from the questionnaire) are found in Folder 13.

25. Immodest though it may seem, I think I can claim (with Wooley) to have invented the term *prospective elder,* still the official LDS term for men who have not yet received the Melchizedek priesthood. I am not sure when our recommendations were actually implemented, for there is often quite a long bureaucratic lag between such recommendations and actual implementation. Articles in the *Church News* indicate that in this case several years elapsed. See "Elders Presidency Magnified," CN Week Ending 29 January 1972, 3, which indicates that the idea was extensively pilot tested during the

previous year. See also David Croft, "Inactive and Prospective Elders Need to Be Needed," CN Week Ending 14 December 1974, 5.

26. See, for example, Robert Merton, *Social Theory and Social Structure* (New York: Free Press, 1968), 319–25. I actually first came across the idea in Merton's 1957 edition.

27. "Anticipatory Socialization toward College as a Factor in Adolescent Marijuana Use," *Social Problems* 16, no. 3 (1969): 357–64.

28. See Folder 12 in Box 22 of the above-cited archive at the USHS.

29. I had already been very much involved with Aaronic youth at the ward level, for my most substantial calling in the Walnut Creek Ward after release from the bishopric had been as head ("general secretary") of the ward's Aaronic priesthood program. In that capacity I prepared, at the request of the new bishopric, the *Handbook for Quorum Officers in the Aaronic Priesthood* (1964), which was used for several years by adult advisers to train the youthful presidencies to operate as much as possible without the intervention of the adult leaders. A copy of this "handbook" is in my personal papers.

30. Much to the irritation of staff members whose otherwise neat desks had usually been somewhat disturbed during our work sessions by the time they returned to work on Monday morning!

31. See Box 22, Folder 1, of my archive at the USHS for these documents.

32. See the instrument, an eleven-page questionnaire, and related documents, in Folder 2 of Box 22. The questionnaires were sent out during September 1968, along with a cover letter from the Presiding Bishopric, to the local bishops of seventy-seven different wards in various western states with instructions to see that all the boys in their charge filled out the questionnaire during a regular Sunday priesthood meeting, under circumstances protecting the boys' identities. Virtually all the questionnaires were returned anonymously, either in plain envelopes dropped in boxes as the boys left the meeting or mailed in later by those who were absent from the meeting. Thousands of questionnaires were received, key-punched, and analyzed through cross-tabulations of certain major variables of interest.

33. Interest in further analyses of our data apparently did not survive the change in Presiding Bishoprics that occurred in 1972, as Bishop John H. Vandenberg was replaced by Bishop Victor L. Brown. Finally, in 1999, I delivered my copies of the punched cards and printouts to Lynn Payne of the Research Information Division (by then the major research arm of the church) in hopes that RID might find a way to get the data translated into electronic form and analyze them for historical or "benchmark" data to be compared with later RID surveys of Mormon youth, but by then it seemed impossible to find a machine or other means for converting card punches into electronic impulses.

34. See, for example, Vaughn K. Featherstone (then bishopric counselor), "Adult leaders . . . now have to provide a sort of shadow leadership . . . [that is,] . . . heavier involvement in all youth activities by bishoprics and branch presidencies," in "News of the Church," *Ensign*, September 1973, 30. See also an important article by Bishop Victor L. Brown, "Our Youth: Modern Sons of Helaman," explaining how the Aaronic priesthood program would operate under the new "correlation" movement of the church: "The

youth, with shadow leadership from adults, will plan and execute their own programs and activities" (*Ensign,* January 1974, 108).

35. Actually, it was not only the PBO where ad hoc social research projects were carried on by staff. The same thing had been occurring in other church departments and auxiliaries, such as the Missionary Department and the Public Affairs Department. The decision to pull together all such research functions under a single agency like RID was a natural part of the "correlation" process under way more generally.

36. For a little additional information on this development, see my "Flowers, Weeds, and Thistles: The State of Social Science Literature on the Mormons," in *Mormon History,* edited by Ronald W. Walker, David J. Whittaker, and James B. Allen (Urbana: University of Illinois Press, 2001), 162–63. See also Marie Cornwall and Perry H. Cunningham, "Surveying Latter-day Saints: A Review of Methodological Issues," *Review of Religious Research* 31 (December 1989): 162–72.

37. I will elaborate a bit more in a later chapter on the episode surrounding Arrington, whose "New Mormon History" project, while he was church historian, led to his replacement and the transfer of his research unit to BYU, with instructions to avoid publications containing sensitive topics in LDS history. Accordingly, the RID staff has always made sure that no such topics have been aired outside their circle. For a list of a few RID-sponsored works that did enter the public domain in various forms, see my above-mentioned "Flowers, Weeds, and Thistles," 189n45.

38. Stark visited RID a couple of times in its early years and made a number of helpful observations and suggestions to its staff. His assessment, published in 1984: "I have consulted with many denominational research departments and have read countless reports of their results. . . . Yet [their] research efforts . . . shrink to insignificance when compared with the quality, scope, and sophistication of the work of the Mormon social research department." Rodney Stark, "The Rise of a New World Faith," *Review of Religious Research* 26, no. 1 (1984): 26.

39. In my files is a letter dated March 23, 1982, from Perry H. Cunningham, study director for this RID project, thanking me for my participation in the workshop on March 12.

40. This was my 1969 "Dimensions of Religious Defection" article, cited above.

41. See again my archive at USHS, Box 23, Folder 7, proposal for a "Religious Activity Study," February 1982, prepared by "Correlation Evaluation."

42. See, for example, Stan L. Albrecht and Howard M. Bahr, "Patterns of Religious Disaffiliation: A Study of Lifelong Mormons, Mormon Converts, and Former Mormons," *Journal for the Scientific Study of Religion* 22, no. 4 (1983): 366–79; and Bahr and Albrecht, "Strangers Once More: Patterns of Disaffiliation from Mormonism," *Journal for the Scientific Study of Religion* 28, no. 2 (1989): 180–200.

43. See Box 23, Folders 1–3, for copies of the staff's "The Conversion Process: A Prospectus for Research" and my critique thereof. In those days the RID staff still identified itself as "Correlation Evaluation" or simply as part of the "Correlation Department."

44. See "Proposal for a Longitudinal Study of Investigators and Converts," February 10, 1982, by the staff of "Correlation Evaluation," my USHS Archive, Box 23, Folder 6.

45. Some of the other BYU faculty participants in this study whom I can still remember would include Gordon Whiting, Department of Communications; Ken Hardy and

Kay Smith, Department of Psychology; and Marie Cornwall, Department of Sociology.

46. My participation in this project was formally solicited by Elder Carlos Asay, one of the general authorities over RID at this point, in a letter to me dated June 17, 1982, and this was followed by one dated July 7, 1982, from Dr. Gordon Whiting, a professor in the Department of Communications at BYU and one of the project directors, and finally by yet another letter from Elder Derek Cuthbert dated July 27, 1982, assigning me as a field director for data collection on this project in eastern Washington. As matters developed, I never actually assumed this role because of changes made later in the research strategy. For these letters and related materials, see Box 23, Folder 4, of my USHS archive.

47. For drafts of some of the questionnaires that were developed, see my USHS Archive, Box 23, Folder 17.

48. The dissertation was by Linda Ann Charney, "Religious Conversion: A Longitudinal Study," PhD diss., University of Utah, 1986. As a permanent member of the RID staff, she was a major participant in the study. As an example of a reference to the study in a church magazine, see M. Russell Ballard, "Members Are the Key," *Ensign,* September 2000, 8–10, where, however, the level of member-missionary participation is incorrectly given as 35 percent, rather than 3–5 percent.

49. In standard social science jargon, the term *myth* in this context carries no connotation of disrespect or debunking.

50. The reference here is to Moroni 10:4–6 in the Book of Mormon.

3. Touring Academia in Search of New Realities

1. Professor Woodbridge Bingham, and my other mentors in the Department of History at UC-Berkeley, had awarded me a master's degree in history and Asian studies (1957), but were unwilling for me to continue on for a doctorate in that department except as a full-time student. Such would have been impossible in my circumstances, namely, as the father of five (with more to come). Fortunately, the Department of Sociology there was relatively new, seeking additional graduate students, and willing to let me (and many others) continue doctoral studies on a part-time basis at my own expense. The change of disciplines proved comfortable for me, since my main interest in history had always been sociological anyway.

2. *Ideology and Utopia: An Introduction to the Sociology of Knowledge* was first published in Germany in 1929 and has appeared in many subsequent editions in German, English, and other languages. The one I read was a 1967 paperback in English (New York: Harcourt Harvest Book).

3. Peter L. Berger and Thomas Luckmann, *The Social Construction of Reality* (New York: Doubleday, 1966); Peter L. Berger, *Sacred Canopy* (New York: Doubleday, 1967).

4. Perhaps the best-known analysis of the cultural consequences of these and related developments was *The Culture of Narcissism* by social critic Christopher Lasch (New York: W. W. Norton, 1979).

5. In Michigan it was named Students for a Democratic Society and in Berkeley the Free

Speech Movement. The two do not seem to have been related except in similar ideological perspectives.

6. Candid disclosure: I cannot claim much high-mindedness myself in this assessment of the protesting students. Having spent two years on a Mormon mission and four years in the military, and never having benefited by a scholarship, a fellowship, or a student assistantship, I took almost a personal offense at the time and money wasted by most of those twenty-year-old world reformers.

7. "The New Left and the Old," *Journal of Social Issues* 27, no. 1 (1971). In a letter to me dated January 26, 1972, Smelser asked my assistance in getting a half-dozen copies of this issue of the journal to place on special reserve in the library for use by students in his course on collective behavior. In addition to my introductory and concluding essays, this volume contained contributions from the following young scholars, several of whom later gained considerable national visibility with distinguished careers in sociology: Gilbert Abcarian, Michael T. Aiken, N. J. (Jay) Demerath, James M. Elden, Henry Finney, Richard Flacks, Nathan Hakman, Arthur Liebman, Gerald Marwell, Gary T. Marx, David R. Schweitzer, and Michael Useem.

8. See especially my concluding essay in that collection, "On Being Strangled by the Stars and Stripes."

9. For example, Richard Fuller and Richard Myers, "The Natural History of a Social Problem," *American Sociological Review* 6 (December 1941): 320–28; and Herbert Blumer, "Social Problems as Collective Behavior," *Social Problems* 18 (Winter 1971): 298–306.

10. See my argument to this effect in "Research in Social Movements and in New Religious Movements: The Prospects for Convergence," in *Handbook of Cults and Sects in America,* edited by David G. Bromley and Jeffrey K. Hadden, vol. 3, pt. A, 127–51 (Greenwich, CT: JAI Press, 1993).

11. These redefinitions have taken place in the medical establishment as well as elsewhere and produced by the usual political processes, even among medical professionals. See, for example, Wilbur J. Scott, "PTSD in *DSM-III:* A Case Study in the Politics of Diagnosis and Disease," *Social Problems* 37, no. 3 (1990): 294–310. The redefinition of homosexuality is discussed on page 304. See also Ronald Bayer, *Homosexuality and American Psychiatry: The Politics of Diagnosis* (New York: Basic Books, 1981).

12. See, for example, Eric L. Jensen and Jurg Gerber, "State Efforts to Construct a Social Problem: The 1986 War on Drugs in Canada," *Canadian Journal of Sociology* 18, no. 4 (1986); Eric L. Jensen, "Politics and White Collar Crime: Explaining Government Intervention in the Savings and Loan Scandal," *Critical Criminology* 7, no. 2 (1986); and Jurg Gerber and Eric L. Jensen, eds., *Drug War, American Style: The Internationalization of Failed Policy and Its Alternatives* (New York: Garland, 2001).

13. Bruce D. Johnson, untitled review of *Social Problems as Social Movements, Contemporary Sociology* 6, no. 6 (1977): 743–44, where the only criticism seemed to be that my book had not considered other theoretical perspectives on social problems besides my own. Actually, my book did, in fact, argue that all other contemporary theories were flawed because they were "objectivist" in nature and therefore ignored the social and political (re)construction of reality as itself the main origin of "social problems."

14. I was called upon to defend my thesis in the summer 1984 issue of the *Newsletter of the SSSP Theory Section* (see my article there, "The Myth of Social Problems Theory"). See also subsequent examples of varied discussions of my theoretical position in, for example, Joseph W. Schneider, "Social Problems Theory: The Constructionist View," *Annual Review of Sociology* 11 (1985): 209–29; Stephen Hilgartner and Charles L. Bosk, "The Rise and Fall of Social Problems," *American Journal of Sociology* 94, no. 1 (1988): 53–78, esp. 70–72; A. L. Mauss, "Beyond the Illusion of Social Problems Theory," in *Perspectives on Social Problems,* edited by Gale Miller and James A. Holstein, 1:19–39 (Greenwich, CT: JAI Press, 1989) (followed by a counter from Ronald J. Troyer); and Erich Goode and Nachman Ben-Yehuda, "Moral Panics, Culture, Politics, and Social Construction," *Annual Review of Sociology* 20 (1994): 149–71. See also references to my conceptualization in *Wikibooks,* "Introduction to Sociology/Social Movements," and in *Wikipedia,* "Social Movements." By Googling "Mauss, movements, problems," one will also encounter other references to this theoretical discussion.

15. John I. Kitsuse and Malcolm Spector, "Toward a Sociology of Social Problems: Social Conditions, Value Judgments, and Social Problems," *Social Problems* 20 (Spring 1973): 407–19; and then Spector and Kitsuse, "Social Problems: A Reformulation," *Social Problems* 21 (Fall 1973): 2–10. See Richard Fuller and Richard Myers, "The Natural History of a Social Problem," *American Sociological Review* 6 (December 1941): 320–28.

16. Malcolm Spector and John I. Kitsuse, *Constructing Social Problems* (Menlo Park, CA: Cummings, 1977) (and later editions).

17. See review of the Spector and Kitsuse book by Leonard Gordon (untitled in "Theory" section), *Contemporary Sociology* 8, no. 4 (1979): 641–42, but also the memorial tribute to the work of Kitsuse by Joel I. Best, "Constructing the Sociology of Social Problems: Spector and Kitsuse Twenty-Five Years Later," *Sociological Forum* 17, no. 4 (2002): 699–706.

18. Letters in my personal files: Blumer to A. Richard Heffron, October 29, 1976; and Gusfield to Heffron, November 2, 1976. These letters had been solicited by Heffron, editor at the Higher Education Division of the Lippincott Company, at my suggestion, but neither of these scholars knew me well enough to feel any obligation to exaggerate their assessments of my book.

19. Letters in my files from Professors John D. McCarthy (July 10, 1984) and Louis A. Zurcher (July 13, 1984) provide important examples of appreciative statements by my contemporaries.

20. Since my book was out of print in only a few years, there were scores of these requests during the 1980s and 1990s for permission to reprint portions of it, mainly from the first two chapters laying out my basic theory. I did not keep track systematically of these requests but was informed of them periodically by the publisher, who sent me modest royalties for the reprints. (For these purposes, incidentally, the "publisher" became HarperCollins, which bought out the sociology list from my original publisher, Lippincott.) These requests for reprints continued for at least twenty years after the book was originally published. They included, for example, requests for reprints in

the following textbooks: Jon M. Shepard, *Sociology,* 2nd ed. (West Publishing, 1984), 626–27 in chap. 18; Steven Vago, *Social Change,* 2nd ed. (Prentice-Hall, 1989), fig. 2-1; Richard Schaefer and Robert Lamm, *Sociology,* 3rd ed. (McGraw-Hill, 1989), 64–66; John D. Hewitt, *Delinquency in Society* (McGraw-Hill, 1990), 66; and many others. See also the monograph Valerie Jenness and Kendal Broad, *Hate Crimes: New Social Movements and the Politics of Violence* (New Brunswick, NJ: Aldine Transaction, 1997, reprinted in 2005 and 2009), 1–10, esp. 7.

21. P. A. Paul-Shaheen and Harry Perlstadt, "Class Action Suits and Social Change: The Organization and Impact of the Hill-Burton Cases," *Indiana Law Journal* 57 (1982): 385–423, esp. 387, 388, 398; and G. Bammer and B. Martin, "Sociopolitical Aspects of RSI" (musculoskeletal problems), in *Work with Display Units 92: Selected Proceedings of the Third International Scientific Conference on Work with Display Units, Berlin, Germany, September 1–4, 1992,* edited by Holger Luczak et al., 532–36 (Amsterdam: Elsevier Science Publishers, 1993).

22. Founded in 1952, the SSSP has defined its mission primarily as research on issues of *applied* sociology, rather than theoretical sociology (the presumed focus of the larger American Sociological Association, founded in the 1930s). Operationally, this means that the SSSP has favored research on whatever "social problems" have risen to the top of the national agenda (for example, poverty, racism, gender differences, alcohol and drug abuse), giving its membership and discourse a decidedly meliorist—and leftist— political orientation. Yet its journal, *Social Problems,* ranks near the top of prestigious journals in the discipline of sociology.

23. He cites my book in his second paragraph. See *SSSP Newsletter* 16, no. 3 (1985): 4, and *SSSP Call for Papers and Program Participation, 36th Annual Meeting,* August 26–29, 1986.

24. See the final paragraph, p. 6, in Gusfield's announcement of the theme for the forth-coming 1989 annual conference in the 1988 program booklet, *Society for the Study of Social Problems, 38th Annual Meeting,* August 21–23, 1988. These publications would presumably be available in the archives of the SSSP. Copies are in my files.

25. The invitation came from Professor Robert Emerson (sociology, UCLA), then acting for the SSSP as chairman of its Editorial and Publications Committee. Emerson's letter to me, dated May 15, 1995, was quite extensive in urging on me an affirmative response.

26. Armand L. Mauss, "Social Problems," in *Encyclopedia of Sociology,* edited by Edgar F. and Marie L. Borgatta, 1st ed. (New York: Macmillan, 1992); and "Social Problems," in *Encyclopedia of Sociology,* edited by Edgar F. Borgatta and Rhonda J. V. Montgomery, 2759–66, 2nd ed. (New York: Macmillan, 2000); the revised version of this article for the second edition was coauthored with Valerie Jenness.

4. REVISITING THE MORMONS:
NEW PERSPECTIVES ENCOUNTER NARROWER BOUNDARIES

1. I have often reflected on the eventual implications of this decision to change disci-plines. Had I been able to remain somehow in Asian studies, I would almost certainly

never have found the time or opportunity later to enter Mormon studies as a specialization. My CV would look very different by now.

2. My teaching load then at Diablo Valley College in Pleasant Hill, California, where I taught social science for the next five years, was fifteen semester hours, and I usually taught six more hours each week in the evenings at other colleges nearby. Of course, these times refer only to hours *in the classroom,* not to all the hours in an academic workweek.

3. In 2001 Glock self-published a long autobiography of his own (326 pages, single-spaced): Charles Y. Glock, *A Life Fully Lived: An Autobiography*, a copy of which is in my files. In this autobiography, Glock devotes considerable attention to his own graduate education, acknowledging in particular his debt to his graduate mentor, Paul F. Lazarsfeld, in the Bureau of Applied Social Research at Columbia University. (On Lazarsfeld, see the entry about him in *Wikipedia.*)

4. Besides a few books on anti-Semitism, Glock and Stark had collaborated on a study of "American piety," a three-volume study of the sources, nature, and consequences of religious commitment. Only the first of these projected volumes was ever published (Rodney Stark and Charles Y. Glock, *American Piety* [Berkeley and Los Angeles: University of California Press, 1968]). In conversations with the authors, I have learned that each of them has a somewhat different explanation for why the second and third volumes never came to fruition.

5. Rodney Stark and William Sims Bainbridge, *The Future of Religion: Secularization, Revival, and Cult Formation* (Berkeley and Los Angeles: University of California Press, 1985). A complementary volume by the same authors, setting forth the formal theory on which their empirical work was based, was *A Theory of Religion* (1987; reprint, New Brunswick, NJ: Rutgers University Press, 1996).

6. For example, Roger Finke and Rodney Stark, *The Churching of America, 1776–1990: Winners and Losers in Our Religious Economy* (New Brunswick, NJ: Rutgers University Press, 1992).

7. See R. Stephen Warner, "Work in Progress toward a New Paradigm for the Sociological Study of Religion in the United States," *American Journal of Sociology* 98, no. 5 (1993): 1044–93.

8. Stark has outlined the history of his connections with various collaborators in the eventual development of the theory for which he is now so well known. See his "Bringing Theory Back In," chap. 1 in Lawrence A. Young, *Rational Choice Theory and Religion* (New York: Routledge, 1997).

9. Rodney Stark, *The Rise of Christianity: A Sociologist Reconsiders History* (Princeton, NJ: Princeton University Press, 1996).

10. Rodney Stark, "Extracting Social Scientific Models from Mormon History," *Journal of Mormon History* 25, no. 1 (1999): 174–94.

11. See Stark's extensive personal web page, http://www.rodneystark.com, and his entry in *Wikipedia.*

12. Armand L. Mauss, "Rodney Stark: The Berkeley Years," *Journal for the Scientific Study of Religion* 29, no. 3 (1990): 362–66.

13. See the acknowledgments in his Tanner Lecture (cited above in the *Journal of Mor-*

mon History, 180), and in his book (edited by Reid Neilson), *The Rise of Mormonism* (New York: Columbia University Press, 2005), x, 1, 24, 33, and 130 (though not by name on 130).

14. Acknowledged in Rodney Stark and Roger Finke, introduction to *Acts of Faith: Explaining the Human Side of Religion* (Berkeley and Los Angeles: University of California Press, 2000), 17, 287–88.

15. And I will immodestly claim to have one of the more substantial publication records among those whom Stark names in the "Berkeley Circle."

16. What I call "empirical regularities" here might be called "laws of nature" in the natural sciences, but in the social sciences that would be claiming too much, given the kinds of data and methods accessible to us.

17. I use the "Age of Aquarius" here as it is sometimes used in popular culture, namely, in reference "the heyday of the hippy and New Age movements of the 1960s and 1970s." http://en.wikipedia.org/wiki/Age_of_Aquarius.

18. I confess that I lean toward the analysis in *The Culture of Narcissism* by social critic Christopher Lasch (see chap. 3, n. 4).

19. For examples of "liberal" Mormons expressing themselves on the race issue and civil rights during the 1950s and 1960s, see the articles by David Brewer, L. H. Kirkpatrick, Sterling McMurrin, and Lowry Nelson in the bibliography to L. E. Bush and A. L. Mauss, *Neither White nor Black: Mormon Scholars Confront the Race Issue in a Universal Church* (Salt Lake City: Signature Books, 1984). In that same book, see my opening essay, "Introduction: Conflict and Commitment in an Age of Civil Turmoil," for a review of how conservative was general American (including LDS) opinion on racial issues in this era. It is noteworthy that in 1957 Thomas F. O'Dea, in his book *The Mormons,* did not even mention the race issue among his potential sources of tension in the LDS Church.

20. We kept minutes for these meetings, now preserved in a document cited at the end of chapter 1.

21. "Priesthood leaders" would be the equivalent of the professional clergy in most religious denominations.

22. Even in 1967, I was promising readers of my first *Dialogue* article a dissertation titled "Mormonism and Urbanism," and I used that phrase still in a 1972 article to describe the set of survey data I had collected and already used by then for my completed dissertation on the race issue. I was clearly loath to abandon the broader topic. I had been intrigued by the doctoral dissertation of G. Byron Done, "The Participation of the Latter-day Saints in the Community Life of Los Angeles" (University of Southern California, 1939) and was hoping to replicate and extend his analysis with more systematic data. When the fall 1968 issue of *Dialogue* was devoted to the theme "Mormons in the Secular City," that was an additional incentive for me to make my own contribution to this topic, which I also did in the pages of *Dialogue* a few years later (see below).

23. I learned later that his doctorate was an EdD from BYU and that his dissertation had been the creation of a curriculum in religious instruction for American Indian church members.

24. Elder Packer had recently replaced Truman Madsen as mission president, and I have sometimes wondered in retrospect if my encounter on this occasion would have been more productive a year earlier with Madsen, who had served his mission under Dilworth Young during the same period as I did and had since earned a PhD in philosophy from Harvard.

25. These two articles in *Dialogue: A Journal of Mormon Thought* were "Moderation in All Things: Political and Social Outlooks of Modern Urban Mormons," 7, no. 1 (1972): 57–69; and "Saints, Cities, and Secularism: Religious Attitudes and Behavior of Modern Urban Mormons," 7, no. 2 (1972): 8–27. I chose to publish them in *Dialogue,* rather than in a mainstream social science journal, because they were mainly descriptive in nature, rather than analytical, and likely to be of far greater interest to Mormon readers than to others.

26. I did succeed in getting out one more brief article in the 1970s based on my survey data from Utah and California Mormons: "Shall the Youth of Zion Falter? Mormon Youth and Sex—a Two-City Comparison," *Dialogue* 10, no. 2 (1976): 82–84. I published almost nothing else on Mormons for another decade.

27. As explained in chapter 1, my research interests in alcohol abuse and other so-called social problems were motivated less by any personal altruism about what I might contribute to public policy issues than by pragmatic considerations, such as the political relevance attached to such problems on the national agenda, which translated into the *research grants* that my university expected all faculty to seek. To make such research relevant to my own scholarly interests, I found ways to relate it to my work on *social movements,* given that the national interest in various kinds of deviant behavior frequently expressed itself in strong social movements to change or institute laws controlling such behavior, as I explained in chapter 3. See my *Social Problems as Social Movements* (Philadelphia: Lippincott, 1976) and my assessment in particular of the national campaigns and interest groups around alcohol use and abuse in "Science, Social Movements, and Cynicism: Appreciating the Political Context of Sociological Research in Alcohol Studies," in *Alcohol: The Development of Sociological Perspectives on Use and Abuse,* edited by Paul M. Roman, 187–204 (New Brunswick, NJ: Rutgers University Press).

28. A perusal of my publication record during the 1970s and 1980s reveals articles on such topics as the new "Jesus Freaks" movement, skid road rescue missions, the conversion process, and religious opposition to abortion, most of them as a coauthor with my students.

29. The Mormon Social Science Association, which has never had as many as even a hundred active members, was founded originally as the Society for the Sociological Study of Mormon Life, a name that seemed to become increasingly cumbersome until it was changed in 1995. This organization actually grew out of a predecessor founded in 1974 by John Sorenson at BYU as the Committee on Mormon Society and Culture. See the MSSA website, http://www.mormonsocialscience.org.

30. We had in common also a friendship with Charles Y. Glock, who had been a mentor for Hammond at Columbia before becoming my mentor at Berkeley.

31. "ISKCON" stands for International Society for Krishna Consciousness.

32. The broader theoretical significance of this widespread phenomenon is the major underlying rationale for *The Future of Religion,* by Stark and Bainbridge, cited earlier in this chapter.

33. Thus, the designation "NRMs" tended to be preferred by sociologists and anthropologists, rather than the more popular but inherently pejorative term *cults.*

34. In my own case, I turned down many invitations to attend Unification (Moonie)-sponsored conferences in Europe and Asia, partly for fear of at least the appearance of intellectual compromise, given such lavish treatment, but also just because I did not want to devote that much time to conferences not central to my academic interests. During the 1980s, I did, however, attend short Unification-sponsored conferences in Quebec City, in San Diego, and at the Unification Theological Seminary in Barrytown, New York, as well as the two-day conference sponsored by Scientology in Los Angeles, where I encountered Phil Hammond, as explained above. From one of those conferences, I believe the one in Quebec City, a collection of papers was published that included one of my own: "God of Gods: Some Social Consequences of Belief in God among the Mormons," chapter 3 in *Social Consequences of Belief in God: The Influence of Religious Belief on the Individual and Societal Levels of Social Reality,* edited by William R. Garrett (New York: Paragon House, 1989), later published also in paperback.

35. An enlightening and representative confrontation between these two "camps" of social scientists in the study of new religious movements, cults, "brainwashing," and so on will be found in Benjamin Zablocki and Thomas Robbins, eds., *Misunderstanding Cults: Searching for Objectivity in a Controversial Field* (Toronto: University of Toronto Press, 2001).

36. I served twice on the Council of the ASR, once as treasurer of the SSSR (1985–88) and as editor of the *Journal for the Scientific Study of Religion* (the major national journal in religion for social scientists) for a four-year term, 1989–92. In 1990 I was nominated as a candidate for the office of ASR president, in 1993 for SSSR president, and finally in 1997 for RRA president, but I was not successful in the actual elections for any of the three.

37. The creation and meaning of this logo are explained at the beginning of my very first issue of that journal in "From the Editor" (28, no. 1 [1989]), and the logo has remained, in some form, on the covers of each succeeding issue through several editors (at least as of 2012).

38. Rodney Stark, active in the same scholarly circles, once observed, "I'm quite aware how easy it is for one person's faith to be another's heresy. Indeed, that was the basis of my early work on religion and anti-Semitism. Nevertheless, one does not really expect to find hard-line particularism among scholars of religion. Thus I continue to be astonished at the extent to which colleagues who would *never* utter anti-Semitic, anti-Catholic, or even anti-Moslem remarks, unself-consciously and self-righteously condemn Mormons." Stark, "The Rise of a New World Faith," *Review of Religious Research* 26, no. 1 (1984): 18–27. The quotation is found at the conclusion of this article, on p. 27.

39. Among my most cherished experiences occurred toward the end of my father's life,

when he privately conceded that I had been right all along in my rejection of the popular Mormon justifications for the race policy and that he was glad I had persisted with the race issue.

40. A fuller treatment of President Young's wariness about *Dialogue* is provided by Devery Anderson in "A History of *Dialogue,* Part One: The Early Years, 1965–1971," *Dialogue* 32, no. 2 (1999): 36–37.

41. I have observed that even geography might be as influential as strict religious conformity in qualifying one for leadership positions in the LDS Church. I recall clearly the cases of two men in my Pullman ward, both faculty members at Washington State University, who were not very active in the church and certainly not abstinent from alcohol and tobacco, but who were both called as bishops (and later even in stake presidencies) shortly after moving to new locations in the southeastern United States, where the need for experienced leadership was much greater than in the Far West. I have no doubt, of course, that their appointments were preceded by a full (if sudden) return to orthodox observances.

42. The first issue of *Sunstone* was dated winter 1975 but had been in preparation for a year or more before that.

43. The *Wikipedia* article on *Sunstone* lists its first editor and publisher as Scott Kenney, 1975–78, with Allen Roberts and Peggy Fletcher jointly as publishers and editors, 1978–80, and then Peggy herself as editor (without a separate publisher), 1980–86.

44. I believe that my first article in *Sunstone* was "Alternate Voices: The Calling and Its Implications," *Sunstone* 14, no. 2 (1990): 7–10.

45. This grand old hotel has since been converted to LDS Church uses as the Joseph Smith Building.

46. Over the years, the annual summer symposium in Salt Lake City has spun off smaller regional counterparts in various locations and seasons of the year. Perhaps the most enduring have been spring Sunstone Symposia in California (alternating between North and South) and in Seattle (usually October). Others have occurred from time to time in Chicago and other Midwest venues, plus Boston, Washington, DC, and a few other places.

47. A more or less complete set of the monthly program announcements for our TSSG will be found among my personal papers (later to be deposited in the archives of the Utah State Historical Society).

48. I should note with gratitude that during two visits we made back to Pullman (2003 and 2008), some of our friends there called together the survivors of the TSSG for gatherings where I was invited to promote my new book (2003) and to update them on my latest academic activities (2008). Robert Wilson and Terry Day were, I believe, chiefly responsible for organizing these gatherings for our follow-up visits.

49. Schwendiman revealed this and related matters to me much later in a private interview that I had with him on March 18, 1991, long after he himself had become a regular participant in the TSSG. Interview notes are in my personal files.

50. In the case of this "Roberts," and of his colleague "Spicer," mentioned below, their surnames have been slightly altered in order to accord them a degree of privacy, since both are still alive but have been living elsewhere in the West for many years.

51. The two-page "Proposal for a New Institute Course (Graduate Level)" was submitted by Armand Mauss and Billy Ward, September 16, 1975. Copy in my personal files.

52. Yet Spicer, as branch president, aided and abetted by a superstitious wife, imposed on his young flock an unusually severe doctrine of "sacrifice" that inculcated guilt and increased the already difficult burdens on these college students—or so it was reported to me by my son and other students in this branch. I have long had the opinion that among CES teachers, there is a strong tendency to regard themselves as the chief arbiters of true orthodoxy, while, ironically, they are actually the most prolific purveyors of dubious doctrine in the church!

53. One of the most enduring of these informal groups during this period was (and still is) the Miller-Eccles Study Group, which emerged in the late 1970s and now has two large chapters in Southern California. I was not among the founders of this group, but I was one of its earliest (and recurrent) speakers whenever I happened to be visiting Southern California from Washington. Now actually residents of Southern California, my wife, Ruth, and I are on the board of directors. See the website, http://www.millereccles.org.

54. Dallin H. Oaks, "Alternate Voices," *Ensign,* May 1989, 27–30. During the 1980s and 1990s, I was a speaker more than once at two different groups of this kind in western Washington, both of which were under regular surveillance and pressure from unsympathetic local church leaders, even though the group members were faithful and active in the church. One of these was led by Patrick McKenzie and another by Devery Anderson. See, for example, the account in Lavina Fielding Anderson, "The LDS Intellectual Community and Church Leadership: A Contemporary Chronology," *Dialogue* 26, no. 1 (1993): 34, 57.

5. TRAVELING BACK AND FORTH WITH A NEW THEORY ABOUT MORMON HISTORY

1. Actually, Arrington had recently stepped down as founding director of the Redd Center and had been succeeded as director by Thomas G. Alexander, who actually issued the invitation to me. Both were obviously instrumental in the decision to invite me, and I do not mean to slight the part played by Alexander, who has also been a good friend for many years.

2. The B. H. Roberts Society, rather short-lived, was another of the private study groups mentioned in the previous chapter. Founded around 1980 by Arrington and some associates, it met periodically in Salt Lake City to hear lectures and book reviews. The gatherings were not small: almost two hundred people turned out for my lecture. However, the organization did not survive the increasing pressure from church leaders during that period to discourage such forums that were not held under church auspices.

3. Arrington is well known for having sponsored and supported the careers and accomplishments of his younger colleagues in Mormon studies, both formally and informally, across many years. Besides his sponsorship of my lecture at the Redd Center and at the B. H. Roberts Society, he was also responsible for my later honor (1995) in

receiving the Mormon History Association's Grace Fort Arrington Award for Historical Excellence.

4. See my "The Angel and the Beehive: The Mormon Quest for Peculiarity and Struggle with Secularization," *BYU Today* 37 (August 1983): 12–15, for the version that survived editorial cuts.

5. My derivative articles were "Assimilation and Ambivalence: The Mormon Reaction to Americanization," *Dialogue* 22, no. 1 (1989): 20–67; and "The Mormon Struggle with Assimilation and Identity: Trends and Developments since Midcentury," *Dialogue* 27, no. 1 (1994): 129–49. The eventual book was *The Angel and the Beehive: The Mormon Struggle with Assimilation* (see chap. 2, n. 17).

6. Warner, "Work in Progress" (see chap. 4, n. 7).

7. My memory on this matter has been augmented somewhat by a review of the main citations to the work of others in my publications during the 1970s and 1980s.

8. Wilbert E. Moore, *Social Change* (Englewood Cliffs, NJ: Prentice-Hall, 1963).

9. Charles Y. Glock and Rodney Stark, *Religion and Society in Tension* (Chicago: Rand-McNally, 1965).

10. Where Sorokin's work is concerned, I am thinking mainly of his multivolume *Social and Cultural Dynamics: A Study of Change in Major Systems of Art, Truth, Ethics, Law, and Social Relationships* (Boston: Porter Sargent, 1957). His massive macrocosmic sweep of history was quite controversial, and one need not embrace the entire historical interpretation to appreciate his analysis of recurrent tension as a dynamic element in history.

11. See my "On Being Strangled by the Stars and Stripes: The New Left, the Old Left, and the Natural History of American Radical Movements," *Journal of Social Issues* 27, no. 1 (1971): 183–202; and *Social Problems as Social Movements,* chaps. 1–2 (see chap. 4, n. 27).

12. Eventually, I employed the term *optimum tension* to refer to the condition that any radical religion (or other movement) would have to seek in order to maintain its existence and identity. A cognate concept (but not the exact term) is prominently discussed at the end of an article about the Mormons by Laurence Iannaccone and Carrie Miles, "Dealing with Social Change: The Mormon Church's Response to Change in Women's Roles," *Social Forces* 68 (1990): 1231–50, esp. 1247. A couple of my colleagues have wondered if I "borrowed" the concept or the term or both from this 1990 article. In fact, this concept had become part of my analytical repertory through my work during the 1970s on social movements (cited above), and I had already used *both the concept and the term* in my 1989 *Dialogue* article (also cited above), pp. 31 and 61, and again in my article (with Barlow), written in 1990 and published the next year, as "Church, Sect, and Scripture: The Protestant Bible and Mormon Sectarian Retrenchment," *Sociological Analysis* 52, no. 4 (1991): 411. In any case, both the concept and the term are obviously quite natural derivatives from the wider academic literature on social change, as well as from the general theory of religion put forth by Stark and Bainbridge in the 1980s, all mentioned above and cited in earlier articles both by Iannaccone and by me.

13. As described by R. Stephen Warner in the article "Work in Progress."

14. Stark and Bainbridge, *Future of Religion* (see chap. 4, n. 5). This collection of empirical studies was followed by a second volume setting forth the more abstract, formal theory on which they were all based. See *A Theory of Religion* (see chap. 4, n. 5).

15. Stark and Bainbridge, *Future of Religion,* chap. 2.

16. Ibid., 125. See also chaps. 5 and 7 more generally.

17. Ibid., 454 and chap. 19 more generally.

18. Rosabeth Moss Kanter, *Commitment and Community: Communes and Utopias in Sociological Perspective* (Cambridge, MA: Harvard University Press, 1972); Dean M. Kelley, *Why Conservative Churches Are Growing* (New York: Harper and Row, 1972). Kelley was an official with the National Council of Churches rather than an academic sociologist.

19. Finke and Stark, *Churching of America* (see chap. 4, n. 6), which was based upon Finke's 1984 doctoral dissertation.

20. I would judge that Iannaccone's most direct and explicit contributions to this new paradigm can be found in his "A Formal Model of Church and Sect," *American Journal of Sociology* (Supplement) 94 (1988): S241–68; "Sacrifice and Stigma: Reducing Free-Riding in Cults, Communes, and Other Collectives," *Journal of Political Economy* 100, no. 2 (1992): 271–92; and "Why Strict Churches Are Strong," *American Journal of Sociology* 99 (1994): 1180–1211. To be sure, though, his contributions to this general theoretical direction are numerous.

21. Benton Johnson's observation that such a reversal was "conceivable" will be found in "On Church and Sect," *American Sociological Review* 28, no. 4 (1963): 543. Kelley's ideas about strictness are found in his 1972 book cited above.

22. Stark and Finke, *Acts of Faith,* 259 (emphasis added) (see chap. 4, n. 14).

23. I know that Stark had a copy of my 1994 book, for I gave it to him personally, though I do not know if he ever read it. He also told me by telephone during 1991 that he had been a reviewer for my manuscript (with Barlow) that was eventually published that year as "Church, Sect, and Scripture," in which I highlighted the Mormon case as an explicit example of a "reversal" on the conventional sect-church continuum (400–404). Stark's coauthor Finke, furthermore, certainly did read my book, for he gave it a fair review in *BYU Studies* 35, no. 2 (1995): 190–94, while explicitly noting its relevance to church-sect theory.

24. At the Albuquerque SSSR conference, *The Angel and the Beehive* actually shared the focus of a well-attended "author meets critics" session with *Contemporary Mormonism,* an edited collection published the same year by the same publisher. The panel of critics for these two books consisted of James T. Duke, Steven Epperson, and non-Mormon scholars Roger Finke and Patrick McNamara.

25. Among the most favorable reviews of the book were those in the *Journal for the Scientific Study of Religion* (Landres, December 1995) and in *Sunstone* (White, June 1996). The reviews in the *Sociology of Religion* (Brinkerhoff, Spring 1997), the *Journal of Mormon History* (Alexander, Spring 1995), *BYU Studies* (Finke, 35, no. 2 [1995]), and *Contemporary Sociology* (Richardson, May 1996) were also, on balance, quite favorable. Several reviews occurred in other journals as well. *Dialogue* failed to review this book (and many others deserving of review), since its book review editor fell seriously ill

during this period and eventually died. Regarding my MHA prize, note that I say *a* best book prize, rather than *the* best book prize. MHA does give an award each year for *the* best single book of the previous year, but it also gives awards for the "best biography," "best documentary," and so on. In my case, the award was for the "best first book," since it was the first one I had personally published in the field of Mormon history (the earlier one with Lester Bush had been simply a collection of our previous articles). My later 2003 book, however, was awarded *the* best book prize by the MHA.

26. Richard D. Ouellette, "Mormon Studies," *Religious Studies Review* 25, no. 2 (1999): 161–69.

27. Matthew Bowman, *The Mormon People: The Making of an American Faith* (New York: Random House, 2012), 290.

28. See article by Carrie Moore, "S. L. Conference Will Focus on LDS Sociology," *Deseret News,* October 31–November 1, 2002, B3.

29. By their very nature, of course, sessions of this kind in academia tend to be "lovefests" in which the person and work being honored receive exaggerated praise for their contributions to certain fields of study, to professional societies, or to the careers of younger scholars. Even while making due allowance for all that, I was pleasantly surprised at the assessments of my work and career on that occasion by two of the panelists in particular, who left with me written copies of their remarks. Both had clearly done considerable bibliographical research and had consulted third-party reviews of my work as a basis for their own thoughtful assessments. See Charles Y. Glock (my esteemed mentor), "Contributions of Armand L. Mauss to Mormon and Other Religious Studies"; and Gary Shepherd (distinguished senior colleague), "The Contributions of Armand Mauss to Mormon Studies." Both essays are in my personal files for the time being.

30. For example, Jan Shipps made such a recommendation to me some years ago, though she herself has been hard at work on her own long-awaited treatment of recent Mormon history.

31. The article appears in the winter 2011 issue of *Dialogue:* "Rethinking Retrenchment: Course Corrections in the Ongoing Campaign for Respectability," a shorter version of which I presented at "Mormonism in Cultural Context: A Symposium in Honor of Richard Lyman Bushman" (on the occasion of his eightieth birthday), Springville Museum of Art, Springville, UT, June 18, 2011.

32. A partial "rollback" of retrenchment is, in fact, the main thesis of the above-mentioned *Dialogue* article.

33. Especially, the unexpected "blowback" the church has received for its intervention in political campaigns over same-sex marriage has taken its toll on the already problematic public image of the church, and the church has recently moderated its earlier public condemnations of the homosexual way of life. See, for example, http://beta-newsroom. lds.org/article/church-mormon-responds-to-human-rights-campaign-petition-same-sex-attraction. See also articles by Peggy Fletcher Stack in the *Salt Lake Tribune* during the fall of 2010: "Mormons Divided on Apostle's Speech on Gays," October 6; and "Official Mormon 'Handbook' Made Public," November 30.

34. This preoccupation of LDS Public Affairs is discussed, among other matters, by Ryan

T. Cragun and Michael Nielsen in "Fighting over 'Mormon': Media Coverage of the FLDS and LDS Churches," *Dialogue* 42, no. 1 (2009): 65–104.

35. At the invitation of an Italian Catholic scholar, I have set these relationships between LDS leaders and intellectuals in a longer historical context. See "The Mormon Church and Its Intellectuals: Traditions and Transitions," *Archivo Teologico Torinese* 15, no. 2 (2009): 358–85, submitted at the request of the Dr. Ermis Segatti of the board of editors. This biannual periodical is published by the Facolta Teologica dell'Italia Settentrionale in Torino.

36. All these recent developments are detailed in my 2011 *Dialogue* article mentioned above. In response to that article, LDS publicist Neylan McBaine concurred in my general assertion about the importance of public relations in the contemporary church, while also offering a very important corrective to my limited focus specifically on the role of the church's Public Affairs Department. From McBaine's personal and professional experience with the LDS Missionary Department and other agencies, it is clear that the new public outreach and image-making efforts of the LDS Church permeate much of the bureaucracy, and not just the professionals at Public Affairs. See her informative letter to the editor, "Insider's Vantage Point," *Dialogue,* 45, 1 (2012): xxiii–xxv.

37. Though still relatively small as a proportion of LDS membership, especially in the United States, LDS African Americans are increasingly influential, as exemplified in the activities sponsored by the Genesis Group, http://www.ldsgenesisgroup.org, not only in Utah, but also in California and elsewhere.

38. This watering-down process was helpfully reviewed on an ex-Mormon website, Green Oasis, http://www.blakeclan.org/jon/greenoasis/2009/08/11/the-new-gospel-principles/index.html.

39. This important insight, expressed in somewhat different ways, will be found in a paper by Ryan T. Cragun, "Moving Targets: Mormon Retrenchment toward the 'New Mainstream,'" presented at the 2008 annual conference of the Society for the Scientific Study of Religion in Louisville, Kentucky. All this is very theoretical, of course, and leaves aside the hard empirical question of how we might measure degrees of assimilation or retrenchment.

40. The last several paragraphs here have been taken in large part from my essay "Mormonism in the New Century," which appeared in the Patheos collection *The Future of Mormonism* featured during the week of August 9, 2010. See http://www.patheos.com/Topics/Future-of-World-Religions/Mormonism.html.

6. Recurrent Visits with the Race Issue

1. "Reflections on a Lifetime with the Race Issue," *Sunstone,* March 2003, 28–30. After writing this article, I learned by contacting the sister in question that her sealing did not occur by special arrangement at the time of her marriage, as I had erroneously remembered, but only in 1973, when the general race policy was already on the verge of being overturned in preparation for the building of an LDS temple in Brazil.

2. See the "guest post" of June 11, 2010, which I was asked to write for the *By Common*

Consent blog on the thirty-second anniversary of the priesthood policy change, plus the dozens of follow-up comments by the blog readers. http://bycommonconsent. com/2010/06/11/reflections-on-another-anniversary/.

3. O'Dea, *The Mormons* (see chap. 2, n. 4). See also the discussion of this irony in my "The Peril and Promise of Social Prognosis: O'Dea and the Race Issue," in *Revisiting O'Dea's "The Mormons": Persistent Themes and Contemporary Perspectives,* edited by Cardell Jacobson, Tim Heaton, and John Hoffman (Salt Lake City: University of Utah Press, 2008).

4. "Mormonism and the Negro: Faith, Folklore, and Civil Rights," *Dialogue: A Journal of Mormon Thought* 2, no. 4 (1967): 19–39. My evidence that racism among Mormons was not unusually high (compared to non-Mormon averages) had been good enough for publication in the peer-reviewed *Pacific Sociological Review* 9, no. 2 (1966): 91–99, as "Mormonism and Secular Attitudes toward Negroes."

5. Kinsolving is a sometime Episcopal priest, sometime radio talk show host, sometime White House reporter, and all-around gadfly. See accounts of his career at http:// en.wikipedia.org/wiki/Lester_Kinsolving, http://leskinsolving.com/bio.html, and http://www.citypaper.com/news/story.asp?id=11089.

6. A clipping of the announcement is in my possession. Given the organizational retrenchment, centralization, and correlation that took place in LDS ecclesiastical culture after this time, it might seem odd to modern church members that an individual like myself, who neither sought nor received authorization from any church leader, would feel free to attempt to represent the church on this occasion (and would, in fact, receive an advance announcement in a local church newspaper). This incident bespeaks the freedom that ordinary LDS scholars and other members still felt in the 1960s to speak and write publicly on topics that were somewhat controversial in the church, usually with total impunity.

7. Also, I have the entire transcript of this broadcast on reel-to-reel tape, which might still be audible with the right equipment.

8. The main product resulting from this research grant was Charles Y. Glock and Rodney Stark, *Christian Beliefs and Anti-Semitism* (New York: Harper, 1966).

9. The questionnaires had gone alternately to the male and the female heads of households and to all single adults. Nonresponse bias was estimated from consultations with ward clerks about demographic traits of nonrespondents.

10. "Mormonism and Secular Attitudes toward Negroes."

11. I received the first such assessment from Professor Hanan Selvin in praise of a graduate seminar paper I had written for him in 1962. At that time, however, I simply took his statement as a gracious and encouraging comment, not as an actual recommendation that I should submit the paper for publication. Accordingly, that paper simply languished in my files until I realized from the above-mentioned experience with the PSR that my work really could be published. Eventually, I submitted the Selvin seminar paper too, and it became my second academic publication: "The Reluctant Right: Right-Wing Anti-communism among Libertarian University Students," *Sociology of Education* 40, no. 1 (1967): 39–54.

12. It was "Mormon Semitism and Anti-Semitism," *Sociological Analysis* (later renamed *Sociology of Religion*) 29, no. 1 (1968): 11–27.

13. I surmised that the sociologist in question was John R. Christiansen, sometime chairman of the Sociology Department at BYU and son of Elray L. Christiansen, then an assistant to the Twelve. Apparently, this Christiansen study was never published; I learned about it from a BYU colleague. The study "already done" might also have referred to John Christiansen's "Contemporary Mormons' Attitudes toward Polygynous Practices," *Journal of Marriage and the Family* 25 (May 1963): 167–70, or to a 1960 survey of 287 LDS high school seniors in three central Utah counties: J. R. Christiansen, J. R. Payne, and K. J. Brown, "Church Participation and College Desires of Rural Youth in Utah," *Rural Sociology* 28, no. 2 (1963): 176–85, which a footnote suggests was, in turn, derived from a larger project by the same authors for the Utah Agricultural Experiment Station in 1959. I searched a few other journals where any surveys on Mormons might have been reported during 1955–65 and could find none by any LDS or Utah authors.

14. The brevity of my stay in Utah was only partly attributable to my discovery that at that time USU did not have a very modern sociology department (or research equipment), as I explained in chapter 1. The move to WSU was definitely a career advancement.

15. "Mormonism and Minorities" (PhD diss., University of California–Berkeley, 1970).

16. See the entry "Johnnetta B. Cole" in *Wikipedia*. She left WSU in 1970 for the University of Massachusetts.

17. My own eldest son, recently returned from his mission, was one of the YSA leaders in Pullman at this time. The director of the institute there was the same stake high councilor who had earlier admonished our monthly study group (TSSG) that we would do better "to concentrate on the basics" than to have our own study group. Recall my account of this in chapter 4.

18. Recall my discussion of this period in earlier chapters.

19. In the unlikely event that anyone would like to see this very rough draft, its various chapters can be found in separate folders in Box 27 of my archive at the Utah State Historical Society. Three articles based on my dissertation data were published in *Dialogue:* "Moderation in All Things: Political and Social Outlooks of Modern Urban Mormons," 7, no. 1 (1972): 57–69; "Saints, Cities, and Secularism: Religious Attitudes and Behavior of Modern Urban Mormons," 7, no. 2 (1972): 8–27; and "Shall the Youth of Zion Falter? Mormon Youth and Sex—a Two-City Comparison," 10, no. 2 (1976): 82–84.

20. Here I refer, of course, to my *All Abraham's Children: Changing Mormon Conceptions of Race and Lineage* (Urbana: University of Illinois Press, 2003).

21. This was "The Fading of the Pharoahs' Curse: The Decline and Fall of the Priesthood Ban against Blacks in the Mormon Church," *Dialogue* 14, no. 3 (1981): 10–45. Until 2008 my article remained the only systematic account of the process by which the race policies were finally dismantled. Since then it has been joined by the thorough treatment in Edward L. Kimball, "Spencer W. Kimball and the Revelation on the Priesthood," *BYU Studies* 47, no. 2 (2008): 5–78. Kimball's article emphasizes internal

church developments, especially the role and struggles of his father, the president. My article has more to say about the outside political context and public relations of the church before, during, and after the 1978 policy change. (See also the appropriate sections of Edward Kimball's *Lengthen Your Stride: The Presidency of President Spencer W. Kimball* (Salt Lake City: Deseret Book, 2005).

22. By that time, we were fortunate to be able to include also a chapter on Elijah Abel that had been published in 1979 by Newell G. Bringhurst.

23. Lester E. Bush Jr. and Armand L. Mauss, *Neither White nor Black: Mormon Scholars Confront the Race Issue in a Universal Church* (Salt Lake City: Signature Books, 1984).

24. For an engaging account of the efforts of some of these leaders a decade earlier to cope with the publication of Bush's original historical research on the church's race policy, see his article "Writing 'Mormonism's Negro Doctrine: An Historical Overview' (1973): Context and Reflections, 1998," *Journal of Mormon History* 25, no. 1 (1999): 229–71.

25. Kimball, *Lengthen Your Stride.* Our ongoing mutual interest in President Kimball's role in this historic policy change is indicated by the frequency with which Ed cites my work or our correspondence in his 2005 book, especially in the "working draft" found on the searchable CD at the end of the book.

26. I have referred to this group many times in my writing on the race issue in the church, and some of its early members, especially Ruffin Bridgeforth, were important informants as I did my research on black LDS members. See the current Genesis Group website, http://www.ldsgenesisgroup.org.

27. This account was shared with me by both Jackson and Gladwell independently on different occasions.

28. Gladwell's public comments on the damage being done by racial folklore among the Mormons were quoted in press accounts even much later: John H. Bunzel, "Is America Ready for a Mormon President?," op-ed, *Boston Globe,* February 19, 2006.

29. My inclusion on this committee was a product of the awareness of the Bush and Mauss book not only by Gladwell and the Jacksons but also by Elder Jensen himself, who had earlier had it called to his attention by my brother, Gordon, whom Jensen had succeeded as president of the New York Rochester Mission.

30. As far as I know, our ad hoc committee never saw the final "brief" or document that Elder Jensen sent up through the leadership channels, but the 1997 document that I submitted to him as reflecting our committee's consensus is in my personal papers with the title "Racial Ideas as a Continuing Problem in the Church."

31. A fuller description of this campaign, along with its abortive outcome, is given by the journalists Richard and Joan Ostling in their *Mormon America: The Power and the Promise* (New York: HarperCollins, 1999), 103–5. Undoubtedly, President Hinckley had not, in fact, heard about the proposal from Elder Jensen, for it had not yet worked its way that far up the hierarchy.

32. See "All Are Alike unto God," address by Bruce R. McConkie to the annual CES Religious Educators Symposium, August 18, 1978. It is clear from any but the most superficial reading of this speech that it is in no way intended as a repudiation of all previous doctrine and policy relating to black members. Rather, it is primarily an argument that

God bestows rights and blessings differentially on different peoples and that those of African lineage simply got their "turn" at the priesthood sooner than expected. McConkie's later writings, including even later editions of his *Mormon Doctrine,* continued to perpetuate all the other racial doctrines common in the Mormon heritage. See also my *All Abraham's Children,* 248–49.

33. I am assuming that President Hinckley would have meant to include such racist folklore in the "disparaging remarks" he referred to in the following passage on that occasion: "I remind you that no man who makes disparaging remarks concerning those of another race can consider himself a true disciple of Christ, nor can he consider himself to be in harmony with the Church of Christ. How can any man holding the Melchizedek Priesthood arrogantly assume that he is eligible for the priesthood, whereas another who lives a righteous life, but whose skin is a different color, is ineligible?" (One wonders if President Hinckley would have agreed also with a *retroactive* implication of his remarks to mean "How could any man holding the . . . priesthood *ever have arrogantly assumed* that . . . one whose skin is a different color was ineligible?")

34. See Peggy Fletcher Stack, "Landmark *Mormon Doctrine* Goes Out of Print," *Salt Lake Tribune,* May 21, 2010.

35. Of course, this folklore has continued to tarnish the public image of the church long after the restriction on priesthood was itself finally dropped in 1978. It was periodically raised against Mitt Romney even as late as his second presidential campaign in 2012. See, for example, Daniel Burke, "Will Mormons' Racial History Be a Problem for Mitt Romney?," *Washington Post,* January 31, 2012, http://www.washingtonpost.com/national/on-faith/will-mormons-racial-history-be-a-problem-for mittromney/2012/01/31/gIQAdtK1fQ_story.html. The same article, with a slightly revised title, appeared the next day in the *Salt Lake Tribune:* http://www.sltrib.com/sltrib/lifestyle/53422107-80/church-romney-mormonblack.html.csp. Any vindication I feel for my 1967 prescience about the danger of this folklore is overwhelmed by my sadness that it has so unnecessarily been allowed to haunt the church's public image even at this writing, just because church leaders would never officially repudiate it.

36. Bringhurst's own highly regarded book on the history of the LDS race issue is *Saints, Slaves, and Blacks: The Changing Place of Black People within Mormonism* (Westport, CT: Greenwood Press, 1981).

37. I consulted especially the *Journal of Discourses, Millennial Star,* and *Utah Genealogical and Historical Magazine.*

38. See my "In Search of Ephraim: Traditional Mormon Conceptions of Lineage and Race," *Journal of Mormon History* 25, no. 1 (1999): 131–73.

39. Reviews, most of them very timely, and some of them very generous, were published in *Contemporary Sociology* (Phillips, May 2004); *Journal for the Scientific Study of Religion* (Loomis, December 2003); *Sociology of Religion* (Martins, Winter 2004); *Journal of Religion* (Barlow, April–June 2005); *Nova Religio* (Annus, 2004); *Dialogue* (Murphy, Winter 2003); *Journal of Mormon History* (Ingoldsby, Spring 2004); *BYU Studies* (Jacobson, 45, no. 2 [2006]); *Utah Historical Quarterly* (Alexander, Spring 2004); *Theological Book Review* (Davies, March 2004); *Choice* (Jorgensen, April 2004), and others—even the *Register of the Kentucky Historical Society* (Taylor, Summer 2003)!

The book also finally brought me even a little vindication at my erstwhile academic home at Washington State University, where my work on religion and race had never been much appreciated: During WSU's Homecoming Week in October 2003, I was invited back to participate with other WSU authors in book-signing sessions at the university bookstore and to present a colloquium on the book with some two dozen graduate students and faculty at my erstwhile Department of Sociology. Then, in the Spring 2004 alumni magazine (*Washington State Magazine*), my book received a brief but decent review.

40. One happy exception is the case of Colin Kidd's book *The Forging of Races: Race and Scripture in the Protestant Atlantic World, 1600–2000* (Cambridge: Cambridge University Press, 2006), where his treatment of Mormon racialism in chapter 7 (226–37) is based largely on my book (with appropriate attribution, of course).

41. Following are articles on the race issue that I have published since the book came out. Most of them were solicited for encyclopedias or edited collections: "Dispelling the Curse of Cain; or, How to Explain the Old Priesthood Ban without Looking Ridiculous," *Sunstone*, October 2004, 54–59 (originally presented as a paper at the 2003 annual conference of the Foundation for Apologetics Information and Research, Salt Lake City); "Casting Off the 'Curse of Cain': The Extent and Limits of Progress since 1978," in *Black and Mormon*, edited by Newell G. Bringhurst and Darron T. Smith, 82–115 (Urbana: University of Illinois Press, 2004); "Children of Ham and Children of Abraham: The Construction and Deconstruction of Ethnic Identities in the Mormon Heartland," in *Race, Religion, Region: Landscapes of Encounter in the American West,* edited by Fay Botham and Sara M. Patterson, 115–24 (Tucson: University of Arizona Press, 2006); "Mormons and Race," in vol. 2 of *Encyclopedia of Race, Ethnicity, and Society,* edited by Richard T. Schaefer (Thousand Oaks, CA: Sage, 2008); "The Perils and Promise of Social Prognosis: O'Dea and the Race Issue," in *Revisiting O'Dea's "The Mormons": Persistent Themes and Contemporary Perspectives,* edited by Jacobson, Heaton, and Hoffman; and "Mormonism and Race," in *Mormonism: A Historical Encyclopedia,* edited by W. Paul Reeve and Ardis E. Parshall (Santa Barbara, CA: ABC-Clio, 2010). In press is still another piece commissioned for a reference work, forthcoming in 2012: "Mormons and Race," in pt. 5 of *The Mormon World,* edited by Richard Sherlock and Carl Mosser (New York and London: Routledge, 2012), a volume in Routledge's Modern World series.

42. Elsewhere I have put forth the conjecture that Young's 1852 declaration about the church's racial restriction was simply part of his larger program (also taken up in that legislature) for a benign form of slavery in Utah. See my "Dispelling the Curse of Cain," *Sunstone*, October 2004, 56–61. My thinking has evolved somewhat since publishing this article. I would now argue that the whole question of race relations, whether civil or ecclesiastical, was driven by the sense of urgency about getting statehood for Utah. The priesthood restriction would simply have been part of the campaign for that larger objective (and certainly in accord with Young's own prejudices). Even though Young and his apostolic colleagues would have preferred entry into the Union without slavery, they were willing to enter as a slave state if that would allow Utah to be next (after California, admitted as a free state in 1850). Recently, I came

across a new article by Christopher B. Rich Jr., "The True Policy for Utah: Servitude, Slavery, and 'An Act in Relation to Service,'" *Utah Historical Quarterly* 80, no. 1 (2012): 54–74, which indeed argues (for example, p. 55) that one of three goals of Young and the Utah Territorial Legislature in passing the 1852 "Act in Relation to Service" was to enhance the chances for early Utah statehood by mollifying the southern states (although other goals of the act were even more important, in that author's opinion). See also my essay "Mormons and Race."

43. See Gregory A. Prince, "David O. McKay and Blacks: Building the Foundation for the 1978 Revelation," *Dialogue* 35, no. 1 (2002): 145–53; and his book (with William R. Wright) *David O. McKay and the Rise of Modern Mormonism* (Salt Lake City: University of Utah Press, 2005).

44. See Kimball, *Lengthen Your Stride*.

45. A somewhat humorous saying among many Mormon scholars since about the 1970s is to the effect that "The Catholic Church still holds the claim of papal infallibility, but nobody really believes it. By contrast, the Mormon Church officially disclaims infalliblity for its prophets, but nobody really believes it!"

46. In this respect, the church's "scandal" over race was far more avoidable than its even more pervasive and enduring scandal over polygamy, which, indeed, continues to have its origin in the LDS scriptural canon. But that is a subject for another time.

47. As recently as February 2012, this predicament produced another black eye for the LDS public image when Randall Bott, a popular religion professor at BYU, was quoted in a *Washington Post* article as "explaining" the traditional LDS policies toward black people by reference to all the old folklore. See the original *Post* article and derivative accounts and discussion in the Utah press: for example, Jason Horowitz, "Genesis of a Church's Stand on Race," *Washington Post,* February 28, 2012, Politics section, http://www.washingtonpost.com/politics/the-genesis-of-a-churchs-stand-onrace/2012/02/22/gIQAQZXyfR_story.html; and reprinted the next day in the *Salt Lake Tribune,* http://www.sltrib.com/sltrib/world/53618680-68/church-romney-banmormon.html.csp; Nathan B. Oman, "Race, Folklore, and Mormon Doctrine," *Deseret News,* February 29, 2012, Opinion section, http://www.deseretnews.com/article/765555343/Racefolklore-and-Mormon-doctrine.html; Joseph Walker, "LDS Church Condemns Past Racism 'Inside and Outside the Church,'" *Deseret News,* February 29, 2012, Faith section, http://www.deseretnews.com/article/765555339/LDS-Church-condemns-past-racisminside-and-outside-the-church.html; Peggy Fletcher Stack, "Mormon Church Disputes BYU Prof's Remarks about Blacks," *Salt Lake Tribune,* February 29, 2012, Faith blog, http://www.sltrib.com/sltrib/blogsfaithblog/53617297-180/churchbott-mormon-priesthood.html.csp; and Peggy Fletcher Stack, "Mormon Church Denounces Folk Beliefs about Blacks and Priesthood," *Salt Lake Tribune,* March 5, 2012, Religion section, http://www.sltrib.com/sltrib/news/53618613-78/church-priesthoodblacks-lds.html.csp. If any good came from this outrageous incident, it was that LDS Public Affairs was forced to issue a statement refuting Bott, a BYU professor, by name, and implicitly disowning such folklore, but without any specifics: "Church Statement Regarding 'Washington Post' Article on Race and the Church," *LDS Newsroom* news release,

February 29, 2012, http://www.mormonnewsroom.org/article/racial-remarks-in-washington-post-article. This was the closest the church has ever come to a formal repudiation of such folklore, although in 2011, it had issued an even fuller statement condemning all "racism" inside and outside the church: http://www.mormonnewsroom.org/article/race-church.

48. Elsewhere I have written of this posture as based on a couple of common organizational myths about history. See *All Abraham's Children,* 262–64.

7. My Journey with Dialogue

1. For an account of the founding and earliest years of the MHA, see Leonard J. Arrington, "Reflections on the Founding and Purpose of the Mormon History Association, 1965–1983," *Journal of Mormon History* 10 (1983): 91–103. For a somewhat fuller counterpart article on the founding of *Dialogue,* see Anderson, "History of *Dialogue,* Part One," 15–66 (see chap. 4, n. 40). Anderson has also authored three additional installments, which cover the history of *Dialogue* through 1992, with yet more sequels to come: "A History of *Dialogue,* Part Two: Struggle toward Maturity, 1971–1982," *Dialogue* 33, no. 2 (2000): 1–96; "A History of *Dialogue,* Part Three: 'Coming of Age' in Utah, 1982–1987," *Dialogue* 35, no. 2 (2002): 1–71; and "A History of *Dialogue,* Part Four: A Tale in Two Cities, 1987–1992," *Dialogue* 41, no. 3 (2008): 1–54.

2. Yet I am pleased that my early participation as a founding member of the MHA is memorialized in a group photo on the cover of the 1983 issue (vol. 10) of the *Journal of Mormon History*, and I felt highly honored to have been elected president of the MHA much later in my career (1997–98).

3. President Young's admonitions about the *Dialogue* enterprise will be found in Anderson, "History of *Dialogue,* Part One," 36–37. Such admonitions surprised founder Eugene England, who (perhaps somewhat naively) had expected a positive reaction from church leaders. President Young's response here was consistent with his personal comment to me in 1968, while I was visiting his home and inquired about his reactions to my own 1967 article on the race issue. He replied, "It was a good article, but I wish you hadn't published it in *Dialogue.*"

4. One example was Dallin H. Oaks, who left the *Dialogue* Editorial Board after the fourth year and went on to a distinguished career as a scholar, judge, and apostle. All in all, I was actually surprised to see how many of the founders (the earliest members of the editorial team, advisory boards, and so on) dropped their close connections to *Dialogue* after the first few years and rarely (or never) contributed as authors.

5. It has always been remarkable how little documentary evidence exists of this official church disapproval of *Dialogue.* Apparently, it was rare for any directives to be disseminated in writing, but many church employees of my personal acquaintance have told me of warnings distributed orally through the church bureaucracies that they were not to be associated with *Dialogue* or *Sunstone.* For some reason, the same official opprobrium did not attach to activity in the MHA, perhaps because that organization did not have its own publication until 1974, and even then it was quite conservative in content. Eventually, however, even MHA membership became suspect for a few years,

when BYU and CES faculty were discouraged from attending its conferences. The fundamental issue for church leaders has always seemed to be the publication and dissemination of church-related research and commentary that they could not control.

6. In this chaper, when I am referring mainly to *Dialogue* the publication, I use italics. Without italics, Dialogue refers to the entire enterprise, including the foundation that finances and publishes the journal.

7. This donor has always desired strongly to remain anonymous, and he has never injected himself into the editorial or managerial processes in any way.

8. All correspondence and other documents to which I am referring in this section are currently in my own possession, but eventually they will be found in the "Dialogue" file among those in my archive at the Utah State Historical Society. Other relevant documents can be found in the Dialogue archives maintained at the Marriott Library of the University of Utah.

9. See the correspondence in my Dialogue folders dated between December 19, 1986, and May 8, 1987, including minutes of the search committee meetings.

10. An announcement with the heading "A Nationwide Search Is On . . . ," dated November 17, 1991, was circulated by Randall Mackey and Lavina Fielding Anderson on behalf of a much larger search committee listed at the bottom of the announcement. All the applicants and nominees were expected to respond to an extensive list of questions, which included some obvious ones (for example, "How would you define the mission of the editor(s) of *Dialogue*?"), and some that were products of the tense times (for example, "In what ways are you vulnerable or not vulnerable to ecclesiastical or social pressure?"). My own responses to those questions required fifteen typed pages, single-spaced.

11. As per a letter to me of April 21, 1992, signed by Martha Bradley (in my "Dialogue" file).

12. I base this statement on an exchange between me and Allen Roberts in which he described three levels of manuscript review, the first two levels of which were entirely internal (within the editorial team), and only the third level, reserved for the "more significant or controversial" manuscripts, involved external reviewers. See Mauss to Roberts, e-mail, August 4, 2006, subject "Your Corrections to My Dialogue Chronology," page 3 of 4, in my "Dialogue" file.

13. The brief and abortive episode in the 1970s of a truly professional historical department in church headquarters is recounted by Leonard J. Arrington, official church historian for only about five years, in chapter 10 of his *Adventures of a Church Historian* (Urbana: University of Illinois Press, 1998), and by his close associate Davis Bitton in "Ten Years in Camelot: A Personal Memoir," *Dialogue: A Journal of Mormon Thought* 16, no. 3 (1983): 9–33. It seems apparent in retrospect that an especially difficult time for LDS scholars began in 1974, when Elder Ezra Taft Benson became president of the Quorum of Twelve Apostles under an enfeebled church president, Spencer W. Kimball. That Benson was a determined antagonist of independent scholarship (as contrasted with apologetics) is clear from Arrington's account, and Benson had the support of several other conservative apostles. Their influence only increased when Benson himself became church president from 1985 to 1994. Thus, during these entire

two decades, 1974–94, Mormon scholars, including many employed by the church, as well as those independently publishing in organs such as *Dialogue,* worked under a more or less constant threat of criticism and even discipline from ecclesiastical leaders.

14. Known subsequently as the "September Six," these scholars had become especially visible in publishing and speaking on topics regarded as particularly sensitive by certain conservative church leaders or in publicly criticizing leaders. See "September Six," *Wikipedia,* http://en.wikipedia.org/wiki/September_Six; and "Six Intellectuals Disciplined for Apostasy," *Sunstone,* November 1993, 65–73. Actually, there were considerably more scholars than six disciplined during the next few years, including a few BYU professors who were terminated. See Bryan Waterman and Brian Kagel, *The Lord's University: Freedom and Authority at BYU* (Salt Lake City: Signature Books, 1998), 258–367. See also Philip Lindholm, *Latter-day Dissent: At the Crossroads of Intellectual Inquiry and Ecclesiastical Authority* (Salt Lake City: Greg Kofford Books, 2011). Of the various other excommunications of intellectuals during the 1990s, few experienced the notoriety of the September Six.

15. See Lavina's "The LDS Intellectual Community and Church Leadership: A Contemporary Chronology," *Dialogue* 26, no. 1 (1993): 7–64, followed by a response from Richard D. Poll in the same issue (67–75). Poll's article, "A Supporting View," was actually a more moderate commentary on the topic of the kind that might have appeared in earlier issues of *Dialogue.* His ideas in fact converged a lot with those in my own earlier article "Alternate Voices" (see chap. 4, n. 44). In a tenth anniversary reprise of her 1993 article at the annual Sunstone Symposium in August 2003, Lavina asked me to follow with a commentary of my own, which clearly was not appreciated by the audience nearly so much as was her continuing criticism of the church leadership. See the published versions: Anderson, "The Church and Its Scholars: Ten Years After," *Sunstone,* July 2003, 13–19, and Mauss, "Seeing the Church as a Human Institution," *Sunstone,* July 2003, 20–23.

16. See copy in my "Dialogue" file of Allen's statement of "Dialogue Philosophy and Approach," as part of the "Portfolio of Brief Essays" submitted by the Bradley-Roberts-Bergera team to the editorial selection committee in early 1992.

17. "The Times—They Are a'Changin," *Dialogue* 26, no. 1 (1993): 1–2.

18. Allen D. Roberts, "A *Dialogue* Retrospective," *Dialogue* 31, no. 3 (1998): 5–8.

19. Martha S. Bradley, in her farewell reflections, "The Times—They Are Still a'Changin," *Dialogue* 31, no. 3 (1998): 1–4, pointed to the editorial difficulty in achieving intellectual diversity when those who might provide alternative views are unwilling or unable to contribute for fear of antagonizing church leaders.

20. I base this claim on the statement of the previous editorial regime (the Petersons) that *Dialogue* had some thirty-six hundred subscribers at the end of their term (as per Devery Anderson's "History of *Dialogue,* Part Four," 40), as compared to only about twenty-two hundred that could be discovered when I joined the board of directors in 1999.

21. I wrote a more detailed review and critique of the Roberts and Bradley editorship on pages 14–18 of an unpublished document, "*Dialogue* Chronology," dated August 2006, which has been typically included since then in the orientation packets of new

members when they join the *Dialogue* Board of Directors. A copy has also been retained in my own "Dialogue" file. This overview actually covers all the editorial periods up through 2006, so some of it parallels the *Dialogue* histories written in phases by Devery Anderson. Since my review of the Roberts-Bradley period was quite critical in places, I asked Allen to review and criticize what I had written. I made several changes in response to his critique. In concluding his critique of my account, Allen wrote, "I don't know what should be done with [your] summary. It is a combination of positive and negative assessments, but overall I think it does not adequately treat the spirit and extent of what we tried to do and did. It is certainly not how Marti, Gary, or I would have summarized our work, had we been afforded the opportunity." Since I was able to document, from his and Marti's own statements, much that I had originally written, I stand by the latest (August 2006) version in the "*Dialogue* Chronology," as well as the somewhat shorter version of that account that appears in my chapter here.

22. This was the Spring 1996 issue. I think it was the first of its kind in the history of *Dialogue* (that is, the first devoted entirely to an international focus). Actually, I cannot now recall how I got the responsibility for producing it—whether the editors invited me, someone else suggested me, or I offered my services. In any case, I think it was a very successful issue of the journal in most respects, and through this project (and subsequent travels in Europe), I formed valuable friendships with LDS scholars and members in Europe and Asia that continue to this day.

23. I might add that I found these to be very pleasant luncheons, since Allen or Marti or both always knew some great places to eat. During these few years, I was also freer to travel, since I had dropped to a half-time appointment at Washington State University, which kept me there only during the fall. I retired completely in 1999.

24. Until the end of 1970, a board of trustees was always listed separately from the board of editors on the inside front cover of *Dialogue,* though the editor or coeditors were also listed as "ex-officio" members of the board of trustees. This would have been in accord with the 1965 founding articles of incorporation. Somehow, as the journal was handed off (1970–71) by Gene England, Wes Johnson, and the founding team to a somewhat divided successor team in California (headed by Robert Rees) and in Utah (headed by Edward Geary), the editorial and trustee responsibilities seem to have gotten merged, so that the editors found themselves responsible for the financial and business affairs as well as the editorial duties. It is clear from Devery Anderson's "History of *Dialogue,* Part Two" that this was a rather messy process, and it certainly proved detrimental to the future business management of Dialogue. Starting in 1971, the board of trustees was apparently replaced by a board of advisers containing about the same people, but apparently signifying some loss of function and authority for this board. Thereafter, in any case, the editor(s) always seem to have acted *for* the trustees, if not, indeed, *as* the trustees. It was this de facto merger of functions and interests, still operative by 1998, that I found so troubling.

25. See my 1997 "Proposal for the Restructuring of Dialogue" in my "Dialogue" file.

26. This was also the year in which I was elected incoming president of the Mormon History Association.

27. Neal and Rebecca had each published a few articles earlier in *Dialogue*. Neal was a professor of creative writing at Cleveland State University and author of a charming collection of short stories titled *Benediction* (Salt Lake City: University of Utah Press, 1989). Rebecca taught English in a private secondary school. As new editors of *Dialogue,* they introduced themselves in the second issue of the journal (Summer 1999) with a colorful and delightful essay titled "Bearing Your Sanctimony."

28. Their first issue did not actually appear until October and was, in fact, the only issue of the journal to be published that year.

29. See "Agenda, *Dialogue* Board of Trustees, August 4, 1997, 6:PM" in my "Dialogue" file. Even in that meeting, the reorganization did not yet call for a total separation of the editors from the board of trustees (directors). Such a separation finally emerged out of board deliberations during 1998, as other members were added to the board and some of those named in 1997 dropped off or never actually functioned.

30. See Eugene England to Marti Bradley, August 12, 1997, in my "Dialogue" file.

31. Allen explained the process of selecting the Chandlers as editorial successors in this way: "We did consider various individuals and teams, but not through a formal, complicated search process. The [choice] . . . was up to the [retiring] editors, and since the Chandlers appeared qualified, interested, and available, and since there was nearly unanimous support for their selection . . . , we decided that it was not useful to conduct an extensive, time-consuming process when it did not seem needed." Mauss to Roberts, e-mail, August 4, 2006, subject, "Your Corrections to My Dialogue Chronology," page 4 of 4, in my "Dialogue" file.

32. From mid-1999 to the present, members of the board of directors (formerly trustees) have been listed on the inside front cover of each issue of *Dialogue.*

33. See my copy of the Homer draft and my own comments on it, dated August 11, 1998, in my "Dialogue" file.

34. Particularly sensitive was the board's proposal that the Chandlers reduce the sixty thousand dollars in salaries, which had been the precedent with the previous editorial team, to forty thousand, so that the rest could cover a part-time salary for a business manager, among other things.

35. Actually, I had begun offering the Chandlers suggestions and advice as soon as I learned of their appointment as the new editors. In my files is a copy of what I labeled a "Mega-Memo," dated July 15, 1998, from "Armand Mauss, Interested Old-Timer" (in my "Dialogue" file). The six-page memo was titled "Unsolicited Advice, Suggestions, Admonitions, and Other Impertinences," in which I offered the Chandlers extensive recommendations on four topics: content, editorial policies and procedures, management and communication, and special projects. I do not know if they welcomed this missive, but they never responded. They might have seen it as presumptuous. I also recommended a long list of potential "peer reviewers" for incoming manuscripts, which was apparently lacking in the records they had received from their predecessors.

36. I thought that a partial and unnecessary return to stridency occurred (for example) with D. Michael Quinn's long and angry article (Fall 2000) on the church's campaign against same-sex marriage and that the collection of past articles for the thirty-fifth anniversary double commemorative issue (Spring-Summer 2001) was, on the whole, a

selectively and unnecessarily controversial one (though it was actually put together by guest editor Gary Bergera, from the previous editorial team).

37. To be sure that all parties in the negotiations would understand the new division of responsibility between the board of directors and the editors, the board had prepared and circulated, early in the process, a "Memorandum of Understanding" to all concerned, so that this division would be clear from the beginning. This document set forth the "mutual obligations and expectations" of the board, on the one hand, and of the editors, on the other. We discussed this memo with all candidates for the editorship and secured their acceptance of it. (A copy of this memo is in my "Dialogue" file.)

38. As editor of the *Journal for the Scientific Study of Religion,* for example, I was responsible to the governing council and executive officer of the Society for the Scientific Study of Religion—which incidentally paid me the grand sum of thirty-five hundred dollars per year as my stipend. In my negotiations for *Dialogue,* I was clearly influenced by both these realities from my own professional experience.

39. A copy of this letter is in my "Dialogue" file. It sets forth the general terms that we understood the new team to have accepted, including compensation and the division of responsibilities between the editors and the board of directors.

40. This document will be found in my "Dialogue" file as "Memorandum of Agreement," dated October 1, 2003, between the board and the two editors. This memorandum was more specific to the new editorial team than had been the generic "Memorandum of Understanding" used during the spring in interviewing all the candidates.

41. Letter from me to "Dear Karen," November 30, 2003, copy in my "Dialogue" file.

42. Letter from me to "Dear Colleagues on the Dialogue Board of Directors," December 1, 2003, copy in my "Dialogue" file.

43. The quoted excerpts that follow here are taken from Levi's letter to Karen dated December 4, 2003, copy in my "Dialogue" file.

44. Karen's papers covering her brief Dialogue experience are housed in the archives at the Marriott Library of the University of Utah. Some of the board members have compared their own correspondence files with Karen's for the years in question and have found some crucial copies not included in hers. See the Karen M. Moloney Collection at the Marriott Library.

45. Of course, the same would be true of the *Journal of Mormon History* and *Sunstone,* and probably almost as true even of *BYU Studies*—to say nothing of the several smaller, more recent, and even lesser-known independent publications produced by Mormons. Yet, perhaps somewhat ironically, these older publications from the 1960s and 1970s are apparently gaining greater notoriety among the grandchildren of the founding generation than they have ever had, thanks mainly to their citations on the numerous websites founded and frequented by this younger generation! Even those websites, however, are scarcely known among the great majority of LDS Church members.

46. This generalization is true so far only in the English language. Millions of rank-and-file Mormons who do not read that language, and especially the few intellectuals

among them, sometimes complain about their lack of access to this large secondary literature.

47. *Dialogue* and other such "outside" literature would be included in what Leonard Arrington and others have dubbed "the unsponsored sector" of Mormon publications and conferences.

48. It was these whom Edward Geary called "Mormonism's Lost Generation" in an article by that name in *BYU Studies* (Fall 1977): 89–98.

49. For some overviews of this literature in the "New Mormon History" and other disciplines, see some of the chapters (especially 3 and 5) in Walker, Whittaker, and Allen, *Mormon History* (see chap. 2, n. 36).

50. *BYU Studies,* which started in 1959, is a rich product of the same generation, of course, but it has never been independent of the church, either organizationally or intellectually, least of all during the Wilkinson administration at BYU (1951–71).

51. Even as recently as 2005, I received firsthand information from two outstanding scholars whose recruitment to the BYU faculty had been cleared by all levels of the BYU administration, only to be overturned at the level of the trustees because these scholars had published articles in *Dialogue* (at least according to feedback to them from the departmental chairpersons involved in the negotiations).

52. I have said little here about my participation in these other organizations, because it has never been on the same scale as my involvements with Dialogue. I have published a few times in both *Sunstone* and the *Journal of Mormon History,* and I have participated as a speaker in numerous conferences of these and other organizations. In the Mormon History Association, I have also served on committees responsible for making annual awards, received three special awards of my own, spent three years on the MHA governing council, and served as MHA president, 1997–98. All such involvements were relatively brief and unexceptional, so I think of them as quite routine contributions, especially for an academic.

53. And in the past two or three years, some of these board meetings have been only "virtual"—that is, via electronic media such as Skype, which seem always to encounter technical glitches and, in any case, cannot replicate the sense of collegial bonding that our boards had during my decade of service.

54. Armand L. Mauss, John R. Tarjan, and Martha D. Esplin, "The Unfettered Faithful: An Analysis of the *Dialogue* Subscribers Survey," *Dialogue* 20, no. 1 (1987): 27–65; and Robert W. Reynolds, John D. Remy, and Armand L. Mauss, "Maturing and Enduring: *Dialogue* and Its Readers after Forty Years," *Dialogue* 39, no. 4 (2006): 82–106.

55. See this 2008 article in the official LDS Newsroom as an indication of this new posture by the LDS Church: http://beta-newsroom.lds.org/article/academic-interest-in-mormonism-rises. See also my article "Rethinking Retrenchment" (see chap. 5, n. 31).

56. In this connection, it was actually fortunate that the board member scheduled to become president in 2011 suddenly decided to resign (as noted above), since it turned out that he had, already in 2006, in effect left the LDS Church as a disaffected member. A similarly serious predicament was avoided when one of the candidates for the *Dialogue* editorship (to start in 2009) angrily and publicly left the church later that year. Fortunately, the board of directors had by then chosen a different candidate as

the new editor. With these observations, I do not mean to be passing any judgment on the decisions made by anyone leaving the church, for many factors, often including painful family events and relationships, enter into such decisions. I am concerned only that those who serve as editors or directors at Dialogue should already have found some sort of peace, resolution, and equilibrium in their personal relationship to the LDS Church—whether or not they remain devout believers.

8. Bridging the Chasm between Academics and Apologetics: The Claremont Experiment

1. A general analysis of this period and process in Mormon history will be found in Thomas G. Alexander's *Mormonism in Transition: A History of the Latter-day Saints, 1890–1930* (Urbana: University of Illinois Press, 1986).

2. The major document promulgating the new pedagogy is known, and published variously, as "The Charted Course of the Church in Education," dated August 8, 1938.

3. See Russel B. Swensen, "Mormons at the University of Chicago Divinity School: A Personal Reminiscence," *Dialogue: A Journal of Mormon Thought* 7, no. 2 (1972): 37–47; and Casey Paul Griffiths, "The Chicago Experiment: Finding the Voice and Charting the Course of Religious Education in the Church," *BYU Studies* 49, no. 4 (2010): 91–130. Even in retirement, Swensen remained enthusiastic about his Chicago days. The Griffiths essay is fairly well balanced but ends up as a kind of cautionary tale about the hazards of such an "experiment."

4. I have traced the changing relationship between the scholars and the ecclesiastical leaders of the LDS Church in my book *The Angel and the Beehive* (see chap. 2, n. 17), esp. 170–72, 182–85, and more recently in "The Mormon Church and Its Intellectuals" (see chap. 5, n. 35). An article updating my analysis in *Angel and Beehive* appears in the Winter 2011 issue of *Dialogue,* "Rethinking Retrenchment."

5. All of this seems abundantly clear from the 2009 interview of the BCC blogsite with Otterson. See http://bycommonconsent.com/2009/06/09/interview-with-michael-otterson/.

6. As a few examples of this academic outreach, I would cite the following conferences: "The Worlds of Joseph Smith," held at the Library of Congress in May 2005, where Elder Dallin H. Oaks, of the Quorum of Twelve Apostles, was a featured speaker (http://beta-newsroom.lds.org/article/the-worlds-of-joseph-smith—conference); "Mainstreaming and Marginalization of Religious Movements," held under the auspices of the Center for Studies on New Religions in Salt Lake City in June 2009, where Elder Robert S. Wood, Second Quorum of the Seventy, was a featured speaker (http://www.cesnur.org/2009/slc_prg.ht); the Third Congress of Traditional and World Religions, held in Kazakhstan in July 2009, where Elder Paul Pieper, First Quorum of the Seventy, presented a paper (http://beta-newsroom.lds.org/article/church-represented-at-world-religions-conference-in-kazakhstan); and the conference "The Mormon Engagement with World Religions," under the auspices of the Foundation for Interreligious Diplomacy, held at the University of Southern California in June 2010, at which Elder Bruce Porter, First Quorum of the Seventy, presented a paper

(http://fidweb.org/projects/fid-events/2010/mormonism-and-world-religions/con-ference-presenters). Elder Quentin L. Cook, of the Quorum of the Twelve, even joined a "conversation" about the future of Mormonism during September 2010 on the Patheos website (http://www.patheos.com/Topics/Future-of-World-Religions/Mormonism.html).

7. http://www.uvu.edu/religiousstudies/mormonstudies/.

8. I recall attending probably the first planning meeting to organize a drive for the Arrington Chair at USU, called by Jan Shipps during the 2002 conference of the Mormon History Association, I believe. I attended two or three others subsequently and made a significant financial contribution to the Arrington endowment, but I cannot claim any involvement in that process otherwise. At Utah Valley University, I attended a planning meeting called by Eugene England in 2000 about developing a Mormon studies program there, and I gave one of the first lectures in the series named for him (http://www.uvu.edu/religiousstudies/mormonstudies/england/index.html). I was also a speaker at conferences sponsored there by the Mormon studies program in 2005 and again in 2009. At the University of Wyoming in the fall of 2008, I gave one of the lectures under the auspices of the "LDS World" series there and spent some time in consultation with both the library and the religious studies faculty about their plans for an emphasis on Mormon studies, perhaps with an endowed chair, as the first "pillar" in a new Center for the Study and Teaching on Religion in the American West. (http://www.uwyo.edu/RELSTDS/lds-lecture-series/index.html). In August 2006, a letter (copy in my files) was sent to LDS opinion leaders throughout Wyoming, signed by the director of religious studies, the local Laramie stake president, and several others, announcing plans to establish a special chair in Mormon studies and soliciting support for the same. At least 5 percent of Wyoming's population is Mormon.

9. All things considered, I have regarded my participation in the affairs of the Claremont Mormon studies program as the most important (and time-consuming) avocation of my retirement years, with my work on the board of directors at the Dialogue Foundation (1998–2008) as a close second.

10. CGU is a free-standing graduate university of about two thousand students, located among (but independent of) the larger Claremont complex of several small liberal arts colleges (http://www.claremont.edu).

11. Despite a relatively small faculty, the creation of this school was made more feasible by an arrangement for widespread collaboration with the nearby (but totally separate) Methodist divinity school, the Claremont School of Theology (CST).

12. See http://www.cgu.edu/pages/6805.asp. The rationale and vision for this system of councils was set forth in an article in the Summer 2006 issue of the CGU Graduate School's official magazine: *Flame* 7, no. 2: 16–19. See also "The School of Religion Goes Global," *Flame* 8, no. 3 (2008): 21–23.

13. Much in these two paragraphs comes from a letter sent to me during September 2004 from Amy Hoyt.

14. In fact, the field of available candidates, especially at the senior level, was, to be sure, very limited.

15. It was probably helpful that similar moral support from the LDS leadership had already been tacitly received by the effort to endow the Leonard J. Arrington Chair of Mormon History and Culture at Utah State University.

16. Since this foundation was established, there has been some turnover among its officers, one of whom, John Hunter, its first president and elder son of Howard W. Hunter, unexpectedly died in 2008. Also, from the very beginning, Howard Hunter's adopted daughter, Elayne Allebest, and her husband, Edward, have been ardent supporters of the entire project.

17. Holland was the only apostle ordained during the short tenure of President Howard W. Hunter. His personal interest in the Claremont project could be attributed partly to that connection and partly to his own earlier doctoral training in American studies (including religion) at Yale University and a term as president of BYU.

18. Organized as the Claremont Mormon Studies Student Association. See http://www.claremontmormonstudies.org/cmssa.

19. Except that the fourth time, strictly speaking, I taught it in collaboration with Richard L. Bushman, since he had arrived in 2008–9 to take the Howard W. Hunter professorship.

20. http://www.cgu.edu/pages/5937.asp.

21. Given the late stage in my own career, I did not wish to be a candidate for this position myself.

22. Strictly speaking, the LDS *Council* became an agent of the Howard W. Hunter *Foundation,* each with a chairman and board of its own, when the latter was established in early 2006 to fund in perpetuity the Howard W. Hunter Chair in Mormon Studies and its associated program of courses, lectures, conferences, and related academic activities.

23. Because of turnovers in the office of CGU president during this period, the LDS Council had actually had to negotiate with three different presidents, of whom Klitgaard was the third, having arrived only in 2005 and been officially inaugurated at the 2006 commencement exercises: See *Flame* 17, no. 2 (2006): 2021. From the beginning, however, he proved a staunch supporter of the Hunter Chair and Foundation. (Coincidentally, Klitgaard had been a student of mine in a seventh-grade class I had taught during my salad days as a secondary level teacher. We enjoyed a very cordial reunion and several visits during his brief tenure.)

24. Carrie A. Moore, "Funding of LDS Post Starts," *Deseret News,* April 28, 3006, http://deseretnews.com/dn/print/1,1442,635203177,00,html.

25. See http://www.cgu.edu/print/4144.asp; http://www.ldschurchnews.com/articles/48912/Mormon-studies—Drive-launched-to-endow-Howard-W-Hunter-Chair.html; and http://www.ldschurchnews.com/articles/49747/Academic-chair-honors-14th-president.html.

26. According to the terms negotiated with CGU and the Hunter Foundation, the new HWH Chair would be considered permanently funded only after the endowment had reached $2.5 million, and a search for the occupant of that chair could then begin. The endowment did not reach this figure until the spring of 2007, so the first person recruited for this position (Richard Bushman), strictly speaking, was considered the

"Howard W. Hunter Professor," not the holder of the chair. By the time of the formal agreement between the foundation and CGU in the spring of 2006, half of the basic $5 million had been raised or pledged, based on the "book value" of CGU's investment portfolio. After the recession two years later, however, the actual "market value" had been reduced by a third.

27. Apparently, the process was no easier in funding the Arrington Chair at Utah State University, despite the clout supposedly available from the university's regular capital development apparatus. From my contacts at USU, I gather that the chair was finally established only with the help of a temporary allocation of general university funds, which would have to be replaced by continued fund-raising for the chair after it was established and occupied by its first professor.

28. At this writing, planning is under way in the San Francisco and Oakland Bay Area to finance a Mormon studies program at Berkeley's Graduate Theological Union, perhaps including an endowed chair. As of 2011, courses in Mormon studies were actually being taught at the GTU on an adjunct basis by Professor Robert Rees, with support from local Bay Area donors.

29. See http://www.loc.gov/today/pr/2005/05-038.html.

30. For some years, the small faculty of the CGU School of Religion had been augmented by a mutually beneficial collaborative agreement with the CST to share faculty, courses, libraries, and other resources. More recently, however, that collaboration has been greatly reduced, and the faculty in the School of Religion itself consists of only seven full-time members—often supplemented, however, by some courses shared with CST and various faculty adjuncts or crossovers from the other Claremont colleges in the consortium. See http://www.cgu.edu/pages/1036.asp. Finally, in 2010 CST was absorbed by the newly created Claremont Lincoln University, further attenuating its ties to CGU's School of Religion. See the Claremont Lincoln website, http://www.claremontlincoln.org/about/.

31. See some of the publicity about his arrival in, for example, http://www.cgu.edu/pages/4546.asp?item=1549. Since this is a reminiscence mainly about my own personal experiences and involvements, it is not the place for an assessment of the enormous contributions of Richard and Claudia Bushman. These deserve a full treatment elsewhere.

32. See the first two issues of the *CMSSA Newsletter* for listings and details on these special events, as well as on courses taught and academic papers and publications by both faculty and students during the preparatory and inaugural years of the Mormon studies program at CGU: http://www.claremontmormonstudies.org/newsletter/index.html.

33. See the general CMSSA website for more information on this impressive organization: http://www.claremontmormonstudies.org.

34. This course was taught jointly with me and replicated in large part the course by similar title that I had taught during a couple of earlier semesters.

35. During the spring semester of 2008, just before Richard took over, Dr. Brian Birch, on leave from Utah Valley University, also taught a course comparing Mormon theology with that of mainstream Christianity.

36. See the account, discussion, and documents about this transition in the CGU presidency in the *Claremont Insider* blogsite during February 2009: http://claremontca. blogspot.com/2009/02/cgu-update.html.

37. The CGU magazine the *Flame* (11, no. 2 [2010]) featured the new president on its cover and provided a nice article about her (14–18), giving some emphasis especially to her interdisciplinary focus and her success at garnering funds for "sponsored research" across disciplinary lines—all of which would fit well with the special needs of CGU. (Incidentally, page 8 also featured an article about the research of one of the LDS students in the School of Religion, Caroline Kline, who had been working with Claudia Bushman in research on feminist themes.)

38. The "upfront" expenses for these events, such as meals, lodging, and honoraria for the key participants, were always covered by the foundation through the council, but the School of Religion still had to provide the space for these events, manage the funds, and provide publicity.

39. There were two special lectures offered during the fall of 2010, but these were presented by the two finalists selected to succeed Bushman in the Hunter professorship, so they were under the direct auspices of the School of Religion. The two conferences during the spring of 2011 were "Mormon Lives, Women's Voices: Agency in the Lives of Mormon Women," held on February 5, and "War and Peace in Our Times: Mormon Perspectives," held March 18–19.

40. The resulting memorandum, written by Dean Min, was followed by some editorial negotiations with Randall Huff, and then concluded on August 6, 2010. A copy is in my files.

41. The agreements specified in this memorandum obtained throughout the two years of Dr. Min's deanship but were modified in various ways under the subsequent dean.

42. I did not serve on this second search committee, that is, for Bushman's successor, since by then Bushman, as regular faculty, was himself available for that role, but I remained close to the process in an advisory capacity.

43. See the announcement, for example, in the bulletin of the Organization of American Historians: *OAH Jobs Online,* June 18, 2010, 2.

44. As a comparable hypothetical predicament, think of someone hired for a Jewish studies chair who turned out to be a "Holocaust denier."

45. This qualification was to be determined by consultation with the management of the LDS Church archives. Of course, the owners of any private library or archives (religious or otherwise) would have the right to determine qualifications for access to their materials.

46. These were "Approaches to Mormonism" (via different academic methodologies) in the fall 2011 semester and "Mormons and Gender" in the spring 2012 semester.

47. Daniel Golden, "In Religion Studies, Universities Bend to Views of Faithful," *Wall Street Journal,* April 6, 2006.

48. "Prelude to Claremont: Faithful Scholarship and the Mainstreaming of Mormon Studies," April 22, 2006.

49. This 2004 conference, "Positioning Mormonism in Religious Studies," was intended to inaugurate the campaign to establish a chair and program in Mormon studies at CGU. It was intended to cultivate interest and support in the local LDS community,

as well as among skeptical academics, so among its speakers were several "heavy hitters" respected by both interest groups (for example, Catherine Albanese, Richard Bushman, Ann Taves, and Philip Barlow). See http://www.cgu.edu/pages/1621.asp.

50. Furthermore, in modern times, sociological studies have shown that among Mormons, religious belief and commitment are positively correlated with advanced education, unlike the case in many other Christian religions: Stan L. Albrecht and Tim Heaton, "Secularization, Higher Education, and Religiosity," *Review of Religious Research* 26, no. 1 (1984): 43–58.

51. O'Dea, *The Mormons,* esp. 241–45 (see chap. 2, n. 4); Terryl L. Givens, *People of Paradox: A History of Mormon Culture* (Oxford: Oxford University Press, 2007), pt. 1, 3–62.

52. Bushman tells me that he answered, "I find that I am more nearly the man I want to be when I live in the Mormon way." Probably expecting a more intellectual rationale, his questioner had no follow-up, and the issue was not pursued (Bushman to me, e-mail, January 11, 2011).

53. President Deborah Freund's official report to the CGU community and alumni can be found in her "President's Notebook" article in the CGU magazine the *Flame* 12, no. 2 (2012): 4–5, or on the CGU website at http://www.cgu.edu/pages/4546. asp?item=5879. Page 31 of the same issue of the *Flame* contains an appreciative introduction of Patrick Mason as a new member of the religion faculty.

9. PERIODIC PASSPORT CHECKS WITH GATEKEEPERS IN THE HOMELAND

1. By the time the rest of my sons received their mission calls, the Missionary Training Center in Provo was functioning, and the setting apart had been delegated to stake presidents.

2. In earlier chapters, I referred to passing and superficial personal encounters I had during the 1960s both with Elder Boyd K. Packer and with the Presiding Bishopric of the church while working on some projects under their auspices.

3. Oaks, "Alternate Voices" (see chap. 4, n. 54).

4. Mauss, "Alternate Voices" (see chap. 4, n. 44).

5. This paper was published first in volume 1 (2008) of the *International Journal of Mormon Studies* and then in the Winter 2008 issue of *Dialogue,* with the title "Can There Be a 'Second Harvest' in Europe?"

6. This article was titled "In Europe, God Is (Not) Dead," *Wall Street Journal,* July 14, 2007, A1, which strongly confirmed the theory of religious economics that I was using in my EMSA paper and published article.

7. Hafen to Mauss, e-mail, July 15, 2007, in my files.

8. See Givens, *People of Paradox,* chap. 11, esp. 211–40 (see chap. 8, n. 51); my book *The Angel and the Beehive,* 159–72, 181–84 (see chap. 2, n. 17); and my articles "Assimilation and Ambivalence" and "Mormon Struggle with Assimilation and Identity" (for both, see chap. 5, n. 5).

9. The significance of this relatively large generation of new scholars is the subject of

"The New Mormon History," chap. 3 in *Mormon History*, edited by Walker, Whittaker, and Allen (see chap. 2, n. 36).

10. Perhaps the most notorious example was the 1946 excommunication of Fawn McKay Brodie for her biography of Joseph Smith, *No Man Knows My History* (New York: Alfred A. Knopf, 1945). Juanita Brooks, in the wake of her classic *The Mountain Meadows Massacre* (Stanford: Stanford University Press, 1950), experienced a certain amount of criticism, and even shunning, but not any formal church discipline. See her biography by Levi S. Peterson, *Juanita Brooks: Mormon Woman Historian* (Salt Lake City: University of Utah Press, 1988).

11. Blakely, "Swearing Elders" (see chap. 2, n. 3).

12. This whole episode is described in detail by Arrington in chapter 10 of his *Adventures of a Church Historian* and by his close associate Davis Bitton in "Ten Years in Camelot" (for both, see chap. 7, n. 13). The Joseph Fielding Smith Institute of LDS History was created at BYU as the new home of Arrington's team. The move was obviously a political compromise between those apostles who had supported Arrington's academic approach to Mormon history at church headquarters and those who believed that church-sponsored historical studies should be a form of apologetics. The Smith Institute itself was finally closed in 2005 as its original members began to reach retirement age.

13. The confidential letter in my personal files is dated May 23, 1983, from stake president Weldon R. Tovey, in Moscow, ID, to Elder Mark E. Petersen, 47 East South Temple, Salt Lake City. It is a strongly supportive letter, describing my influence as constructive and pointing to my family's important activities in the church.

14. On the origins of this committee, see D. Michael Quinn, *The Mormon Hierarchy: Extensions of Power* (Salt Lake City: Signature Books and Smith Research Associates, 1997), 311–12, and accompanying notes, 568; and the article "Committee to Strengthen Church Members," *Wikipedia,* http://en.wikipedia.org/wiki/Strengthening_Church_Members_Committee.

15. In a personal e-mail letter to me many years later, Elder Jensen still recalled appreciatively our encounter on this 1998 occasion and acknowledged that ever since then he had "admired your mind and its output" (Jensen to author, January 29, 2012).

16. This gap in institutional memory would be largely attributable to his relative youth. He was probably still in his teens or twenties during the rise of the Arrington project and the contemporaneous publications.

17. The most recent case to receive any public notice was that of Grant H. Palmer in late 2004, who had written *An Insider's View of Mormon Origins* (Salt Lake City: Signature Books, 2002). With the trappings of scholarship, this book was nevertheless, in effect, an exposé of serious inaccuracies in the official church narrative of Mormonism's founding (inaccuracies, however, already well known to Mormon historians). Palmer was eventually disfellowshiped from the church for his efforts, and his case received considerable public attention because he had recently retired from decades of service in the Church Education System. Apparently, the Committee to Strengthen Church Members had provided a dossier on Palmer to his stake president. A brief news account of the Palmer case can be found in the archives of his publisher, Signa-

ture Books, for December 12, 2004, which, in turn, cites an Associated Press account. See http://web.archive.org/web/20050306102953/www.signaturebooks.com/news. htm and scroll down to December 12, 2004.

18. A glimpse into this process for several intellectuals excommunicated or otherwise disciplined during the 1990s is provided by the interviews of the so-called September Six (and a few others) by Philip Lindholm in his *Latter-day Dissent* (see chap. 7, n. 14). Since these interviews provide only one side of the disciplinary process, they naturally tend to give somewhat self-serving—or at least exculpatory—accounts. Nevertheless, they suggest the variety of attitudes, on the parts both of the church authorities and of the summoned scholars, with which the disciplinary encounters took place.

19. I see here an analogy to the account by Edward A. Geary, "Mormondom's Lost Generation: The Novelists of the 1940s," *BYU Studies* 18 (Fall 1977): 89–98.

20. In that question-and-answer session with students in a class at Utah State University, Elder Jensen's remarks were recorded. Listen at http://www.fileswap.com/dl/5iKOuShH9D/ElderJensenQandAInterlacedEdited.mp3. A written summary, provided in a blogspot by the anonymous blogger "Simple Mormon Spectator," was posted only temporarily during January 2012. Some of Jensen's most pointed remarks were, however, included in at least two news articles: Peggy Fletcher Stack, "Mormons Tackling Tough Questions in Their History," *Salt Lake Tribune,* January 30, 2012, http://www.sltrib.com/sltrib/news/53408134-78/church-lds-mormon-faith.html.csp; and Peter Henderson and Kristina Cole, "Special Report: Mormonism Besieged by the Modern Age," Reuters, US edition, January 30, 2012, http://reut.rs/xCcGs9.

21. My friend and colleague D. Michael Quinn has taken me to task for affecting such detachment in a theoretical analysis that I once did of Mormon dissenters and apostates ("Apostasy and the Management of a Spoiled Identity," in *The Politics of Religious Apostasy: The Role of Apostates in the Transformation of Religious Movements,* edited by David G. Bromley, 51–73 [Westport, CT: Praeger, 1998]). Quite to my surprise, Quinn implies (without specifics) that my "academic detachment" in this case involved language that was somehow dismissive and condescending toward doubters and apostates, and he seems to include me among "self-confident academics [who] should all stop devaluating the anguish of people they do not understand" (Quinn, "'To Whom Shall We Go?': Historical Patterns of Restoration Believers with Serious Doubts," *John Whitmer Historical Association Journal* 24 [2004]: 75–91, esp. 90–91). In response, I would plead only that there are many who live in perpetual doubt but manage to avoid a complete break with the institutional church or its religion, but that does not mean that we have not experienced the anguish of those who, for whatever reasons, have finally made the break. For some it can at times be a greater struggle to stay in than to leave. Even "detached academics" can have strong personal feelings!

Concluding Apologia

1. http://www.mormonscholarstestify.org. Several dozen other scholars have contributed. Testimonies and photos are listed alphabetically.

2. In the social sciences, or indeed in any science, an "unfalsifiable" premise or hypothesis is not usually considered useful (perhaps not even meaningful), for it is framed in

such a way that it cannot be tested empirically. That is, there is no way that it can be demonstrated to be either true or false. This would obviously be true of any propositions involving supernatural factors or variables.

3. In these comments, I am obviously influenced by the "new paradigm" in the sociology of religion, discussed in an earlier chapter, and particularly by the work of Stark and colleagues mentioned there. See Stark and Bainbridge, *The Future of Religion,* chap. 1; Young, *Rational Choice Theory,* chap. 1; and Stark and Finke, *Acts of Faith,* chaps. 1–2, all cited more fully in chapter 4 (notes 5, 8, and 14, respectively). In effect, I am simply applying to myself what I have come to understand in the sociology of religion more generally.

4. I have explored such cultural transformations elsewhere. See my "Feelings, Faith, and Folkways: A Personal Essay on Mormon Popular Culture," in *Proving Contraries: A Collection of Writings in Honor of Eugene England,* edited by Robert A. Rees, 23–38 (Salt Lake City: Signature Books, 2005). In this essay I drew also on the work of Warrick N. Kear, who analyzes the "feminization" of music in the LDS Church during recent decades. See his "The LDS Sound World and Global Mormonism," *Dialogue: A Journal of Mormon Thought* 34, nos. 3–4 (2001): 77–93.

5. As I am using the term here, *disillusionment* connotes a degree of *disaffection,* in addition to simple disenchantment or disenthrallment.

6. Indeed, with the collapse of the Soviet Union and the end of the Cold War, I have moved ever closer to libertarian thinking, largely in response to the continued (and, in my view, destructive) imperialist foreign policy of the United States and the failed domestic drug war. I soon joined the Libertarian Party and have continued to vote mostly for Libertarian candidates.

7. Gordon B. Hinckley, *Standing for Something: Ten Neglected Virtues That Will Heal Our Hearts and Homes* (Salt Lake City: Three Rivers Press, 2000).

8. Such is certainly the perception of many of those intellectuals interviewed by Lindholm in his *Latter-day Dissent* (see chap. 7, n. 14).

9. The widespread attempts of general and local church leaders to participate in this campaign surreptitiously were readily discovered and widely resented inside and outside the church. See Martha Sonntag Bradley, *Pedestals and Podiums: Utah Women, Religious Authority, and Equal Rights* (Salt Lake City: Signature Books, 2005). See also Sonia Johnson, *From Housewife to Heretic: One Woman's Spiritual Awakening and Her Excommunication from the Mormon Church* (New York: Doubleday, 1981); and Quinn, *Mormon Hierarchy: Extensions of Power,* 373–406 (see chap. 9, n. 14). In later campaigns against same-sex marriage, the church intervention was perhaps less surreptitious but, of course, still resented.

10. I have deliberately chosen not to enter the public debate (inside or outside the LDS Church) over the complicated and emotional issue of same-sex marriage, since I lack any real competence to do so. The single exception is the rejoinder I wrote to a strident article by Mike Quinn in *Dialogue* 33, no. 3 (2000): 53–65.

11. http://www.mormonlawyers.com/2008/10/prop-8-divides-mormon-faithful.html.

12. I have elaborated on this idea in a recent essay, "Living Indefinitely with Ambiguity," in *Why I Stay: The Challenges of Discipleship for Contemporary Mormons,* edited by Robert A. Rees, 39–44 (Salt Lake City: Signature Books, 2011).

Index